THE EXISTENTIALIST REVOLT

The Existentialist Revolt

THE MAIN THEMES AND PHASES OF EXISTENTIALISM

Kierkegaard · Nietzsche · Heidegger
Jaspers · Sartre · Marcel

KURT F. REINHARDT

THE BRUCE PUBLISHING COMPANY
MILWAUKEE

PREFACE

THE writing of this book has been anything but an "academic" affair. The main themes of Existentialism have occupied the author for at least the past three decades. His first acquaintance with Kierkegaard dates back to the years of World War I. In the early postwar years he read and reviewed some of Theodor Haecker's German translations of the Danish thinker. From 1919 to 1922 Karl Jaspers at the University of Heidelberg, and Edmund Husserl and Martin Heidegger at the University of Freiburg were among his teachers in philosophy. Their personalities as much as their works have left an indelible impression on his mind.

It was at about the same time that the author took the first timid steps in his approach to the thinking of Aristotle, St. Augustine, and St. Thomas Aquinas under the guidance of Joseph Geyser (who was a Thomist) and Martin Heidegger, who taught a "Philosophy of Existence" long before "existentialism" became a fad and a fashion.

After many years of philosophic study and after having familiarized himself with the thought of such "existentialists" as Unamuno, Ortega y Gasset, Albert Camus, Jean-Paul Sartre, and Gabriel Marcel, the writing of this book became in the end what Heidegger calls "a necessity of thought," that is, a matter of compelling personal urgency.

It has long been the author's conviction (which he shares with many contemporary Thomists) that in their emphasis (and often overemphasis) on the concrete "historicity" of human existence and in their revolt against an abstract "essentialism" (or idealism), the modern "existentialists" may aid in the rediscovery of long-forgotten or neglected philosophic truths. It is by "testing all and retaining the best" that the *philosophia perennis* remains "existentially" alive in the timeless validity of its essential principles.

The author thus hopes that he may have succeeded to some extent in placing the "existentialist revolt" in its proper temporal and histori-

cal perspective. He has attempted to interpret the challenge of "existentialism" in such a way that its significance for the human individual
and his personal predicament in this age of crisis stands clearly and
cogently revealed.

*   *   *

The author and the publisher gratefully acknowledge their indebtedness for the generously granted permission to quote from the original
works and translations which are cited throughout this book. If not
otherwise indicated, the translations are those of the author. A debt
of gratitude is also due to Dr. Mary Williams, of Stanford University,
for her aid in the reading of the page proofs.

KURT F. REINHARDT

Stanford University, California
December 28, 1951

Contents

THE EXISTENTIALIST REVOLT

The Crisis of Human Existence

"Homo abyssus est" (St. Augustine).

No ONE, even if he should live in the most remote and least disturbed corner of the globe, can escape the disquieting effects of the revolutionary transformations which human civilization is now undergoing. The most astute leaders of the thinking in East and West are well aware that the "modern" crisis affects not only certain sectors or aspects of life and civilization but their totality and thus the total existence of man.

In this "progressive" age it is both pitiful and tragic to see the ever increasing discrepancy between the plenitude of scientific knowledge and the helplessness with which governments, peoples, and individuals face the intellectual and moral problems of human life. It is this tragic plight of modern man that was summarily stated by General Douglas MacArthur in 1945, in the brief but memorable radio address he delivered after the fall of the Japanese Empire. "The problem," the General said, "is basically *theological,* because it involves a spiritual improvement of human character, an improvement which must synchronize with our advance in science, art, literature, and all our material and cultural development of the past two thousand years. It is of the spirit and of the spirit alone that the flesh can be healed."

Speculative thinkers of such widely differing philosophical and religious outlook as Jacques Maritain and F. S. C. Northrop[1] share the conviction voiced by the man of action that the present age stands in need of a radical spiritual revolution and re-formation. They are equally perturbed by the undeniable fact that the most advanced scientific and technical civilization the world has ever known presents itself, to use Albert Schweitzer's words, as "a strange medley of civilization and barbarism."

This precarious situation in which contemporary man and con-

---

[1] Cf. F. S. C. Northrop, *The Meeting of East and West* (New York: Macmillan, 1946), Chap. I.

I

temporary civilization in general, but the Western world in particular, find themselves, suggests that all the manifold social and political upheavals in every part of the globe are merely the external manifestations, the symptoms and outbursts of a creeping and prolonged spiritual and moral disease. Modern civilization, it seems, is gravely threatened because the perennial values of intellectual and moral verities have increasingly been divorced from the realities of matter and nature, so that material reality, deprived of the guidance of right reason and a rationally enlightened will, is being handed over to the blind forces of chance and the biological urges of the will to power.

From the centuries of the Christian past the nineteenth century had inherited certain basic convictions as to the nature of man, the structure of state and society, the rights and obligations of man as an individual and social being, the destiny of man, and the meaning of human existence and human civilization. The questions which the men and women of these past centuries had asked concerning these matters had been answered for them by theology and philosophy, which had ranked as the two supreme sciences in the hierarchy of knowledge. But in the course of the nineteenth century and with the adoption of the "scientific method" by historians, jurists, sociologists, and "humanists," the Western mind began to reject the guiding principles provided by these two disciplines. "Truth" henceforth was to be found exclusively in and by those sciences which analyzed and described extended and measurable physical reality. Sense knowledge was termed the only valid kind of knowledge, while rational or intellectual knowledge was declared synonymous with meaningless abstractions and fictitious beliefs. Theology became another name for superstition, and philosophy abandoned its ambition to arrive at universally indubitable certitude concerning the nature and destiny of man and human civilization. Instead of continuing as a normative discipline, laying down rules of human thought and conduct, philosophy became either a mere adjunct of the natural sciences or a purely historically minded discipline, relishing the re-telling of the past exploits of the human mind. Positivism and neopositivism made philosophy the handmaid of natural science, while idealism relegated it to an abstract sphere of pure thought, apart from the universe of material realities.

In either case philosophy ungrudgingly surrendered its supreme prerogative of dealing creatively with fundamental human problems.

And thus that discipline which Plato had once described as humanity's "best guardian," because "it comes and takes its abode in man, and is the savior of his virtue throughout life," largely lost the understanding of its legitimate function. It subsequently had to abandon also its guiding role in the institutions of higher learning and was forced into an inferior position in the curriculum. And such a consequence was quite natural and unavoidable, simply because a philosophy which has lost the power of translating itself into significant forms of human existence has surrendered its birthright and lost its aboriginal "existential" significance.

*   *   *

The crisis toward which the modern world was slowly but surely moving was early diagnosed as a disease of the human mind by some advanced thinkers who dared to take their stand against the "spirit of the age" and some of whom fell as victims in a valiant struggle against forces which were as powerfully alive within their own selves as in their surrounding world. The German poet Goethe, usually given to optimism, grew doubtful and melancholy when he weighed the progressive trends of the early nineteenth century against the chances of human happiness. "Men," he wrote, "will become more shrewd and clever, but they will not be better or happier. I see a time approaching when God will no longer be pleased with man, when He will have to smash His creation to pieces in order to rejuvenate it." And Friedrich Nietzsche was to write half a century later: "Oh thou proud European of the nineteenth century, art thou not mad? Thy knowledge does not complete Nature, it only kills thine own nature. . . . Thou climbest toward heaven on the sunbeams of thy knowledge — but also down toward chaos. Thy manner of going is fatal to thee; the ground slips from under thy feet into the dark unknown; thy life has no stay but spiders' webs torn assunder by every new stroke of thy knowledge."[2]

In the interval between these apprehensive warnings of Goethe and Nietzsche, the imposing system of G. F. Hegel's metaphysical idealism had risen as a final attempt to unify science, philosophy, and religion. But Hegel's own "dialectical method" was seized upon by the radical "Young Hegelians" in Germany and England to destroy their master's

[2] Friedrich Nietzsche, *Thoughts out of Season, II: The Use and Abuse of History* (translated by A. Collins; Edinburgh and London: T. N. Foulis, 1910), p. 76 f. [In *The Complete Works of Friedrich Nietzsche*, ed. by Dr. Oscar Levy, Vol. V.]

idealistic premises. Taking their cue from Auguste Comte's positivism, they developed a dialectical "historic materialism" which saw in history no longer any issues involving problems of true and false, right and wrong, good and evil, but merely questions of fact and material force. Even while Hegel was still alive, the inductive method of the natural sciences began to replace the deductive reasoning of the Hegelian system. Comte's positivism became first a powerful rival of Hegelianism and then its triumphant conqueror.

With a thoroughly Germanic consistency, German positivism developed Comte's positivistic premises to the extreme conclusions of an integral philosophy of materialism. In 1855, the German Darwinist Karl Vogt published his famous essay on Superstition and Science (*Köhlerglaube und Wissenschaft*), a cynical and witty attempt to dispense with the problem of a human soul. *Thought* he described as a secretion of the brain, in the manner in which the digestive juices are secretions of the stomach, bile a secretion of the liver, and urine a secretion of the kidneys.

The most crucial blow against Hegel, however, was struck not by the materialists but by a representative of the religious individualism of the Protestant-Christian tradition. The Danish religious philosopher Sören Kierkegaard (1813–1855) regarded Hegel's philosophy on the one hand and the teachings of liberal Protestantism on the other as the two most dangerous anti-Christian forces in modern times. Against Hegel's pantheistic identification of God and world, divine mind and human mind, Kierkegaard insisted that the Creator and the creature, God and the world, supernature and nature were separated by an unbridgeable gulf. Against Hegel's secularization of Christian dogma he preached the absolute sovereignty of the Deity. And against Hegel's deification of the omnipotent State he proclaimed the "inward-ness" of the individual. But, following Martin Luther's lead, Kierke-gaard proposed to discard reason for the sake of "Faith." He thus unwittingly contributed his own weighty share to the self-destruction of philosophy in the nineteenth century.

Nevertheless, Kierkegaard diagnosed the spiritual and moral sick-ness of the modern age more profoundly and accurately perhaps than any other modern author, with the possible exception of Friedrich Nietzsche. Again and again he inveighed against the half-heartedness and the intellectual and moral slovenliness of those of his contemporaries who lacked the courage and consistency to face the far-reaching consequences of their philosophical and religious opinions. He regretfully stated that with the aid of Hegelian philosophy and liberal Protestant theology, it had become an easy and comfortable thing to call oneself a Christian and actually be a pagan. And he drew a sharp dividing line between "Christianity" and "Christendom," asserting that whereas the former was and remained a resplendent reality, the latter was in danger of becoming but an "optical illusion." With his demand of an all-decisive "choice," an unconditional "either-or" he furnished the weapons with which Henrik Ibsen fought in his philosophico-religious dramas *Brand* and *Peer Gynt* against the half-heartedness and irresponsibility of liberal politicos and social phrase-mongers. In the symbolic characters of these two plays Ibsen presented his own version of the demand "All — or Nothing."

"I want honesty," Kierkegaard wrote in a political pamphlet, shortly before his death. "If that is what this race and generation wants, if it will uprightly, honestly, frankly, openly, directly rebel against Christianity and say to God, 'We can but we will not subject ourselves to this authority' — but remember that it must be done uprightly, honestly, frankly, directly — well then, strange as it may seem, I am for it; for honesty is what I want. . . . But an honest rebellion against Christianity can only be made when one honestly admits what Christianity is and how one is related to it."[3] It is understandable that the Danish liberal left-wing writer and famous literary critic Georg Brandes ventured the opinion that Kierkegaard had led the intellectual life of Denmark to a juncture at which there remained as the only alternative "a leap either into the black abyss of Catholicism, or over to the point where freedom beckons."

It is his rejection of compromise, his call for an intellectual honesty that emanates from the deepest roots of human existence, which constitutes one of the reasons for Kierkegaard's hold on many prominent thinkers of the present day. In the "existentialisms" of Heidegger, Jaspers, Sartre, Marcel, etc., no less than in the "dialectical" or "crisis" theology of Karl Barth and his associates, Kierkegaard's thought lives on as a challenge to the twentieth century. "There must be another Reformation," the Danish thinker wrote in one of the eighteen thousand pages of his *Journals,* "and this time it will be a horrible reformation. Compared with it that of Luther will appear as a mere jest. Its battle cry will clamor for the remnants of Faith on earth. And we shall witness millions becoming apostates: truly a

---

[3] Cf. Walter Lowrie, *Kierkegaard* (New York: Oxford University Press, 1938), p. 574.

fearful reformation. We shall recognize that Christianity is practically nonexistent, and it will be a horrible sight to behold this generation, pampered and lulled to sleep by a childishly deformed Christianity — to see this generation wounded once again by the thought of what it means to become a Christian, to be a Christian."

*   *   *

About a generation after Kierkegaard had thus predicted a mammoth apostasy and a second reformation, Friedrich Nietzsche (1844–1900) lamented "the unspeakable impoverishment and exhaustion of human existence." In the first part of his *Thoughts out of Season* (*Unzeitgemässe Betrachtungen*, 1873) he wrote: "We are living in an atomic age, an atomistic chaos. Today everything is determined by the coarsest and most evil forces, by the egotism of an acquisitive society and by military potentates. . . . A revolution is unavoidable, and it will be an atomistic revolution." And the preface of *The Will to Power* (*Der Wille zur Macht*) contains the following prophetic message: "My work will pass a summary judgment on this century, on the entire modern age, on the kind of civilization which we have attained. . . . What I am going to narrate is the history of the next two centuries. I shall describe what will of necessity come about: *the advent of Nihilism.* — Our entire European civilization has long been moving with a tortuous tension, a tension growing from decade to decade, toward the final catastrophe."

Nietzsche was perhaps the first among European thinkers of great format to realize to the fullest extent the dangers inherent in a *scientism* that had thrown off the guardianship and guidance of human wisdom. In the preface to the second edition of *The Birth of Tragedy from the Spirit of Music* (*Die Geburt der Tragödie aus dem Geiste der Musik*, 1886), he wrote: "What I got hold of at that time was something terrible and dangerous, a problem with horns, not necessarily a bull, but certainly a new problem: the problem of science itself, science comprehended for the first time as something problematical and highly questionable." Though never a systematic philosopher himself, Nietzsche first discerned the essential difference between science and philosophy and categorically emphasized the basic distinction between the scientific and philosophic aims and methods.

In Nietzsche's sensitive mind and passionate heart all the intellectual vibrations, radiations, and dissonances of the modern age are reflected as in a focus. His lonely fight against the tremendous odds of an "atomized" society and a disintegrating civilization, his ever growing isolation, and his final descent into the listless night of insanity make him both a witness and a victim of the modern crisis, the crisis of human existence. Philosophy was for him "love of wisdom" in the strictly Socratic sense, and the philosopher, if he was deserving of his title, was the friend and lover of wisdom. Possessed of the distinctive philosophic character marks of integrity (*Redlichkeit*), serenity (*Heiterkeit*), and steadfast consistency (*Beständigkeit*), the philosopher was first of all called to realize in his own life the virtues of a philosophic existence, and then to shape human conduct in the image and likeness of the true philosopher, whose supreme task was the consummation of a reintegration of thought, life, and civilization. This is why he calls the philosopher: "the physician of culture."

Nietzsche was not only convinced that Western humanistic culture had utterly failed to live up to its original promises but also (owing to the slanted view of Christianity which he had rather uncritically accepted from Luther and Schopenhauer) that the originally Christian impulses of Humanism fully shared in this failure and were ultimately responsible for it. To escape, however, the snares of skepticism, cynicism, and nihilism, he called upon Western man to let the dead bury their dead and look toward a future in which the youth of the world would wrest new values from the vital forces of *the earth*, values which were once more to determine "the measure, currency, and weight of all things."

The final phase of Nietzsche's battle with the "spirit of the age" and with the menacing forces of darkness in his own mind was marked by his despairing outcry for a synthesis of "Dionysos and Christ," the personification of the splendor of this life and the glory of the life beyond, and the profoundest longing of his complex soul was perhaps revealed in his call for "a Caesar with the soul of Christ."

Nietzsche's message to the modern age, like that of Kierkegaard, was above all a great challenge: his deification of telluric forces and his simultaneous merciless dissection of the actually existing civilization signalized the crossroads to which modern mankind had advanced. The alternative was either an unequivocal new paganism or a wholehearted, integral Christian Humanism.

*   *   *

Again, a generation later, Nietzsche's attempt to diagnose the modern crisis and "to narrate the history of the next two centuries" was repeated by Oswald Spengler (1880–1936) in the two volumes of *The End of the West* (*Der Untergang des Abendlandes,* 1917, 1922). The crisis of Western man and Western civilization, born of a growing lack of confidence in long established spiritual values and moral standards, was recognized by both Nietzsche and Spengler as involving the totality of human existence and its cultural *milieu:* the state, society, economics, education, art, literature, philosophy, and religion. But whereas for Nietzsche's basic cultural optimism the mind of Western man was still capable of advancing to new shores by means of the vitalization of its unused recuperative resources, by means of a "transvaluation of all values," for Spengler's biologically determined cultural pessimism the modern crisis was caused by the biological exhaustion of the organism of Western culture and therefore indicative not of a transition but of the impending *finale.* To both thinkers, however, it appeared as the tragedy of human existence in its most critical stage that the modern scientific age, which had promised progress, peace, security, and liberation from all illusions and superstitions, was producing on all sides a growing existential insecurity, accompanied and aggravated by multiplying revolutionary upheavals.

The merit of Spengler's diagnosis of the crisis of human existence and of the crisis of the age lies, notwithstanding his counsels of despair, in his grim and cruel analysis of the "spirit of the age" and in the unrelenting consistency with which he proceeded from certain widely endorsed premises to seemingly inescapable conclusions. That this abysmal pessimism itself was one of the symptoms of the crisis is evidenced by the fact that Spengler remained completely unaware of the major flaws of his own materialistic and naturalistic metaphysics. There is no doubt that if his premises of an all-inclusive materialism and naturalism were correct, the conclusions presented in *The End of the West* are logically conclusive and thus equally correct. If the distinguishing mark of man is indeed "his hand" rather than his head, then such a being might actually achieve its greatest triumphs in the creation of "millions and billions of horsepower." But if man's distinguishing marks are his intellect and free will, then the entire picture changes, and the essentially different premises call for essentially different conclusions and solutions. If in fact the crisis of human existence issues from the confused mind, the sick heart, and the perverted will of modern Western man, then he and his civilization are not irretrievably doomed or lost, because then even at this critical juncture human nature will be able to rouse itself and to rise again, to challenge the "spirit of the age" and to recover the wholeness and balance of a truly human life and civilization.

But it seems that to achieve this ascent modern mankind stands in need of the challenge of such intransigent prophets as Kierkegaard, Nietzsche, Spengler, or some of the contemporary "existentialist" thinkers — men who are highly sensitive to the prevalent disproportion between thought and action, theory and practice, between truths intellectually known and truths actually lived. Their negations no less than their affirmations contain a stern summons to face anew the narrowness of a path marked by the dramatic possibilities of existence, by the unquestionable realities of "choice," of good and evil, of sin, death, and judgment.

Whereas a century ago the large majority of Western men were still either convinced Christians or convinced rationalists, the present generation is in the gravest peril of losing both the "tragic optimism of Christianity" (Emmanuel Mounier) and the cheerful self-assurance of rationalism. Intimidated by the unexpected sight of the opened abyss of human existence, man finds himself lost in a world which dangerously closes in upon him from all sides, and he laments the seeming absurdity of his situation. Everything is *"de trop"* (Sartre), gratuitous, superfluous. In a world without God, man may succumb to the temptation of Nietzsche; he may feel tempted to become a god himself or a superman, but the inevitable failure of such an attempt results in *"la nausée"* (Sartre), in existential disgust and the horrifying experience of complete vacuity. Thus human existence in a meaningless world becomes for the French writer Albert Camus the absurdity of all absurdities. The existential "anguish" of Kierkegaard is transformed into the vague fear complexes of a nihilistic forlornness, and nihilism produces as its sociological counterpart the sadistic passion of terror and destruction. The Spanish philosopher Ortega y Gasset compares contemporary man with a traveler in a motorcar the mechanism of which is a complete mystery to him. Man without God resembles the traveler without an experienced chauffeur: the car races at full speed, but the traveler has lost control. The world moves at full speed toward events over which man is no longer master.

The general course of the transformations that were taking place in the West on the stages of the passage from antiquity to modern times was very ingeniously described by Oswald Spengler. Europe had experienced the early phases of its life in the sheltering embrace of a closed cosmos and a universal Church. The cultural and artistic creations of ancient Greece and imperial Rome had reflected the static character of a spatially and temporally limited and self-contained world view. Christianity introduced the dimension of spiritual infinity into this finite universe: it placed history under the dual aspect of eternity and time. The temporal phase of history begins with the divine *"Fiat!"*, with an act of creation *ex nihilo;* and then the irreversible time current of history moves toward a preordained end, in which time and eternity will again converge. But within the temporal span between the beginning and the end the statically closed cosmos remained intact.

With the waning of the Middle Ages a new cosmic consciousness begins to take hold of man: Galilei hurls the globe into infinite space, and the ancient and mediaeval arithmetic and geometric concepts are superseded by the functional dynamism of the infinitesimal calculus and of analytical geometry. The static economics of agrarian feudalism and the corporative economic ethics of the mediaeval guilds give way to the fluid open markets of competitive capitalistic enterprise. The homophony of mediaeval plain chant develops into the richer textures of polyphony and into the intricate mathematical and geometrical musical designs of fugal counterpoint. Balance, harmony, symmetry, and spatial limitation disappear in the *élan vital* of the dramatically antithetic and tragically restless Baroque and finally in the whirlpools of the existential disorientation of the nineteenth century. Human destiny can no longer be read in the symbolism of art and nature and in an objective reality open to reason and faith, but appears now enveloped in impenetrable and incalculable mystery, without a known beginning or a decipherable end. Human existence reaches backward to an indefinite past and forward to an indefinite future, but in either direction toward a time series which no longer carries any recognizable existential meaning.

In individual and social life, in politics and economics, in national and international affairs, contemporary man is confronted with a complexity of facts and events which defies even the best-intentioned efforts of governments and administrators. Although people talk as usual, gather in assemblies, conventions, and committees as usual, they are cynically or despairingly aware of their powerlessness over those events which tomorrow, without any known rhyme or reason, may make havoc of their plans and designs. Thrown back on their precarious momentary situation, men grow skeptical of the tremendous intellectual and material powers which have accumulated in their minds and hands. But even if everything over which they had proudly claimed mastery seems to be slipping away, there still remains the narrow circumference of their actual individual existence with its inevitable challenges and choices. And so they become "existentialists."

At this very moment something unforeseen happens: a new power, more awesome than any of which man had held possession in the past, is handed over to him, the power, namely, to put an end to all human and natural power, the power to annihilate the very planet which he inhabits, to annihilate the past, present, and future of the human race as such. Thus the power released by the splitting of the atom has made the solitary existentialist "choice" a universally human problem and concern. The question is no longer whether I, individually, prefer snuffing out my private personal life to the more arduous task of living it on a high and rational plane, but the question is whether mankind as such prefers the easier way of collective self-destruction to the heroic moral effort required for self-preservation and self-realization.

Thus science has pressed anew into human hands the two-edged sword of *freedom*. A second time man has eagerly seized the fruit of the tree of knowledge, and again, and in the most ominous way, the promise of the Serpent has been fulfilled: he has become "like unto God, knowing good and evil." The freedom of "choice" has reappeared in the fearful armor of atomic power: armed for the attainment of good, and armed for the perpetration of evil.

Emmanuel Mounier[4] distinguishes between two types of nihilism, one of which is creative and "preliminary," while the other is destructive and final. Creative nihilism points to the dark abyss of nothingness in order to warn and to rescue; it calls "nothingness" by name in order to reveal and save the splendor of "being" which lies buried in its hidden depths. This is the nihilism of Nietzsche and of Heidegger. Destructive nihilism, on the other hand, grows out of a frustrated desire to be creative in the attainment of knowledge or in the domination of life and nature. It resembles the primitive reaction of the child taking vengeance on the object or subject which refuses to be subservient to his wishes or whims. The destructive nihilist is possessed by a horrible intoxication, a raving despair which drives him to the demolition of his home, his work, and his self.

---

[4] Cf. Emmanuel Mounier, *Gedanken für eine apokalyptische Zeit*, "Lancelot," I, 8 (Koblenz, 1947), p. 22. Originally published in *Esprit*, January, 1947.

When Nietzsche wrote in 1873, "The great springtide of barbarism is at our door," he thought primarily of the approaching Russian flood, but he was also acutely aware of the barbarism in the hearts of his contemporaries in the Western world, hearts which had been emptied of the strong and noble sentiments of a heroic past. He thought of the barbarism in human minds which had lost their sense of direction and orientation, and of the barbarism in human works and deeds which had become the stillborn children of intellectual and moral chaos. He thought above all of those whom Kierkegaard had identified with the featureless human herd, the anonymous "public," and whom Mounier calls followers of the colorless "everyman's party," the party of indifferentism, the party of those without faith, will, or aspiration. "I have as little desire," writes Mounier, "to deny as to admit that we have entered into those convulsive spasms which according to the Scriptures are to precede the end of our time. But I know that, even if this were the case, we should still be in duty bound to explore our disorder and to attempt for the sake of the honor of man — as did our ancestors of the year 1000 — to build a realm of granite, a realm which, depending on our beliefs, will either defy or anticipate eternity. . . . 'Peace to men of good will' may be read in reverse: 'War to men of ill will!' "[5] This generation as perhaps none other before has learned to know the meaning of peace and of war. The choice is ours.

*   *   *

Human existence achieves its self-realization from day to day in works and accomplishments which have their measure and their justification in the mandate of God. By losing himself and finding himself in his daily tasks, the tasks of the farmer, the laborer, or the artist, man attains to the mastery of the world. There exists no contrast and much less a contradiction between *homo faber* and *homo sapiens* (man, the maker, and man, the thinker). The greatest minds of mankind were perfect artisans, perfect laborers, and their labor was consecrated for all time by the God-Man, who was a carpenter. It does not matter whether the fruits of their labor are visible or invisible: if their labor is inspired and guided by love, their works are perfect: their humanity is informed and transfigured by Christianity. In this way and in this way only human existence opens out toward

---

[5] *Ibid.*, p. 24.

and takes into itself the totality of that creation which owes its generation to the Divine Word. For "in him all created things took their being, heavenly and earthly, visible and invisible . . . , and in him all subsist."[6]

---

[6] Col. 1:16, 17.

CHAPTER ONE

THE PROBLEM OF HUMAN EXISTENCE

HUMAN existence has always been a problem for man, the rational animal, who, in virtue of his faculty of rational reflection, could not help looking searchingly and critically at his own life and at life in general, and comparing his own mode of being with that of other creatures. *Existentialism* in its modern and particularly its contemporary form concentrates this critical reflection on the individual human self. It confronts this individual human existence with those collective claims and forces which threaten to submerge or pulverize individuality and personality in abstract, ideal essences or in such pseudo-absolutes as "the nation," "the fatherland," "the race," "the international proletariat." In view of this danger, man passionately reasserts himself as an *in-dividuum,* as an indivisible unity or substance, conscious of the fact that no valid substitution can ever be made for a human personality. Existentialism has risen in modern Europe because the steadily increasing pressures of collectivism and abstract idealism have forced the individual to a resolute and radical self-affirmation.

The rise of existentialism is thus one of the symptoms of a specifically European crisis, although in its broader ramifications it is indicative of the modern crisis of human existence as such. History offers ample evidence that, as long as human life and culture are healthy and normally integrated, the individual and universal elements balance each other. In times of severe stress and strain, however, when the foundations of human life and of the established system of values have been shaken, when man experiences more acutely the insecurity of life, one or the other of these elements tends to assert itself disproportionately and often pathologically.

In existentialism, then, the weight or burden of life lies heavily on the individual and on the contingent and finite aspects of his "being-in-the-world" (Heidegger). But once contingency and finiteness become the exclusive frame of reference in human existence, man's interest and preoccupation center in increasing measure in his own individual predicaments and uncertainties. In such a self-centered state of mind he is prone to become oblivious to the social components and needs of human nature and, burrowing deeply in the mysterious grounds of his own self, he starts on a dangerous journey of subterranean adventures. A certain kind of existentialism has without doubt succumbed to this kind of narcissic self-centrism, while another kind, taking cognizance of the noncontingent, spiritual component of human nature, has arrived at various possibilities of "transcendence." It is thus, roughly speaking, a different anthropology that accounts for the metaphysical and ontological differences between theistic existentialism (Kierkegaard, Jaspers, Marcel), on the one hand, and the nontheistic or atheistic forms of existentialism (Heidegger, Sartre), on the other. In its ambivalence existentialism mirrors the ambivalence and instability of human nature and both the positive and negative possibilities implicit in man's position in the universe. Beyond this, existentialism offers documentary proof of the desperate seriousness with which some of the best minds of the present age have been wrestling with both the problem of man and the problem of philosophy.

The major theme of existentialism is, as the term indicates, *existence,* this term being understood in the meaning conveyed by the German word *"Existenz,"* as an *ek-stasis,* an *ek-sistence,* a "standing out" from the mere biological vitality by which all subhuman forms of existence are characterized and circumscribed. Martin Heidegger has this etymological root-meaning of "existence" in mind when he distinguishes between three different modes in which existents are or have their being: (1) things are "given" or exist as objects of human knowledge; (2) things are "given" or exist as tools or means of human activity (a hammer, for example, is "given" in this way: it derives its meaning, its signification, from the practical use which man makes of it); (3) the existent called "man" stands out from all other modes of existence in that man *is* not simply and statically like minerals, plants, and animals, or like inanimate tools, but has constantly and dynamically to affirm and actualize his existence in self-knowledge and self-realization. Man is thus a being suspended between nothingness and the plenitude of being. Man is *"homo viator"* (Gabriel Marcel), never at the goal, but always on the way: he may, to use Goethe's words, "become what he is," or he may fall away from his authentic self.

The term "existence" was first understood and used in this sense by Kierkegaard and Nietzsche. Kierkegaard in particular, by the profound analysis of "existence" and existential thinking (in his *Concluding Unscientific Postscript,* 1846), has fathered existentialism in contemporary theology and philosophy. The "crisis theology" or "dialectical theology" of Karl Barth, Emil Brunner, and Reinhold Niebuhr is no less indebted to the Danish thinker than the existential philosophy of Heidegger, Jaspers, Sartre, and Marcel. But while "dialectical theology" is concerned primarily with the precarious existential situation of the individual Christian facing the "Eternal Word" of Christian revelation, Kierkegaard's main concern is the possibility of man's self-realization: to what extent, he asks, can man realize himself and save himself by withdrawing from the irresponsibility, superficiality, and forgetfulness of everyday life? Existence, then, is for Kierkegaard the attainment of self-possession in the spiritually directed and determined life of the individual. And "existential thinking" is the vital thought-process by which the concrete human individual appropriates that Truth which for the armchair philosopher and the systematizer remains an abstract proposition, compelling no existential assent.

The heavy emphasis which Kierkegaard placed on the personal appropriation of the contents of knowledge and truth could have acted as a wholesome corrective of the excesses of Hegelian idealism, which had been both the cause and the object of the existentialist attack on abstract speculation. But in this same emphasis there loomed the danger of subjectivism and irrationalism if the existential thinker in his concentration on the personal attitude of the knower were to lose sight of the objects of knowledge. Kierkegaard — and several existential philosophers with him and after him — did not always escape this danger. By demanding of the philosopher the highest degree of "subjectivity" in the passionate appropriation and vitalization of truth, and by denouncing "objectivity" as irresponsibility and indifferentism, he opened the door to an anti-intellectual voluntarism.

Existentialism in all its forms is keenly aware of an element of insecurity that attaches to all purely philosophical knowledge. This awareness is the strength of existential thinking, but it may become its weakness if the subject's share in the establishment of philosophic certitude is exaggerated. Philosophic knowledge is never as complete and final as an article of theological faith or a mathematical equation.

Far from being allowed to rest securely on its past and present accomplishments, philosophy is thrown back again and again to its original queries, to the initial stages of its struggle for certitude.

Time and again philosophers have tried to emulate theology and science, in attempts to eliminate this element of insecurity and instability. The representatives of the *philosophia perennis* went farthest in laying a solid groundwork for rational certitude, but in the end they too had to resign themselves to the fact that their discipline lacked complete self-sufficiency and remained ultimately *ancilla theologiae*. Descartes, Spinoza, and, to some extent, Kant tried to impart to philosophy the impregnability of mathematics, while modern and contemporary positivists and neopositivists (logical empiricists, semanticists) have aimed at establishing philosophy as a branch of the experimental sciences, and the German idealists proposed to get rid of the troublesome concrete subject by immersing it in a "general consciousness" (Kant) or in an absolute, universal ego (Fichte, Hegel). But the concrete human being eventually rebelled against all these attempts to dispose of his dynamic subjectivity. Existential philosophy poses anew the problem of individuality and personality and the part the philosopher plays in the establishment of philosophic certitude. Existentialism calls attention to the fact that philosophy is a truly human discipline precisely because it always includes venture and risk and reflects in both its sublimity and frailty the ambivalence of human existence.

Existentialism insists that no valid philosophic question can be asked and answered unless both question and answer take into account the concrete existence of the questioner. The query concerning the questioner is the central query of every existential philosophy. That being, called "man," who asks philosophical questions, wants first of all to know what he is and where he stands. And why is he so anxiously and vitally concerned with his own existence? Simply because by his very nature he is a questioning being, a philosophical creature. The irrational animal, on the other hand, is essentially unphilosophical: it does not question the meaning of its existence, nor the meaning of its surrounding world. It merely accepts both and uses them to the best of its ability. But man is that peculiar kind of being which perpetually questions and wonders and doubts. Man is thus, existentialism tells us, at the core of every philosophical quest. With him philosophy begins, and with him it ends. He may cling to it as to a guide, and then it may lead him to the depths of his own self. Or it may beckon to him as a lure to intellectual adventure, and then he may eventually lose his self and be led to existential disintegration. For Plato and Thomas Aquinas philosophy acted as a guide to wisdom and virtue; for Nietzsche and Sartre it was to become a lure into adventure and into the abyss of self-destruction. But there may be greatness even in philosophic negation and existential despair if, as in Nietzsche's case, this attitude is inspired by a passionate sincerity, supported by a willingness to bear all the consequences, and hallowed by self-immolation. In other words, an attitude of existential despair may still be called philosophical as long as this despair does not consume the thinker's *philo-sophia,* his "love of wisdom" or his "wisdom of love," as long as he remains attuned to the mysterious heartbeat of Reality. The uncritical dogmatism of the armchair thinker, and the smug and irreverent skepticism of the nihilist are, on the other hand, equally sterile and unphilosophical.

Peter Wust[1] compares man's genuine philosophic awakening to a *"metánoia,"* a real *conversio* that marks a radical change of mind and lends a new vision of self and of life. The egotistic and merely utilitarian point of view gives way to a larger and broader perspective in which reality appears in its objective and enduring aspects. Thus man's philosophic awakening is an advance from knowledge to wisdom, a wisdom which penetrates to the metaphysical grounds of sensed phenomena and farther beyond to that timeless or eternal Reason or Truth in which all existents are rooted and in which all share. The philosopher's query thus aims at the ultimate meaning of all beings, including his own self. Though his quest may overshoot the capacity of his reason, his thirst for truth is as imperative as his bodily appetite for food and drink. The striving for total truth and total goodness manifests, according to Aristotle and Thomas Aquinas, the universal human desire for happiness, the happiness of self-realization and perfection. This philosophic striving or rational appetite, impelled by the light of reason, gropes for light and shrinks from darkness, and it cannot be at rest until it has illumined that massive

---

[1] Cf. Peter Wust, *Der Mensch und die Philosophie* (Münster, 1946), *passim.*

darkness which veils and shrouds Reality. The human heart is described by St. Augustine as a restless heart, constantly beset by the weight of truth, a truth incarnate in the eternal Source of all Truth and Light and Love.

Because philosophy becomes lightless and listless when it disregards this restlessly striving and loving human heart, the existential philosopher finds in Descartes's *"cogito, ergo sum"* (I think, therefore I am) or *"sum res cogitans"* (I am a thinking substance) a very inexhaustive description of the human self. The "I am," he argues, is much more than the "I think"; the human self is much more than *"res cogitans,"* and the Cartesian formula is therefore inconclusive unless the ego understands himself in Kierkegaard's sense, as a subject discovering in introspection his existential and essential relationship to an Absolute Subject and, by virtue of this discovery, becomes actually what he is potentially: a human being.

This opposition to Cartesian rationalism and idealism explains the predilection shown by some existential thinkers for the pre-Socratic philosophers of ancient Greece, and especially for Heraclitus (*c.* 500 B.C.). While Kierkegaard praises Socrates as a philosopher whose existence fully and adequately expressed the Socratic ideas of truth and goodness, others (Nietzsche, Heidegger) find fault with the Greek philosopher's rationalism and give preference to those thinkers who preceded him and in whom they claim to find a more complete understanding of man and the world. The results of the most recent research[2] seem to confirm this claim.

The major question in the speculation of Heraclitus concerns the self-analysis, the self-understanding of the human being, that is, the basic problem of every anthropology. Unlike Descartes and his successors, but very much like St. Augustine and the leading schoolmen of the Middle Ages, the Greek philosopher was interested in the totality of man and of reality, not primarily in human consciousness and human knowledge. Heraclitus describes the soul of the philosopher as being related to "the eternally living fire," a relationship which enables him to recognize within his own self the reflection of divine wisdom. These anthropological views are grounded in cosmology and theology. "For Heraclitus," writes Werner Jaeger, "the human

---

[2] Cf. Werner Jaeger, *Paideia* I: *The Ideals of Greek Culture* (New York: Oxford University Press, 1947); and Ludwig Binswanger, *Ausgewählte Vorträge und Aufsätze* (Bern: A. Francke, 1947), pp. 98–131.

heart is the passionately feeling and active center in which all the forces of the cosmos meet and fuse." Human existence, to gain a real possession of itself, must gather itself from distraction, and such self-collection cannot pass by the world but must proceed in the world and through the world.

The common characteristic of all men, according to Heraclitus, is the possibility of *phronesis,* that is, reflection or introspection. Man enters into the state of *phronesis* when he collects himself in the tranquil contemplation of truth as it speaks to him in the voice of nature and in the voice of his own deep and enduring selfhood. But while this kind of existence is potentially open to all, it is actually sought and chosen by but a few. The multitude remains immersed in the distractions of life. These few are the *aristoi,* the best, while the many are termed the *hoi polloi* (Kierkegaard's "featureless crowd," Jaspers' "masses," Heidegger's *"das Man"*). The crowd does not understand, learn, know, or remember anything, but it believes it knows everything. As a crowd and in the crowd human beings become forgetful of what it means to listen and to speak. They become like the deaf, of whom it is said that "though present, they are absent."[3] Eyes and ears are poor witnesses in men who have the souls of barbarians. But the most reprehensible feature of their way of life is what Heraclitus calls *hybris,* that is, their presumptuous pride. Although they behave like children or irrational animals, they are really inferior to the animal which moves with instinctive certainty within its natural orbit, whereas a human existence is bound to transcend its natural orbit positively or negatively: choosing, forming, creating, or failing to choose, to form, and to create. For whatever man is or becomes depends on what he chooses to make, or fails to make, of his natural vitality. Karl Jaspers merely elaborates this Heraclitean thesis when he points out that the man who chooses to descend to the level of the brute becomes not an animal but less than an animal, "an existence shaken by despair, lacking that power and certainty which the animal possesses." However, the animal-like gregarious man, the man who has disappeared in the crowd, resembles the brute in that he, too, accepts life without questioning, without authentic choices, without actual command over his destiny.[4]

---

[3] Cf. Hermann Diels, *Fragmente der Vorsokratiker,* Vol. 1, 1922. Cf. Kathleen Freeman's translation (Oxford: B. Blackwell, 1948).

[4] *Ibid.,* fragment 11.

The many resemblances which the Heraclitean concept of man and his "being-in-the-world" bears to the existentialist point of view are obvious. There is lacking, however, in the Heraclitean anthropology the "metaphysical category" of Kierkegaard's "individual," who *ek-sists* (i.e., "stands out") against the universal claims and demands of the *polis* (the state, the world, civilization). For Heraclitus, no less than for Hegel, the individual is ultimately absorbed by the political and social universal.

Phronesis, or the introspective listening to the truth of being in nature and in the self, is in the opinion of Heraclitus the way to gain knowledge of that cosmic norm which he calls *Logos.* "All human laws are nurtured by the one divine law, for this divine law commands whatever it wills, and prevails above all else."[5] Knowledge of the cosmic norm (the *Logos*) teaches men that all cosmic events express in their dialectical movement the eternally changing nature of the aboriginal cosmic "fire." However, the main accent of the Heraclitean metaphysics lies not, as has often been asserted, on the *panta rei,* that is, the eternal flux of all things. For in all this flux the Greek thinker seeks that eternal harmony which underlies all change.[6] Although the world often looks "like a disorderly heap of rubbish,"[7] this foreground appearance merely veils the hidden harmony of being, and true *phronesis* would be impossible if there were not recognizable in all becoming a normative measure, proportion, order, or law. But *phronesis* is not only intellectual insight into the nature of the *Logos:* it also partakes, as does the *Logos* itself, of the "cosmic fire," so that a material and moral parallelism exists between the soul and the world; between microcosm and macrocosm. "The regularity of cosmic phenomena guarantees the ethico-juridical nature of all becoming."[8] This unified and transparent view of the cosmos, as both Heidegger and Binswanger have observed, allows as yet of no distinction between separate philosophic and scientific disciplines, such as metaphysics, ethics, logic, psychology, biology, and physics. It is strictly *monistic,* and the cosmic unity and harmony is maintained in the dialectic of opposites. The *Sophon* (divine reason) itself, to which reference is made in fragment 108 of *Fragmente der Vorsokratiker,* is evidently no transcendent principle but immanent in the cosmic dialectic. This cosmic movement oscillates between two poles: it

---

[5] *Ibid.,* fragment 114. [6] *Ibid.,* fragment 51. [7] *Ibid.,* fragment 124.
[8] Cf. Friedrich Nietzsche, *The Will to Power* (II, 3.); and Diels, *op. cit.* (fragment 94).

swings back and forth between the human *phronesis* and the *Sophon,* but it is impossible to say at which pole the movement begins, for "in the cosmic circumference the beginning and the end coincide."[9] The divine principle is impersonal: it entertains no plans or designs, either regarding man or regarding the world. In the anthropology of Heraclitus, as in the existential "humanism" of Jean-Paul Sartre, man finds himself sufficiently rewarded for his relentless striving by the possibility of freely "making himself."

*   *   *

The discussion of some of the basic concepts in the thinking of Heraclitus seems to warrant the conclusion that existentialism is a new name applied to a philosophic attitude or method that is not only very old but actually timeless in its significance. The existential philosopher, whether ancient or modern, proclaims and teaches a truth which is all too often lost sight of: that it is the end of philosophy to furnish a way of life rather than to present an abstract doctrine, and that the genuine philosopher vouches for the authenticity of his thinking with his existence rather than with his "system." In a lecture delivered at the University of Louvain, Gabriel Marcel told his audience that "not a day passes without someone (generally a woman of culture, but perhaps a janitor or a streetcar conductor) asking me what existentialism is. No one will be surprised that I evade the question. I reply that it is too difficult or too long to explain. All one can do is try to elucidate the key-notion of it, not to formulate a definition." This keynote is stressed by Martin Heidegger when he writes: "We are used to looking for philosophic thought in the form of the extraordinary, which is only accessible to the initiated. We conceive of thought in the way of scientific knowledge and its research projects. . . . It is time to rid ourselves of an overestimation of philosophy which demands of it the impossible. What we need in the present plight of the world is less 'philosophy' and more care in thinking; less 'literature' and a greater care in the cultivation of language and letters." Thought is only "a preliminary tool."[10] It is a tool, however, which, when properly used, will aid man in his self-realization and thus in the fulfillment of his human destiny.

---

9 Diels, *op. cit.,* fragment 103.

10 Martin Heidegger, *Platons Lehre von der Wahrheit* (Bern: A. Francke, 1947); cf. the appended *Brief über den Humanismus,* addressed to Jean Beaufret in Paris, p. 109.

CHAPTER TWO

"EITHER — OR": THE CHALLENGE OF KIERKEGAARD

I

THE biographical data of Sören Kierkegaard's life (1813–1855) and the autobiographical confessions of his *Journals* are of more than ordinary significance for an understanding of his thought, because they demonstrate to what extent the Danish author realized in the successive stages of his personal existence his demand for an "existential" philosophy. He praised *Socrates* so highly because it seemed to him that the Greek archenemy of the Sophists had perfected philosophy by placing the chief emphasis on the philosophic existence as such, that is, on a thorough self-knowledge and self-realization of the philosopher. Only when the philosopher, he argued, has attained this kind of self-knowledge and self-realization, only when he has become existentially rather than professionally a philosopher, *a friend and lover of wisdom* — only then will he be in a position to aid others in achieving the same end. He wanted, in short, to teach his contemporaries what it means "to think existentially," that is, to vouch for one's thought with one's personal life. And this kind of instruction called for the use of the "Socratic method."

The Socratic method consists, according to Kierkegaard, in leading the reader to a point where he finds out for himself what the author has been trying to convey to him, without the need of "direct communication." To accomplish this, Kierkegaard needed a number of sharply profiled individual characters whose thoughts and actions he could experimentally develop to their extreme possibilities. This is the explanation of the use of the many *pseudonyms* in Kierkegaard's works. "With my left hand," he says, "I gave to the world *'Either/Or'* (i.e., pseudonymous "indirect communication"), and with my right hand *'Two Edifying Discourses'*" (i.e., "direct communication" over the signature of his own name).

In the last analysis, to be a philosopher means for Kierkegaard to understand oneself as a creature of God. To be, generally speaking,

means "to be created," but to be a human being means to be created
with the special capacity for the understanding of Truth, that is, to
be created as a rational and spiritual nature. From a self-knowledge of
his true nature Kierkegaard wants to lead man to an understanding of
Christianity, that is, to the consciousness of both the meaning and
the implications of a spiritual and everlasting existence. From this
consciousness derives man's ethical task, his moral imperative. And
he hailed Socrates as "the discoverer of Truth understood as the
transformation of the individual in the depth of his self."

It was Kierkegaard's conviction that in every generation there are
two or three individuals who are marked out as a sacrificial offering
to the rest of humankind: "In my melancholy love of my fellow-men
I pondered how I might help them, how I might console them and,
above all, how I might clarify their thinking *in specie* Christianity.
The thought goes far back in my memory that in every generation
there are two or three who are being sacrificed for the others, who
are made use of, so that their horrible suffering may benefit the
others. This is the way I understood myself: I understood that I
was singled out in this manner."[1]

Gradually but inevitably Kierkegaard centered his existence in the
alternative indicated by the title of his first great book: *Either/Or*
(1843). Either wholehearted obedience to God's law or open rebellion
against it; either for or against Christ, for or against Truth; either
hot or cold, but never lukewarm or halfhearted!

Kierkegaard's father was of Jutland peasant stock. Born in dire
poverty, the elder Kierkegaard had by hard work and thrift managed
to establish himself as a successful and prosperous merchant in Copenhagen, the capital of Denmark. A stern and God-fearing man, he
ruled over his family with severe patriarchal authority, rearing his
children in strict obedience to Lutheran orthodoxy. But once, in his
childhood days, when he had been herding the flocks on the heaths
of Jutland, he had, in hunger and despair, rebelled against his sordid
lot: he had cursed God, and he was unable to forget the enormity
of this offense even when he had reached the age of eighty-two. In
1786, Michael Pedersen Kierkegaard had sold his hosier's business
and had begun to devote himself to the study of theology under the
guidance of Bishop Mynster, who at that time was the most brilliant
and the most cultured among the Lutheran theologians of Denmark

---

[1] Sören Kierkegaard, *Samlede Vaerker*, XIII, p. 605.

and who later on became the Primate of the Danish-Lutheran State Church.

Young Sören soon began to rebel against what he termed his "insane upbringing," and for a time religion itself became "a scandal" to him. Nevertheless, his love and reverence for his father remained undiminished and, in spite of most serious doctrinal disagreements, extended even to the person of Bishop Mynster, to whom he habitually refers as "my father's priest." It was this reverence for his father and "his father's priest" that made him withhold his violent attack on the Danish State Church until Mynster's death.

Outwardly Sören's childhood was happy, but inwardly he was, even as a child, burdened with an inherited melancholy, a fact which in retrospect he registers in his *Journals*. "I was already an old man when I was born," he writes, "but . . . it was granted to me to hide my melancholy under an apparent cheerfulness and *joie de vivre*." He describes himself as "delicate, slender, and weak, deprived of almost every condition for holding my own with other boys," but "one thing I had: an eminently shrewd wit, given me presumably in order that I might not be defenceless."[2] Another autobiographical note adds the characteristic remark, "I constantly prayed to God that He would give me zeal and patience for the work He Himself would point out to me. . . . So I became an author."[3]

In 1831 Sören entered the University of Copenhagen and, in conformity with his father's wishes, he chose the faculty of theology, but devoted a considerable amount of his time to historical, literary, and philosophic studies. At least some of the ten years he spent as a student at the university were years of dissipation and bohemian libertinage. He contracted heavy debts, was frequently drunk, and the *Journals* contain some references to contemplated suicide. He speaks of this period of his life as his "lowest fall"; it was followed by his "repentance," his "conversion," and by the decisive event of his father's death.

To draw again on Kierkegaard's own accounts, he began his career as "a drawing-room hero," who soon became well known for the "dandyism" of his intellectual and moral bearing. He was exceptionally fond of the theater and loved especially the operas of Mozart. His sparkling wit and biting irony were equally prone to charm and offend. Hans Christian Andersen, whose claim that great genius needs

---

[2] Walter Lowrie, *Kierkegaard* (New York: Oxford University Press, 1938), p. 46 f.
[3] *Ibid.*, p. 50.

favorable circumstances for its development had been challenged by Sören ("a genius is like a thunderstorm coming up against the wind"), took his revenge by caricaturing the challenger in *The Galoshes of Fortune* as the conceited parrot with its harsh voice, its sharp beak, and its delight in flattery.

During his student years the *aesthetic* component in Sören's personality and work became quite dominant, and his artistic and poetic talents sought and found an outlet in his *Journals* as well as in his early published works. Intellectually and morally he was seriously unbalanced and headed toward a major crisis. It was at this time that he formulated the question which was to become a kind of nucleus for his "existential" thinking: "What is Truth but to live for an idea?" If he was to go on living, he must needs find a truth which was truth "for him": "Every human action must be preceded by knowledge," he wrote; "it is a question of understanding what I am destined for; of finding out what God wants *me* to do; it is a question of discovering a truth which is truth *for me,* of finding the idea for which I am willing to live and to die." He needed something "related to the deepest root of my existence, something by which I am rooted in the divine, even if the entire world should fall to pieces."

The day came when Sören learned of his father's guilt, and by a combination of circumstances he was led to believe that this guilt weighed on his entire family. Everything that had previously looked like divine blessings — his father's great age and material prosperity, his own exceptional gifts — appeared suddenly as a divine curse. It was this "great earthquake" that helped the young writer to gain a new understanding of the events of his past life. "I was tossed about in life," he wrote, "sorely tempted by much. . . , also unfortunately drawn into errors, and, alas! also into the path of perdition. So in my twenty-fifth year I was for myself an enigmatic, complicated, extraordinary possibility. . . . But I understood one thing, that my life should be most properly employed in doing penance. . . . Then my father died."[4]

Shortly before his death Michael Pedersen Kierkegaard had paid his son's debts and provided for an allowance which should enable Sören to live and work independently. Yet notwithstanding the fact that at the time of his father's death young Kierkegaard found himself in the possession of a sizable fortune, his capital dwindled rapidly and

[4] *Ibid.,* p. 115.

in the year of his own death had reached the vanishing point. Although Sören enjoyed living in comparative luxury, the main beneficiaries were the poor. When he died, there was hardly enough money on hand to pay the expenses of the funeral.

A few weeks after having received the degree of master of arts from the university, Sören became engaged to Regina Olsen. "I owe everything that I am to the wisdom of an old man and to the simplicity of a young girl," Kierkegaard wrote in his *Journals*. The old man was his father, the young girl Regina Olsen. Looking back upon the decisive phases of his life, they appeared to Sören as so many attempts to escape his true and ultimate destiny: the absolute and unconditional devotion to a strictly religious vocation. The escape into an aesthetic fool's paradise of poetic imaginings had led him "unto the path of perdition." The second attempted escape, through marriage, turned out to be, humanly speaking, an even more tragic failure. He had hardly become engaged when he began to realize that there were "further orders," and he felt himself in duty bound to break his engagement and to forsake, again humanly speaking, the greatest love and happiness of his life. These deeper reasons and motivations, however, were not immediately evident to him. What became clear to him almost immediately, and eventually beyond the shadow of a doubt, was the moral impossibility of burdening the girl he loved with his profound melancholy and with the real and imagined sins of his youth.

"The whole of existence frightens me," Kierkegaard wrote in a *Journal* entry of May 12, 1839, "from the tiniest fly to the mystery of the Incarnation. Existence is inexplicable to me in its totality, and the most inexplicable thing of all is my own existence. . . . My suffering is great, boundless. No one knows it but God in heaven, and He does not want to have mercy on me. — Young man, you who stand at the beginning of life's road: if you have gone astray, return; turn back to God, and under His guidance you will be . . . strengthened for manly deeds. Then you shall never learn what he has to suffer who, after having gambled away the courage of his youth in rebellion against God, now starts upon his retreat, exhausted and powerless, passing through destroyed lands and devastated provinces, surrounded on all sides by the horrors of destruction, by burned cities and the smoking ruins of disappointed hopes."

At the time of the engagement Regina was eighteen, Sören twenty-seven, but he felt that he "was an eternity too old for her." When he returned the ring to Regina, he sent along with it a letter in which he begged her to forget him: "Forget above all him who is writing this. Forgive a man who, no matter whatever else he is able to do, is *unable* to make a girl happy." And in *Guilty — Not Guilty,* a section of *Stages on Life's Road,* he describes in some detail what followed: "What happened? Dear Lord, she came to my room while I was out. Upon my return, I find a note written with the passion of despair: she cannot live without me, it will be her death if I leave her; she implores me for God's sake and for my own salvation, in the name of every memory which binds me, by that Sacred Name which I only rarely pronounce (because my doubts have prevented me from appropriating it for me, although precisely for this reason my veneration for this Name is greater than for anything else)." This "Sacred Name" was the name of Christ. "In the name of Jesus Christ and for the sake of your father's memory," Regina had made her appeal. Thus, Sören felt, she had raised the entire question to a higher plane: now he felt bound unless he could persuade Regina to take herself the decisive step. And in order to bring this about he worked out a plan whose execution caused him more suffering than anything else he had hitherto experienced. He took it upon himself to pose publicly as a model of treachery and depravity, as a degenerate libertine, in order to convince Regina that he was thoroughly unworthy of her love and devotion.

Regina was the youngest daughter of State Councillor Olsen of the Ministry of Finance. Kierkegaard's actions caused a tremendous scandal in the Danish capital, but while everyone else took appearances at their face value and condemned the young man as a profligate, Regina understood and forgave. She may not have grasped entirely the complexity of Sören's motivations, but she firmly believed in his moral integrity, and she respected his singular devotion to what he regarded as his religious vocation. Things did not work out therefore exactly as Sören had planned. After two years had passed, Regina married Fritz Schlegel, who in 1855, the year of Kierkegaard's death, was appointed governor of the Danish West Indies. When Sören received the news, he, who at first had tried every possible means to bring about this solution, felt shaken and crushed. Regina found happiness in her married life. She died in 1904.

It was at about the time of his engagement that Christianity appeared to Kierkegaard in a new light, in all its majestic greatness and commanding force. He asked himself many times whether he was justified in imposing upon Regina's innocent youth the harsh demand of an unconditional *"either/or."* It was the same problem that Henrik Ibsen was to pose, later on, in the tragic conflict within the soul of pastor Brand. But Kierkegaard, unlike Brand, chose renunciation and thus steered clear of Brand's tragic guilt.

To Christianity, as Kierkegaard began to understand, the demand *"either/or"* applied absolutely: it must be absolutely true or absolutely false. But he also understood that, because Christianity is such a "radical cure," man is naturally inclined "to postpone it as long as possible." As far as Kierkegaard himself was concerned, to the end of his days he never thought or spoke of himself as "a Christian," but always and emphatically of the unfulfilled task of "becoming a Christian," that is, a follower of Christ. At the time of his engagement he had come to a parting of the ways where he felt it was a question of *"either* choosing this world on a scale that would be dreadful, *or* the cloister. . . . I understood how impossible it was for me to be religious up to a certain point."

"Oh blissful time," Kierkegaard wrote in recollection of these years, "oh sweet disquietude, oh happy sight, when I embellished my hidden existence with the enchantment of love. . . . My sin has never been that I did not love her. . . . My sin was that I did not have real faith, faith to believe that with God all things are possible. . . . And it was his eyes' delight and his heart's desire. And he stretched out his hand for it and grasped it, but he could not retain it; it was proffered to him, but he could not possess it — alas, and it was his eyes' delight and his heart's desire. And his soul was near despair; but he preferred the greater pain of losing it and relinquishing it, to the lesser pain of possessing it wrongfully."[5]

Immediately after the breaking of his engagement Kierkegaard left for Berlin. Six months later he was back in Copenhagen, and for the next four and a half years he worked unceasingly, "almost without a day's break." The *Journals* faithfully reflect his state of mind: "My mind expands and presumably is killing my body. . . . During the past months I have been pumping up a veritable shower-bath; now I have pulled the cord, and the ideas stream down upon me — healthy, happy, plump, merry, blessed children, easily brought to birth, and yet all of them bearing the birthmark of my personality."[6]

A few months after the pseudonymous appearance of *Either/Or*

---

[5] *Ibid.*, p. 226 f.   [6] *Ibid.*, p. 254.

(1843), Kierkegaard published under his own name the first two of his *Edifying Discourses*. In the same year appeared *Fear and Trembling* and *The Concept of Dread*, both again making use of pseudonyms, that is, of "indirect communication." His purpose in writing these works was to demonstrate the insufficiency of both aestheticism and moralism as philosophies of life. Both, he was now convinced, were unable to penetrate to the highest sphere, that of *religious* existence. The *Edifying Discourses* were addressed to the only desirable reader, *"my* reader, *the individual."*

As far as the different characters used dialectically in Kierkegaard's pseudonymous works are concerned, they all represent integral (yet contradictory) elements of the personality of the author. A good example are the five persons attending the banquet described in *In Vino Veritas* (*Stages on Life's Road,* I): Kierkegaard was as bitter and coolly rational as *Constantine Constantius,* as pensively melancholic as *The Young Man,* as lyrico-dialectically reflective as *Johannes de Silentio,* as ironic as *Victor Eremita,* and as cynical as *The Seducer.* By being presented simultaneously these widely divergent characters balance each other off. The author is hiding behind all of them: they are he, and yet not he, because none of them is wholly Sören Kierkegaard.

Fear and Trembling begins with a paraphrase of the Old Testament narrative of Abraham's journey to the mountain of Morija, where he is to sacrifice Isaac. Abraham is hailed as "the father of faith," who believes "in virtue of the absurd." He is thus for Kierkegaard a symbol of both the "Knight of Faith" and the "Knight of Infinite Resignation," the man who undergoes the terrifying adventure of the mystical "dark night," "hoping against hope" (St. Paul's *contra spem in spe*).

The year 1846 was marked by another important change in Kierkegaard's thinking. He was giving serious thought to the possibility of relinquishing his career as a writer and of having himself ordained as a Lutheran minister in the State Church. What finally prevented his going through with this plan was, aside from his "thorn in the flesh" — his almost morbid consciousness of personal guilt — his growing doubts as to the authenticity of modern "Christendom" and the "Established Church."

While 1847 was for Kierkegaard a year of silence, the period from 1848 to 1851 witnessed another literary "evacuation," with works of a strongly religious flavor following each other in rapid succession. He now definitely turned from "indirect" to "direct" communication.

There were few publications after 1851, but a considerable number of works were published posthumously.

Using the Socratic method of "midwifery," Kierkegaard's mature religious works aim at teaching human beings "to take notice" of the prime factors of human existence, namely, the reality of God and of their own immortal souls. To this end the Danish author uses all his brilliant literary gifts: wit, irony, a riotous poetic imagination, the "tactic of surprise," the "skill of wounding from behind." In *leitmotif* fashion these works repeat the identical theme: that it is easy enough *to know what Christianity is* but that it is extremely difficult *to be a Christian,* a follower of Christ, and that the difficulty increases rather than decreases with the individual's acquisition of education and culture.

In his *theological convictions* Kierkegaard was and remained emphatic in his denial that merit can attach to human works in the sight of God, but he was equally outspoken in his rejection of Luther's assertion that man is justified and saved *"sola fide,"* that is, by a faith that bears no fruit in works of love. He likewise rejected the doctrine of absolute predestination as incompatible with human freedom. And he kept insisting that the love of God and one's neighbor must prove its authenticity "existentially," that is, in "living" Christianity.

A concise summary of Kierkegaard's religious and theological significance is found in Theodor Haecker's short treatise on the Danish writer. He points out that it was Kierkegaard's historical mission "to defend the supernatural against the natural, the transcendence of God against the immanence of the rational philosophers, the personal God against pantheism; to urge the absolute uniqueness of the God-Man, the reality of sin and salvation, and the love of God as against the impurity and sentimentality of the 'beautiful soul' of Rousseau."[7]

Perhaps the most controversial point in Kierkegaard's theology is his concept of "existential faith." Regis Jolivet, the French Thomist, says of it that it "rests upon a great truth, corrupted by a grave error." Since faith is a divine *gift,* Kierkegaard is right when he emphatically insists that it can only be *received* but not *acquired,* regardless of any amount of scientific, philosophic, or theological effort. And as the object of supernatural faith is absolutely beyond

---

[7] Theodor Haecker, *Sören Kierkegaard* (translated by Alexander Dru; New York: Oxford University Press, 1937), p. 58.

the capacity of human reason, it may properly be called a "paradox" ("a stumbling block to the Jews, and foolishness to the Greeks"). This is especially true of Christ, the God-made-man. As a believing Christian, therefore, Kierkegaard had to protest against Hegelian rationalism which had proclaimed the primacy of reason over faith.

Kierkegaard's fundamental error, on the other hand, consists, according to Jolivet, in his identifying the following two procedures: "the rational demonstration of the truth of something which transcends reason, and the rational demonstration of the reasons for belief in something which transcends reason." Kierkegaard's confusion, says Jolivet, "is well revealed in the texts where he objects to every attempt to 'prove Christianity' and unremittingly condemns apologetics." But "apologetics does not assume the senseless task of proving mysteries: it applies itself solely to assembling and establishing the proofs of credibility." The motives of credibility "do not produce faith, but they influence the soul and justify it in admitting the gift of faith."[8] Kierkegaard is wrong then when he asserts that one must believe without reason and even against reason and that therefore faith is a blind "leap into the absurd."

Kierkegaard's *The Point of View*, published in 1848, is one of the great autobiographical documents of Christian literature. His outlook seems to have decisively changed once more. He feels "incredibly older and yet eternally young." Silently, he says, he has surrendered everything to God. With divine help, he knows, he will at last become himself; with the help of Christ he will at last triumph over his melancholy. "The thorn in the flesh" has been removed at last. The burden of his own and his father's guilt has been lifted.

The most stirring event of this final period of Kierkegaard's life was the echo caused by his violent attack on the liberal theology of the Danish-Lutheran State Church. With Bishop Mynster's death in 1854 the time to speak had come, and Kierkegaard turned from his "religion of hidden inwardness" to an unequivocal profession of his creed. In the "pure inwardness" taught by Martin Luther he saw now the greatest threat to Christianity because it prevented religion from manifesting itself in "works." "Christendom," he had written in *The Sickness unto Death* (1848), "is so far from being what it calls itself that the life of most men . . . is far too spiritless to be

---

[8] Regis Jolivet, *Introduction to Kierkegaard* (translated by W. H. Barber; London: Frederick Muller, 1950), p. 55 f.

called sinful in the Christian sense."[9] Scornfully he now looked upon his own aesthetic and poetic endeavors: "A poet! Now, of all times, one poet more . . . ; now, when what is needed is . . . martyrs by the thousands."[10] Christianity, he claims, was abolished in "Christendom" by leniency, "but for us there is only one salvation — Christianity. And for Christianity there is only one salvation — severity."[11]

In Kierkegaard's own estimate *The Sickness unto Death* — the sickness of despair, healed by faith — was his greatest religious work. It culminates in the demand that the disciple of today must become "contemporary with Christ." Never, the author contends, was a severely disciplined spiritual life more necessary than in the modern age, because the task of "reintroducing Christianity into Christendom" is a much more difficult one than that of introducing it into paganism. It is more difficult because it requires first of all that the "illusion" be overcome that all who live in "Christendom" are Christians, that Christianity is still a vital force in "Christian" nations and in a "Christian" civilization.

In 1854, the year preceding Kierkegaard's death, the people of Denmark were deeply stirred by a series of nine pamphlets which appeared at monthly intervals; they were entitled *The Instant* and were published over the signature of their famous fellow countryman. Kierkegaard had been provoked to give vent to his pent up resentment by the funeral oration which Professor Hans Larsen Martensen, a pupil of the German philosopher Hegel and a liberal Lutheran theologian of the Danish State Church, had delivered on the occasion of Bishop Mynster's death. What in particular aroused Kierkegaard's wrath was the fact that Martensen had called Mynster "a link in the sacred chain of witnesses to Apostolic Truth." Without questioning the great erudition and the intellectual acumen of either Martensen or Mynster, the Danish thinker saw in them two typical representatives of the prevalent type of nominal Christianity. They represented that "mediocrity of Christendom" which enjoyed such a high reputation "particularly in Protestantism, particularly in Denmark." From the time that Luther had abolished good works in favor of "faith alone," Kierkegaard argued, Christianity had been progressively emptied of its meaning by the gradual removal of all its difficulties. The abolition of the confessional, the suppression of the monasteries and religious orders, the despisal of evangelical poverty and asceticism, and, above

---

[9] Lowrie, *op. cit.*, p. 414 f.   [10] *Ibid.*, p. 417.   [11] *Ibid.*, p. 431.

all, the growing conformance of "Christendom" to the worldliness of the modern environment, were all stages on the same disastrous road to total secularism.

It had long been Kierkegaard's secret hope that Bishop Mynster before his death might make the admission that the kind of Christianity which he had been preaching was seriously defective, lacking in consistency and earnestness. His disappointment was therefore supreme when, after the democratic revolution of 1848, Mynster had enlisted the support of the liberal daily press, the same press of which Kierkegaard had written that it ought to bear on a big signboard the inscription: "Here people are demoralized in the shortest possible time, in the highest possible degree, and at the lowest possible price." Kierkegaard had an almost boundless contempt for the servility, the venality, and the lack of principles which he had encountered among journalists and, it seemed to him, the worst offenders were the spokesmen of the liberal press. "Although I believe," he wrote in his *Journals,* in an entry of the year 1851, ". . . that we shall rise with a transfigured body, I will ask God to let me retain even on my transfigured body a little scar as a reminder that I was killed by journalists." What he particularly revolted against was the power wielded by journalists to the end of inducing millions of human beings to think identically *en masse*. This seemed to him a grievous insult to the eternal dignity of individual man, created in the image of God.

"Bishop Mynster," Kierkegaard wrote, "has a dual aspect. He possesses a religious inwardness, and from this he draws his incomparable sermons. . . . But then he has another aspect — and, alas, the week, as is well known, has seven days. . . . And in the remaining six days worldly shrewdness is his element." "Now he is dead," reads a *Journal* entry of March 1, 1854, "dead without that admission. . . . Now all he has left behind is the fact that he has preached Christianity fast into an illusion. . . . What I have to do now, I do with sorrow; yet it must be done, about that I am perfectly clear; I can find no peace until it is done."[12]

In the last period of his life Kierkegaard expressed himself rather definitely on his concept of the Christian Church. Opposing any democratic-constitutional or presbyterial authority, he sees the Church resting exclusively on divine authorization, and the authority of its ministry derives from apostolic succession and ordination. A priest

---

[12] *Ibid.*, p. 219 f.

is essentially what he is through ordination, we read in the *Concluding Unscientific Postscript;* ordination constitutes a *character indelebilis.* But wherefrom, he asks, derives the authority of the 1000 parsons of Denmark? Simply from the fact that they have behind them the police force. And because the pastors of the State Church are employees of the secular state, Kierkegaard denies them the right to administer the sacraments. Because they are "actors," he adds, it might even be questioned whether they should be buried in consecrated ground!

The case of Christianity versus "Christendom" had already been stated without any equivocation in the stirring essay entitled *The Present Age* (1846). "Christianity," Kierkegaard had written there, "without the following of Christ is merely mythology, poesy. . . . The enlightened nineteenth century treats Christianity as a myth, but it lacks the courage to give it up."[13]

On October 2, 1855, Kierkegaard suffered a stroke on his way home from the bank, from which he had drawn the pitiful amount that remained of his fortune. Partly paralyzed and in great pain, he was taken to Frederick's Hospital. He knew that death was near, but he refused to receive the viaticum from the hands of "an employee of the State." He died on November 11.

According to Kierkegaard's own judgment, it was his providential mission to act as a "corrective," to be "that little pinch of spice, that little touch of red" that was used by the divine housekeeper and artist to impart a particular taste and hue to the rest: "A little pinch of spice! That is to say: Here a man must be sacrificed. . . ." His work had begun with *Either/Or,* and it ended "at the foot of the altar where the author, very conscious of his own imperfection and guilt, in no sense describing himself as a witness to the truth but only as a particular kind of poet and thinker who, 'without authority,' has nothing new to bring, and only 'desires to have read through once again in a more heartfelt way the original document of individual and human existence, the old, the known, as it was handed down by the fathers.' "[14]

Three years before his death Kierkegaard had confided to his *Journals* that he had found the solution of the riddle of his existence in Divine Love. "Love," writes Theodor Haecker, "led Kierkegaard

---

[13] *Ibid.,* p. 539.

[14] Cf. Preface to *Discourses at Communion Service on Friday* (1851); and the epilogue to *Concluding Unscientific Postscript,* in Haecker, *op. cit.,* p. 51.

to profounder, more valuable and more lasting knowledge than faith, which he understood so wrongly and one-sidedly."[15] The *Journals* sound the same dominant chord: "The birds on the branches, the lilies in the field, the deer in the forest, the fishes in the sea, countless hosts of happy men exultantly proclaim: God is Love. But underneath all these sopranos, supporting them as it were, as the bass part does, is audible the *De profundis* which issues from the sacrificed one: God is Love."[16]

"Historically speaking," Kierkegaard writes, referring to his own impending death, "he died of a deadly disease but, poetically speaking, he died of his longing for Eternity, so that henceforth he might do nothing else but thank God unceasingly."

Kierkegaard's message to the present age is eloquently summarized by Johannes Hohlenberg: "What is at stake is the choice between the individual and the collective, between the human person and the crowd, between freedom and slavery, between Christ and Antichrist. *Either:* the life of the individual person, a microcosm as the image of God, capable of free, responsible action, and therefore . . . a life of toil and much suffering and many dangers; *or:* the life of an impersonal, unfree member of a collective, without the possibility of independent knowledge and responsible action, a life in the service of unknown forces —, and as compensation for the loss of freedom at best a false, illusory dream of material welfare in an earthly paradise which can never become a reality."[17]

*   *   *

Kierkegaard's battle cry, "either — or," signalized his valiant fight on two major fronts: on the one hand, he fought against the liberalist secularization of the Danish Lutheran State Church and, on the other, against Hegel's pantheistic idealism with its incumbent dissolution of Christian dogma. The fight against the State Church, however, eventually became part of the more crucial problem which confronted him in the almost undisputed reign of Hegelianism in theology and philosophy. What was at stake was Christianity and Christian revelation as such, in view of Hegel's ultimate denunciation of Christian theology. Driven on by historical circumstances and en-

[15] Haecker, *op. cit.*, p. 51.
[16] Walter Lowrie, *op. cit.*, p. 588.
[17] Johannes Hohlenberg, *Sören Kierkegaard* (translated by Maria Bachmann-Isler; Basel: Benno Schwabe & Co., 1949), p. 417.

vironmental influences, Kierkegaard advanced and defended his own and Luther's fideism against Hegel's gnosticism. His fear of Hegel's extreme rationalism made him recede farther and farther from a rationally grounded theology, until at last he arrived at the position of an integral supranaturalism, approaching and following Luther in his contempt of reason and his denunciation of philosophy.

This was of course not the first time in the history of Christianity that such antithetical positions as those held by Kierkegaard and Hegel had followed and challenged each other. In Christian antiquity, for example, the School of Antioch (John Chrysostom, Theodoret) had opposed its theological positivism (fideism) to the allegorical and gnostic rationalism of the School of Alexandria (Clement, Origen). In the Middle Ages many antidialectical theologians took their stand against that dialectical movement which culminated in Abelard's rationalism. Similarly, but more radically, Luther turned against Aristotle and the scholastics as Kierkegaard turned against Hegel and Schleiermacher. In Thomistic scholasticism, on the other hand, the organic relationship between faith and reason, theology and philosophy, supernature and nature is duly recognized and firmly established, and both the transcendence of faith and the relative autonomy of reason are safeguarded. Thomism, then, strikes a middle path between the extremes of an integral supranaturalism (fideism) and an integral rationalism (gnosticism).

Both of these extreme positions are strangely enough rooted in an almost identical concept of the Deity: they both entertain the idea of a God who creates the world, only to leave it to its own evolution and proliferation: *"creavit et abiit."* As against this "deistic" concept of the Deity the patristic and scholastic theologians and philosophers insisted that God not only creates but also sustains His creation, and that without this sustenance the orphaned universe would immediately sink back into nothingness.

Though representing the exact antithesis of Hegel's theological position, Kierkegaard was in his own spiritual development at least negatively determined by Hegel's dialectical philosophy. As Hegel finally arrived at a complete identification of God and world, Kierkegaard posited the complete and irreconcilable "otherness" of the absolute divine Mind as against all contingent created being, including the created human mind. He thus saw no analogy, but only an abysmal difference between infinite and finite being, between the necessary and the contingent, between the Creator and His creation.

Hegel, starting out as a theologian, had in the end denounced all theology. Step by step he had transformed Christian dogmatics into a gnostic theory of knowledge: Redemption was interpreted as the redeeming force of love; the Holy Trinity became "the dialectic of the Absolute Mind"; the God-Man was transformed into a man who had experienced his identity with the Absolute; and the Holy Spirit appeared as the communal spirit of social life. Was Kierkegaard's view then unduly gloomy when he saw in Hegel the most ingenious and therefore the most dangerous modern enemy of Christianity?

Kierkegaard himself, on the other hand, had started out as a speculative writer and ended as a theologian who denounced philosophy. He became "a Protestant monk," a lonely Christian who deeply, in fear and trembling, experienced the agony of Christ on Mount Calvary, almost forgetting its sequel, the gladness of Easter. He took a forceful stand against Hegel's fatalistic theory of the predetermined evolution of the world spirit. Far from conceiving of Christianity as one phase among others in an evolutionary cosmic process, the Christian dispensation was for him a unique occurrence of absolute and incomparable value and validity. For him, therefore, the individual's concern was with faith and salvation rather than with the "objectivations of the World Spirit."

There is ample justification for accepting as essentially correct Kierkegaard's contention that Hegel's goal, as revealed in the concluding paragraphs of his *Philosophy of History,* was the secularization of religion and the divinization of nature and worldly prudence. God must become man, so that the philosopher may become God, or, to use Hegel's own phraseology, a representation of objective truth, of absolute being, of self-conscious Idea; so that in the end all opposites may be identified and neutralized: God, World, and Man are One Idea.

Against the backdrop of the Kierkegaard-Hegel antithesis, the present condition of Christianity in the world stands out more clearly. The contemporary philosopher who chooses his stand on the side of atheism and paganism is no longer apologetic about it and therefore perhaps more sincere than Hegel. Kierkegaard had tried desperately to resolve the thought — extension, spirit — nature, soul — body dualisms and antinomies which Descartes had bequeathed from one generation of philosophers to the next. But, because the Danish thinker had no access to the scholastic doctrine of the "analogy of being," the antinomies remained, and the self-destruction of philosophy went on apace. In such a situation the Christian philosopher has all the more reason to equal and surpass his atheistic opponent in unequivocal and uncompromising determination. A clarification of the issues at stake can only aid in making both controversy and conversation more fruitful. Nothing is more inducive to generating mutual respect than an increasing emphasis upon the sincerity and integrity of religious and philosophical convictions. And Kierkegaard may well be regarded as the prototype of such an attitude, grounded in the wholeness of human existence, and thus as the "father" of modern "existentialism." It was his historically and circumstantially conditioned fate to be a Christian thinker who felt it his duty to call in question the very concept of a Christian philosophy. It was his merit to have emphasized anew the distinction between the infinite and the finite, and to have defended this basic distinction against any philosophy of immanence and identity. But an aspect of tragedy and frustration was introduced into Kierkegaard's life and work by his inability to recognize that both finite and infinite being partake of the common term of *Being*. Thus he failed to see what St. Augustine described as *"tanta similitudo, tanta dissimilitudo."* His integral supranaturalism thwarted his comprehension of the fullness of life, reality, and human nature: it cut short his vision of a world redeemed and transfigured by Divine Love Incarnate.

II

What is the meaning of "existential truth" in Kierkegaard's life and work? It is a translation of the abstract into the concrete, an ethical and religious appropriation of the ideal, an active practice and realization rather than any doctrinal knowledge; a "how" rather than a "what." It is the actual living of all that one believes, teaches, and preaches. Theodor Haecker calls the separation of the intellect from all the other human faculties in man a special characteristic of European philosophy. "European philosophy," he says, "proceeds from the world through the person, who is but an empty relative point, back to the world; it goes from objects, things, sensations . . . , passing as quickly as possible over the subject, the self, the individual, back to objects, things, and sensations. . . . Kierkegaard does not follow this age-old development, because he aims at something higher. He wishes to reverse the order for both philosophy and thought. He wishes to go from the person by way of the things to the person, and not from the things by way of the person to things."[18]

---

[18] Haecker, *op. cit.*, p. 25 f.

Kierkegaard's writings, hedged in by the dialectics of "double reflection" and pseudonymous mystification, and yet having their center of gravity in existential introspection, present formidable obstacles to objective analysis and interpretation. "If one were to attempt a presentation of Kierkegaard's thoughts," writes Haecker, "he would find himself compelled to repeat step by step and sentence by sentence the original writings. One would, in other words, find himself compelled to refer the reader to the works themselves and to tell him: now go ahead and read!"[19]

While the exposition of the ideas of an author who dreads all objectivity with a genuine *horror vacui* is thus by no means an easy task, it is nevertheless possible to trace the many radiations of Kierkegaard's existential thinking to a focus in which they fuse. This focal convergence and concentration is found in the *Concluding Unscientific Postscript,* a work which was published in 1846 and which represents the promised sequel to *Philosophic Fragments,* published two years earlier. The *Postscript* outweighs the earlier work both in volume and pivotal significance. It marks the transition from "indirect" to "direct" communication (an acknowledgment of Kierkegaard's authorship of the works previously published under pseudonyms, and an explanation of his reasons for the use of the pseudonyms is appended), and it poses *in concreto* the problem to which all the earlier works had been leading up, the problem of "becoming a Christian." The use of the term "unscientific" in the title is explained by an entry in the *Journals* (1846), in which Kierkegaard expresses his apprehensions as to the encroachments of natural science on the human studies, in particular on philosophy and religion. "In the end," the note reads, "all corruption will come about as a consequence of the natural sciences. . . . The scientific method becomes especially dangerous and pernicious when it encroaches upon the realm of the spirit. Let science deal with plants and animals and stars; but to deal in that way with the human spirit is blasphemy."[20]

The *Postscript* bears the subtitle, *An Existential Contribution by Johannes Climacus.* This pseudonym had originally been chosen by Kierkegaard in 1842, in connection with the composition of a polemic fragment against Cartesian rationalism. It was used again in the

---

[19] Theodor Haecker, *Der Buckel Kierkegaards* (Zürich: Thomas Verlag, 1947), p. 8.

[20] Kierkegaard, *Concluding Unscientific Postscript* (translated by David F. Swenson, introduction and notes by Walter Lowrie; Princeton: Princeton University Press, 1944), p. XV.

Philosophic Fragments, and a third time in the *Postscript.* At the time of the publication of the latter two works it had become clear to Kierkegaard that the true enemy of existential thinking was Hegel, not Descartes.

From the outset and to the very end of the book, Johannes Climacus asserts emphatically that he is not a Christian, but a poor, lonely, existing individual who is passionately and infinitely interested in what it means to become a Christian, to be a Christian. Johannes Climacus had made the "leap" from the aesthetical to the ethical, but the more decisive leap from the ethical to the religious still lay ahead. In two later works (*The Sickness unto Death,* 1849; and *Training in Christianity,* 1850), Kierkegaard introduces an "Anti-Climacus," whose existence represents that final leap and who proclaims himself a Christian in the highest degree, a title never claimed by Kierkegaard himself.

In a precious passage the *Postscript* relates how Johannes Climacus became an existential thinker and an author. One Sunday afternoon, while he was sitting as usual at the café in the Frederiksborg Garden ("that wonderful garden where the King dwelt with his Queen") and smoking a cigar, it occurred to him that he had been a student for ten years and had not yet launched himself on any career, while many of his acquaintances had achieved prominence in the realm of thought or in practical life. They knew well how to become benefactors of mankind by making life easier by means of railways, omnibuses, and steamboats, or by telegraphy. Others benefited the age by facilitating public enlightenment by means of textbooks, compendia, and digests, and still others ("the true benefactors of the age") made both thinking and living ever so much easier by neutralizing all difficulties in the comfortable abstractions of Hegelian thought, in the "unity of opposites" of the Hegelian "System." What was there left to do for poor Johannes Climacus, who, though possessed of a keen wit, a sense of irony and humor, was only an idle dreamer? Meanwhile the cigar had burned down, and while he reflectingly lit another, Johannes was struck by the idea that everything had grown so easy that it had become intolerable, and that perhaps someone was needed to make things hard and complicated again. And so, "out of love of mankind, and out of despair at my embarrassing situation . . . , I came to regard it as my task to create difficulties everywhere."

Hegel had carried farthest the rationalistic attempt to understand man, the world, and God by way of a logico-dialectical mediation of contingency and necessity, finiteness and infinitude, matter and mind. He had described human personality and its faculties as a passing, historically conditioned and limited phase in the dialectic evolution of the World Spirit or Universal Reason. In this view the contents of human consciousness could be made intelligible only by first relating them to the totality of human personality, then relating this individual totality to the totality of the human species, and finally relating the human species to the Universal Idea or Reason which contained in itself the sum total of all things.

It is against this Hegelian submersion of the individual in the universal and his consequent virtual annihilation that Kierkegaard protests. He refuses to let the individual self be reduced to "a paragraph in a system." Both "the professor" who espouses such a system and the age which is willing to accept and acclaim it have forgotten what it means *to exist*. The authentically existing individual will always be infinitely interested in himself and in the realization of his destiny. That infinite interest Kierkegaard calls *the passion of human freedom*. This passion forces upon the individual a decisive *choice,* but a choice which always involves the incertitude of a *risk*.

Only the infinite can be desired and chosen with an infinite passion. And as the finite existence of the individual is constantly confronted with the infinite, his decision is a decision for or against the infinite, an absolute "either-or," all or nothing; it is a choice which makes or unmakes the individual, a choice in which he either truly "becomes what he is" or utterly fails to realize his authentic existence. Therefore, Kierkegaard concludes, truth is "subjectivity," that is, the highest degree of personal self-realization.

Subjectivity could, on the other hand, never become conscious of itself and of the decisive choice imposed upon it, if it were not confronted with an infinite "object," an Absolute Being. "The existence of a Christian," Kierkegaard wrote in his *Journals* in 1854, "is his contact with Being." The Christian, in other words, finds himself face to face with God at every moment, but in thus finding himself in his finiteness confronted with the infinite God and the infinite Good, he recognizes himself as a sinner. To exist, therefore, means for a Christian to be a sinner. But to exist as a sinner in the sight of God is not only the mark of human misery but simultaneously the mark of human grandeur: existence in the Christian sense is at once sinfulness and bliss, the annihilation of the individual before God and his rebirth in God, a rebirth which comes about in the supreme venture of a faith which passionately embraces the paradox of the eternal in the temporal, the divine that has entered into history, the Word that has become flesh. It is this faith which is "a scandal to the Jews and folly to the Gentiles."

Johannes Climacus, in the *Postscript,* is not directly concerned with the objective problem of the truth of Christianity; he rather proposes to deal with the subjective problem of the individual's relationship to Christianity. He asks, "How may I, Johannes Climacus, participate in the happiness promised by Christianity?" The first book of the treatise nevertheless deals with the possibilities of an objective approach, but it does so derisively and ironically, with scathing contempt, and with much special pleading for "subjectivity." In Hegel, the author asserts, the passionate question of existential truth does not even arise, since Hegelian philosophy has tricked individuals into becoming "objective." In making everything relative to the dialectic of the world-process Hegel has introduced into modern philosophy the sophistry of Protagoras and has thus made philosophy totally indifferent to the eternal happiness of the individual.

The second book, treating in a preliminary form of "the relation of the subject to the truth of Christianity" and "the problem of becoming a Christian," begins with an expression of gratitude to Gotthold Ephraim Lessing, the famous German critic and playwright of the eighteenth century. In Lessing's cautious rationalism and biblical criticism, Johannes Climacus believes he finds support for his own refusal to base the truth of Christianity on the approximative methods of history and philosophy. He surmises in Lessing the same existential concern with the Deity that stirs his own passionate self. And it seems to him that to the question which had been asked in the *Philosophic Fragments,* "Is it possible to base an eternal happiness on historical knowledge?" Lessing would have replied in the negative as emphatically as he.

In an essay entitled *Uber den Beweis des Geistes und der Kraft* (On the Demonstration of Spirit and Power), Lessing does not deny that the scriptural accounts of miracles and prophecies are as reliable as any other historical testimony, but he asks: "Why, seeing that these accounts are only reliable in this sense, is it proposed to make a use of them that demands an infinitely greater reliability?" Both Johannes Climacus and Lessing are thus opposed to admitting the possibility of a direct transition from the reliability of an historical account to an eternal decision or choice. But both (and Kierkegaard with them) are unaware of the fact that historical reliability rests qualitatively on the authority of "the witness" and that in the case of the scriptural accounts the authority of the witnesses constitutes a motive of credibility. For both Johannes Climacus and Lessing, on the other hand, any transition from the historically contingent to the eternally necessary involves a "leap": "This requires 'a leap,'" says Lessing in his last reported conversation with Friedrich Heinrich Jacobi, "a leap which I can hardly afford to make with my old legs and my heavy head."

Is Lessing speaking seriously or with his tongue in his cheek? Johannes Climacus is not too sure, but at any rate he wishes to believe that for Lessing, too, "all Christianity has its roots in the paradox, whether one accepts it as a believer, or whether one rejects it precisely because it is paradoxical."

A confirmation of his own thesis that the existing individual is constantly in process of becoming, that this process makes all earthly life insecure, and that this existential insecurity in turn finds its expression in the individual's infinite striving for Truth, is found by Johannes Climacus in Lessing's well-known saying: "If God held enclosed in His right hand all truth, and in His left hand the single, ever watchful striving for truth (though with the implication that I am forever bound to err), and if He were to ask me to choose, I should humbly seize upon His left hand and say to Him: Give, Father! Pure Truth is for Thee alone!"[21] Human existence, born of the infinite and the finite, the eternal and the temporal, is then this constant and infinite striving, and it is only the systematizing philosopher who forgets that he himself is such a striving and

---

[21] G. E. Lessing, *Werke* (Leipzig: Göschen, 1864), vol. II, p. 319. Though Lessing declares in this frequently quoted statement of the year 1778 that he would make his hypothetical choice "humbly," his words betray a kind of "humble" presumptuousness which foreshadows the *hybris* of Goethe's *Faust* and Nietzsche's *Übermensch*. For it is nothing but a romantically disguised presumptuousness when a higher value is attributed to an endless human striving ("forever bound to err") than to the possession of the noblest and highest Good. Johannes Climacus (and Kierkegaard) evidently read into Lessing's words a meaning that expresses their own restless striving for infinite Truth, a striving which rather fits the experience of St. Augustine, the God-seeker, than Lessing, the "Faustian" advocate of eternal becoming, who rejects the objective claim and testimony of revealed Truth. What Kierkegaard wanted to stress with his reference to Lessing was the dynamic transforming power of Christian Truth, a power which allows of no complacency and satiety on the part of the individual. But, upon closer analysis, Kierkegaard would certainly have been unwilling to pay the terrific and entirely unwarranted price stipulated by Lessing: to be "bound to err in perpetuity." The Danish thinker was acutely aware that the refusal to accept the Truth spelled the disintegration of the human spirit.

insecure human being, and that his purported explanation of life omits both the existential and essential factors.

The unique historical fact which for Johannes Climacus is not only approximately but infinitely and absolutely certain is the fact of his own existence. This existence includes both positive and negative elements, simply because it is a synthesis of the finite and the infinite, the eternal and the temporal. And it is precisely the perpetual presence of the negative, the contingent, the finite that opens the individual's eyes to the reality of the positive, the necessary, the infinite. Thus, while the existing subject is essentially eternal, *qua* existing he is temporal. *Qua* existing, his positive security is shaken, not only by the negations implicit in his temporality and historicity, but by the reality of *death,* which may terminate this individual earthly existence at any moment.

The preliminary inquiry into the subjective problem of how the individual can share in the eternal happiness promised by Christianity leads Johannes Climacus to the conclusion that (1) a logical system is possible; (2) an existential system is impossible. Reality is a "system" for God, but it cannot be or become a system for an existing human individual, because a system is something final, whereas an existing individual is a constant striving for finality and as such always *in via* or unfinished. The only truly systematic thinker therefore is *God,* who in His eternity is absolutely and forever complete and who also includes in Himself the fullness of existence. To an existing human individual, on the other hand, there applies an unconditional "either-or": he can *either* try to forget that he is an existing individual; and thereby he becomes a ridiculous figure, because existence continually holds him in its grip, whether he remembers this or chooses to forget it. *Or* he can concentrate his total energy on the fact that he is an existing individual; and thereby he realizes his authentic existence. In the "system" of the speculative philosopher (Hegel) subject and object, thought and being are identified, whereas in individual existence they are separated. The "philosophy of identity" thus revokes and abolishes individual existence in a pantheistic unity of opposites. And while the speculative philosopher, by identifying himself with Humanity at large, works under the illusion that he has made himself into something infinitely great, he has actually ceased to be anything at all.

Part Two of the *Postscript* adds further qualifications to the concept of "subjectivity." How does individual existence relate itself to the sphere of moral action? Johannes Climacus anticipates Nietzsche's critique of "historicism" when he asserts that an overdose of historical interest paralyzes the individual's spontaneity and renders him unfit for the exercise of his freedom. The great ethical personality, in devoting all his efforts to the task of self-realization, will in all probability also produce the greatest effects in the external world. But such a person remains from first to last conscious that, as these external results are not in his power, his primary concern must be with his own moral existence. A reformer may entice an entire generation with the zeal of his teaching, but he will nevertheless confound the meaning of existence unless his own life be an adequate expression of his doctrine.

Johannes Climacus compares moral freedom with Aladdin's miraculous lamp: when the lamp is rubbed, some spirit appears, but the Divine Spirit appears only when the lamp is rubbed in the right way, that is, with the highest ethical passion. In the fable of Aladdin the spirit of the lamp is the servant of the owner of the lamp, but whoever rubs the lamp of freedom with the highest ethical resolve becomes himself the servant of the appearing Divine Spirit, the Spirit of the Lord. An individual, bent on "doing good to others, even to the extent of improving the whole human race," may perhaps have the power to make the Spirit appear, but "I think the Spirit would then gather itself together in wrath and say to this individual: 'Stupid man! Do I not exist, I who am omnipotent? . . . Presumptuous man! . . . Do you possess anything of your own, whereof you might give to me? Or is it not a fact that even when you do your utmost you merely give back to me my own, and that sometimes you do it in a paltry enough fashion?' "[22] (The real task and the great venture of the individual is to dare renounce everything so as to become as nothing before God, that is, to become that particular existing individual, of whom God requires everything. Then — and this is the reward — "God can in eternity not get rid of you." Then only will the individual have gained his true significance as a human being, a significance in comparison with which every other significance becomes illusory.)

It is the simplest things in life, Johannes Climacus holds with Socrates, that are the most difficult to understand, and more difficult for the learned and cultured than for the unlettered. Why should

---

[22] Kierkegaard, *Concluding Unscientific Postscript*, p. 124.

any man take pride in his complex scientific knowledge and pursuits as long as he has not learned to understand the simplest? There is, for example, the problem of *death, the problem of what it means to die.* People know of course of death in a general and abstract way. They know that all men are mortal, and they may even have heard of the syllogism which infers from this general knowledge that Socrates, being a man, is mortal also. They know that there are several ways in which one may commit suicide; that one man dies in bed and another on the field of battle; that the hero usually dies in the last act of a tragedy, and that the dead are eulogized in funeral orations and remembered in the prayers of the living. But does this knowledge actually convey to them an understanding of the meaning of death? All my knowledge of "universal history" will likewise contribute very little to such an understanding. And yet my own death, which may occur some years hence or at any moment, is something which concerns me very directly and intimately. It is with me and remains with me as an existential insecurity that imparts a peculiar flavor to everything I am and everything I do or fail to do. It is an impossibility for an individual to gain an understanding of his own self unless this understanding includes the prospect of his own death. He has to ask himself whether the nonbeing of death invades his being as it invades and destroys the being of a dog, or whether his own death rather signalizes a victory of being over nonbeing. The answer — any answer — to this question will have a decisive transforming effect on his entire life.

Reflection on such questions concerning the simple and massive realities of life may teach a man what it means to think "existentially." He may learn that this kind of thinking is very different from the kind engaged in by the speculative philosopher who, seated at his desk, writes about what he has neither done nor ever intends to do. In existential thinking man's very soul is on trial, and his God-relationship is put to the test: If, for example, one who lives in Christendom goes to the house of God, the house of the true God, with the conceptually correct knowledge of God in his mind, and his entire being is not seized and permeated by this knowledge, he cannot be said to have true devotion. If, on the other hand, a man who, having been reared in an idolatrous society, and never having had an opportunity to form a correct concept of the true God, prays to the image of his idol with the infinite passion of his being: he, as much as lies in him and according to the lights given him, prays to the true God, although externally he worships an idol. In this way "subjectivity" may become a more truthful expression and acknowledgment of the truth than a detached nonexistential "objectivity."

Once upon a time, Johannes Climacus reflects, it was a very difficult thing to become a Christian, but nowadays it has become even more difficult because of the fact that in modern Christendom it is taken for granted that everyone is *eo ipso* a Christian. It has remained for the modern age and its speculative thinkers to say the most offensive, revolting, and stupid thing about Christianity: that it is true to a certain degree! Such a statement is worse than blasphemy: let a man be scandalized (as the Jews and Greeks were scandalized); let him despair of his ever becoming a Christian; let him shed his blood in persecuting Christianity; in his hatred there is passion, and there may also be a realization of the great force that Christianity is. But if he says: Christianity is true to a certain degree, he is not only wicked, but plainly stupid. "Whoever is neither hot nor cold is merely nauseating. . . . Had not Pilate asked 'objectively' what truth is, he would never have condemned Christ to be crucified. Had he asked subjectively, the passion of his inwardness, paying heed to what in the decision facing him he had *in truth to do,* would have saved him from doing wrong."[23] The persecutor may defend himself by saying: Yes, I have tried my best to exterminate Christianity; it had set my soul on fire, and I had perceived its hateful tremendous power. And the apostate may say: Yes, I was aware that if I gave Christianity my little finger it would take the whole of me, and I was unable and unwilling to surrender on such terms. But different from these is "the professor" who has explained Christianity and has come to the conclusion that it is true to a certain degree. "Which of these," asks Johannes Climacus, "must be regarded as in the most terrible position?" What makes a man a man is his God-relationship. Outside this relationship he may imitate in a puppet-like fashion human motions and emotions, but at the end of his earthly journey it would have to be said that the one essentially human thing had escaped him: he had taken no notice of God. "Idolatry is indeed a sorry substitute for God, but that God should be entirely omitted is still worse."

"Becoming objective" in the Hegelian sense means to sit down and contemplate in a nobly detached manner Christ's crucifixion, an event

---

[23] Kierkegaard, *Concluding Unscientific Postscript,* p. 206.

"which when it happened did not permit even the temple to remain objective, for its veil was rent in twain, nor the dead, for they rose from their graves; that is to say, what suffices to make even the lifeless and the dead subjective, that is now studied objectively by objective gentlemen."[24] This latter statement is found in an appendix to chapter two of the second part of the *Postscript,* in which Johannes Climacus offers his comments on two of Kierkegaard's earlier pseudonymous works (*Either/Or,* a Fragment of Life by Victor Eremita, 1843; and *Stages on Life's Road,* edited by Hilarius Bookbinder, 1845). The "stages," as described in the later of the two works, are the aesthetic, the ethical, and the religious. While *aesthetic existence* is said to be essentially sensuous enjoyment ("the path of perdition"), and *ethical existence* is essentially struggle and victory, *religious existence* is essentially suffering. In regard to this triple division Johannes Climacus now states that the three stages are intimately related to one another and that in their cumulative sequence they lead up to an unconditional "either-or." The characters who represent the three stages are all "consistent to the point of despair." But in the sphere of abstract thought there is no room for any such existential consistency, and Hegel is quite right when he abolishes the principle of contradiction in his system of purely abstract essences. He is wrong, however, when he extends this annulment to the categories of existence, because by so doing he annuls existence itself.

Could it be, asks Johannes Climacus, that the appearance and increasing popularity of these abstract thinkers has some deeper significance? "An epidemic of cholera is usually signalized by the appearance of a certain kind of fly. . . ; may it not be that the appearance of these fabulous pure thinkers is a sign that some misfortune threatens humanity, as for instance the loss of the ethical and the religious?"[25]

Chapter three of part two of the *Postscript* continues the examination of the existential thinker's relation to reality and proceeds to a critical analysis of the Cartesian *cogito, ergo sum.* The real subject, Johannes Climacus argues, is not the cognitive subject, and it is therefore impossible for an abstract thinker to prove his existence as a human being by the fact that he thinks. "How silly," objects the existential philosopher, "there is no question here of your self or of my self, but solely of a pure ego," an ego which has no real but only a conceptual existence, so that the supposed syllogism becomes

---

[24] *Ibid.,* p. 248. [25] *Ibid.,* p. 272.

nothing but a tautology: I think (abstractly), therefore I am thinking.

Abstract speculation in the Cartesian and Hegelian manner has led to an unspeakable impoverishment of life. People smile at the practices of mediaeval monasticism, but no monk in his cell and no hermit in the desert ever lived so unreal a life as is common in the modern day and age. For while the monk and the hermit abstracted or withdrew from the world, it never occurred to them to abstract or withdraw from their own selves. Human existence, while partaking of the Universal Idea, is not itself an Idea or a purely ideal existence. Abstract thought is thought without a thinker. Concrete thought is thought which is related to an existing thinker.

To be sure, existential thinking is not yet moral action, but it is pregnant with the possibility of moral action. It makes sense to speak of virtue in thought and sin in thought, because the external act is related to an internal moral decision. The good deed I intend to do is certainly not identical with the good deed I have done, but neither is the external act always a valid criterion of the moral disposition of the agent, "for the human being who does not own a penny can be as charitable as one who gives away a kingdom." The moral accent of an action therefore lies rather with the internal decision than with the external execution. But "the professor" takes a different view of the nature of these things: "For six thousand years human beings have loved and poets have sung the praises of love, so that now in the nineteenth century we ought to know surely what love is; our task is to assign to love, and especially to marriage, its proper place in 'the System' — for the professor gets himself married in distraction of mind."[26]

What then is the supreme ethical task of the individual? No more and no less than to become "an entire man." And "if ever so many blind and mediocre and cowardly individuals renounce their own selves in order to become something *en masse* . . . , Ethics does not bargain with them."[27]

Abstract philosophic idealism is a fashionable game that can be easily and comfortably played in the professorial chair and in the lecture hall, but not nearly so easily in real life, because reality and existence posit formidable obstacles. Philosophic idealism expresses on the highest level the peculiar depravity of the modern age: its "dissolute pantheistic contempt for the individual man." And why this

---

[26] *Ibid.,* p. 308.   [27] *Ibid.,* p. 309.

general flight from individuality? Because for an age that lacks religious and moral enthusiasm individual existence becomes a matter of despair; because in an age that has forsaken God and has therefore been forsaken by God, individual existence becomes the prey of fear, and individuals henceforth dare to live only *en masse,* clustering together in the vain hope that *collectively* they may again amount to something. While modern statesmen and politicians are apprehensive of an imminent breakdown of governmental institutions, the threat of a general spiritual bankruptcy is far more serious; for ideas have been emasculated and words have lost their meaning, so that controversies and disputes have become as sterile and ridiculous as common resolutions and mutual agreements.

Chapter four, finally, turns from Ethics to *Religion* and treats in particular of the problem of *how to become a Christian.* Once more the theme of the Hegelian "mediation" of opposites is resumed: mediation, Johannes Climacus states, is "a rebellion of the relative ends against the majesty of the absolute, an attempt to bring the absolute down to the level of everything else, an attack upon the dignity of human life, seeking to make man a mere servant of relative ends."[28] The absolute *"telos"* of man is forgotten, and whenever this happens, men, in a kind of mad frenzy, attach themselves with an absolute and idolatrous devotion to relative ends. For it is nothing but madness when a being whose nature is consecrated to the eternal clings with all the strength of his enthusiasm and passion to the precarious and transitory, to that which is nothing aside from that fleeting moment in which it is possessed, "a moment in time filled with emptiness."

The teacher and preacher of religion must forcefully call attention to this case of mistaken identity, to this confusion of means and ends, to this reversal of man's existential relationship to the absolute and the relative. The religious discourse must point out that it is not man's task to begin with the individual in order to arrive at the human race, but that both the beginning and the end lie with the individual.

Occasional Sunday glimpses into eternity are of no avail for the remaining six days of the week, for it is on the weekdays, in daily life and work, and in the living room, that the decisive Christian battles must be fought. The absolute demand, the absolute standard must be introduced into the life of every day and every hour and,

---

[28] *Ibid.,* p. 375.

though not specifically mentioned, it must always be present. Only if this is done can the conception of God or the conception of a promised eternal happiness transform the entire existence of the individual in relation to this idea. If man in his human frailty thus holds fast to the absolute concept of God at every moment of his life, God will console him in his suffering. And this will be his only consolation, as he can derive no comfort whatsoever from knowing what the crowd knows, from the knowledge of men "who have a shopkeeper's notion of what it means to be a man, and a facile gossipy notion at seventeenth hand of what it means to exist before God."

Has then a man who thus exists before God an eternal certainty? Yes, says Johannes Climacus, he has the eternal certainty that "whatever pleases God prospers in the hands of a devout man." But what is it that pleases God? "Is it this or that, is it this occupation that he ought to choose, this girl he ought to marry, this piece of work he ought to begin? Perhaps, and perhaps not." And precisely because he cannot be too sure in these matters the religious man should not be unduly concerned about these external things, but rather seek those things which always and indubitably please God: peace of mind and his soul's salvation.

The last chapter of the *Postscript* presents a "conclusion." Johannes Climacus recapitulates by repeating that his work has tried to point out the difficulties involved in becoming a Christian. But he adds that it has not been his intention "to make it difficult for laymen to become Christians. First of all, everybody can become a Christian; and, in the second place, it is assumed that everyone who says he is a Christian, and has done the highest things, is actually a Christian and has done the highest things. . . . Woe unto him who would be a judge of hearts."[29] The problem of the difficulties involved in becoming a Christian was raised for a different reason: it was raised because of the suspicion aroused by the ambition of an entire generation to go farther than Christianity would have them go, to aspire to the "objectivity" of speculative philosophy as the highest thing. But in the Christian order of things such a "forward" ambition is in reality a going backward. The claimed "objectivity" of "the System" expresses in reality merely disrespect, irreverence, and indifference. Christ loved the young man who could not make up his mind to give all his possessions to the poor and follow Him. This young

---

[29] *Ibid.,* p. 520.

man showed respect and reverence for that which he could not bring himself to accept. "Better, then, frank sincerity than lukewarmness."

Johannes Climacus is satisfied he has demonstrated that in the modern age it is not easier to become a Christian than it was in the beginning, that, on the contrary, it has become more difficult and will become more difficult from year to year, especially for the learned and cultured. For "the predominance of intellect in the man of culture and the trend towards the objective will in his case constantly cause resistance against becoming a Christian, and this resistance is the sin of the intellect: lukewarmness."[30]

A summary statement of the existential position and message of Johannes Climacus is contained in the final paragraphs of the *Postscript,* in which the author addresses the reader: "My dear reader! If I have to say it myself, I am anything but a devilish good fellow at philosophy, one who is called to direct it into new paths. I am a poor, individual, existing man, with sound natural capacities, not without a certain dialectical dexterity, nor entirely destitute of education. But I have been tried in life's *casibus* and cheerfully appeal to my sufferings, not in an apostolic sense as a title of honor, for they have only too often been self-deserved punishments, but yet I appeal to them as my teachers. . . . I remain what I myself concede is infinitely little. . . ." But "I am prepared for being an apprentice, a learner, which in itself is no small task. I do not give myself out to be more than this: fit to be able to begin in a higher sense to learn. If only among us there were to be found teachers! . . . The teacher of whom I speak . . . is the teacher of the ambiguous art of thinking about existence and existing. . . . And I cannot suppose that such a teacher could believe he had nothing else to do but what a mediocre teacher of religion in the public schools does: set a paragraph for me to learn every day and recite it the next day by rote. . . . In our time, when one says 'I know all,' he is believed; but he who says, 'There is much I do not know,' is suspected of a propensity for lying. . . . Ah, those ungodly and mendacious men who say, 'There is much that I do not know' — they get their just deserts in this best of worlds. . . ."[31]

Here the existential confession of Johannes Climacus ends, but for Kierkegaard himself the problem raised by his *alter ego* called for a

---

[30] *Ibid.,* p. 536.   [31] *Ibid.,* pp. 548–550.

more definite and unambiguous conclusion. In his life and in his last works he demonstrated that he was that teacher for whom Johannes Climacus looked in vain: the teacher who lived his doctrine, who "ventured far out," from the ethical to the religious; who found in divine Love the true identity of subjectivity and objectivity and in the divine "I Am Who Am" the *ens realissimum* for all existence. But before he could discover that ultimate Reality, Kierkegaard had to experience in full measure the depth of the abyss that separates subject and object, thinking and being. Before he could envisage the individual's relation to the infinite he had to experience human existence in its aspects of finiteness and temporality. Human individuality appeared to him as implying both sinfulness and freedom, and while human existence is isolated by individuation and wounded by sin, it is, by virtue of its freedom, capable of opening itself to the life-giving action of the Infinite Spirit, of making the consciousness of sin the first decisive step toward redemption. It is thus the consciousness of sin that opens the way toward *authentic existence* and that distinguishes the religious stage from the aesthetic and ethical stages of human life.

"Authentic" human existence is, however, never a real unity or synthesis but rather a togetherness of opposites, a paradoxical and ambiguous junction of contrasting elements whose vital tension finds its expression in existential *anguish* (Danish, *angest*). This anguish or anxiety, which is distinguished from *fear* by the indefiniteness of its object, is intimately linked with the finiteness and temporality of human existence and results from the fact that man is, as it were, suspended at the danger point between Being and nothingness. Existential anguish is thus generated by the mysterious contact of the temporal and the eternal, the finite and the infinite, the human individual and God.

The religious function which Kierkegaard attributes to existential anguish is most conspicuous in his concept of *faith*. For him as for Martin Luther faith, as has been pointed out, requires a "leap," a plunge into the paradox, a "fighting certitude," a certitude of the uncertain. Kierkegaard thus carries his abhorrence of "mediation" even into the very center of his theology, notwithstanding the fact that his own religious experience could not help but acknowledge the divine mediatorship in the person of Christ.

Kierkegaard's three "stages on life's road" culminate and find their existential fulfillment in the transcendent reality of the supernatural. Farthest removed from the religious existence is the aesthetic mode of life. In the *Diary of the Seducer* (*Either/Or* I) and in *In Vino Veritas* (*Stages* I) Kierkegaard discusses the existential relationship between the aesthetic and the ethical stage, while the interrelation between the ethical and religious stage is the major theme of *Fear and Trembling* and *Guilty — Not Guilty* (*Stages* III). The *Diary of the Seducer* is akin in spirit to the German romanticist Friedrich Schlegel's novel *Lucinde*, and Plato's *Symposium* provides the pattern for *In Vino Veritas*.

Johannes the Seducer shares with Julius, the hero of Schlegel's novel, the conviction that any "conventional" tie, such as engagement or marriage, is incompatible with "love." Johannes thus exemplifies the aesthetic stage of existence, its outward appearance of gaiety and its inward emptiness and despair. It is characterized by a perpetual seeking for moments filled with sensual enjoyment, moments which mutually cancel themselves out, so that the seeking and striving never end in fulfillment. The type of this kind of life is the Don Juan of Mozart's opera: he possesses "the passion of the infinite," but with him this passion attaches itself to the evil infinity of lustful moments which, as soon as they are attained, become shallow and empty and dissolve into nothingness. Don Juan's world is a world of appearance rather than of reality; it is the world of the constant betrayal, a world of nihilistic passion. In it no "existential choice" is possible.

Judge William, the ethicist, the main character in Part Two of *Either/Or*, enumerates five modes of aesthetic existence, differing according to the ascending scale of sophistication. These five modes are represented by the five guests attending the banquet of *In Vino Veritas*. Each of these evades reality and authentic existence by a passionate devotion to relative and transitory values, such as health, beauty, riches, honor, talent, and sensual pleasure. But inwardly every aesthetic mode of life is abysmal despair because finite man, without the vista of the eternal and the infinite, finds himself eventually face to face with nothingness.

Existential despair expresses the *reductio ad absurdum* of the aesthetic mode of life. But this "sickness unto death" may bear within itself its own cure. The shipwreck of the aesthetic life may mean the emergence and growth of the *ethical* life. The ethical is present, according to Kierkegaard, whenever an "authentic choice" becomes possible. And thus, if man *chooses* despair, he chooses himself in his eternal validity. The man who turns away from the glamour and lure of the external world toward the inwardness of his own self, gains with this decision his ethical existence. He learns to know himself and to form himself. The paradigm of this type of existence is Socrates.

The *ethical* stage is discussed at length in Part Two of *Either/Or,* in *Several Observations about Marriage (Stages* II), and in the *Post-script.* Judge William calls the ethical "the universal and as such divine." The ethical life has continuity; its amplitude encompasses hope and recollection, future and past, whereas the aesthetic life is torn to shreds in its attachment to the fleeting moment. Only the ethical life can also enduringly save and preserve aesthetic beauty. And only the ethical life, by virtue of its universality, can bind the individual to the rational and social order of things and thereby awaken in him the consciousness of his calling as a human being. "The great thing," says Judge William, "is not to be this or that, but *to be oneself,* and this is something which every man can if he wills." In choosing himself, man also ethically acknowledges an absolute distinction between *good and evil,* a distinction which Hegel, in his "metaphysical attempt to assassinate all ethics," had tried to "mediate."

But even the *ethical* structure of human existence is still seriously incomplete; although the ethical individual reaches out toward the universal, he is bound to remain within the confines of human immanence unless, by probing even deeper into the hidden layers of his selfhood, he discover in his *sinfulness* and his *faith* the bridges leading to divine transcendence: "An ethics which disregards sin is a perfectly idle science; but if it affirms sin, it is *eo ipso* well beyond itself."

The authentic individual is not only responsible to himself and his fellow men; he is, above all, responsible to God. The ethical mode of life is transformed into the *religious* mode of life when, with a contrite heart, man chooses himself as *guilty* and hopes for divine forgiveness: "There is an 'either/or' which makes a man greater than the angels."

The pseudonymous author of *Fear and Trembling* is Johannes de Silentio, and the principal character of the work is Abraham, the "Knight of Faith." The major theme is the clash between the ethical and the religious "stage." In obedience to God, in fear and trembling, in the detachment of infinite resignation the Jewish Patriarch surrenders his son to God, only to receive him back by virtue of the magnitude of his faith; for with God all things are possible. Thus the religious mode of life suspends or absorbs the ethical. By the "leap of faith" the *homo religiosus* imparts to the finiteness and temporality of his existence an infinite and eternal significance. Every aspect of his life is henceforth determined and permeated by his God-relationship.

In the concluding pages of the *Postscript* Kierkegaard designates the ethical stage as *"religion A"* and the religious stage as *"religion B."* When man stands in the self-annihilation of sinfulness before God, he is in the state of "religion A." In his finiteness he has entered into the crisis of existential despair, the "sickness unto death." But this spiritual sickness, unlike any physical deadly disease, does not have to terminate in death. It is a sickness which can be healed by "existential faith." "The despair," says Kierkegaard, "consists in that despairingly man wants to be himself; that the despair cannot get rid of the self." And when despair turns into its opposite, namely, *faith,* man gains his authentic selfhood in virtue of the Eternal and Infinite. He "leaps" into a nothingness in which the abyss of sin becomes the abyss of faith: "As long as you despair, you sink; as soon as you believe, you are carried by the power of God. . . . The weaker a man is, the stronger is God in him, and the stronger a man is, the weaker is God in him." In faith man has crossed the threshold that marks the entrance to "religion B." He has risked everything, surrendered everything, but he receives back infinitely more than he has been able to give: his union and communion with God's Love. He has gained "authentic existence."

*   *   *

Kierkegaard had started out with the contention that the deadly disease of the modern age was the divorce of thought and life. He had complained that philosophy had become highly abstract, lifeless, and artificial, and that life had been emptied of real content to such a degree that human beings no longer knew what it means "to exist." As for Christianity, it had become "a diluted, enervated sentimentality and a refined epicureanism." In relation to their imposing "systems" the philosophers were living "in a little shack nearby: They do not live in their magnificent edifices. Spiritually speaking, however, a man's thought must be the building in which he lives."

Existential thinking calls for the unity of thought and life. And the eternal pattern of this unity Kierkegaard sees in Christ. He therefore fervently pleads for the "following of Christ": "Thou, the holy pattern of the human race and of each individual, hast left a *footprint* so that, saved by Thy atonement, man might at any moment be willing to strive to follow Thee." Christianity is thus for Kierkegaard essentially *communication of existence*. It can only be taught "existentially," that is, by a teacher whose life has been informed and transformed by Christ.

CHAPTER THREE

MAN-GOD OR GOD-MAN?

THE CASE OF NIETZSCHE

I

THE tragedy of Friedrich Nietzsche (1844–1900) is partly revealed in a brief passage from a letter he wrote to his sister Elisabeth in the year 1886: "A man of spiritual depth needs friends, unless he still has God as a friend. But I have neither God nor friends." The weaknesses and fallacies of Nietzsche's thinking are rather obvious and have frequently been commented upon, while its strength escapes a superficial glance at his life and works and becomes visible only with a more penetrating insight into his complex personality. Never afraid of facing the ultimate consequences of his own ideas, even to the point of self-destruction, Nietzsche carried his relentless search for the plenitude of human existence beyond the shallow and fragmentary views of positivism and naturalism, notwithstanding the fact that these philosophic creeds often refer to Nietzsche's doctrines to support their own claims. But, as in the case of many an outstanding thinker, historical justice demands that one distinguish between those who profess to speak in Nietzsche's name, and the actual implications of Nietzsche's thinking and teaching.

Nietzsche had in fact very little in common with those among his self-styled disciples who in his name have tried to blacken and debase the image of man, with those who indulge in the glorification of the blind forces of instinct and in the calumniation of the spirit. There is no doubt that the motivating force in all of Nietzsche's negations was his passionate will for affirmation. It was his burning desire to remake human existence in its entirety that urged him on to tear down the actual structure of human society in order to build a better one on a truer foundation. His attacks on the hollowness and shallowness of nineteenth-century bourgeois morality were to clear the way for a new existential moral philosophy. Without deviation he maintained his conviction that philosophy is something more real and substantial than a harmless intellectual parlor game or a sophistic juggling of words and concepts, and he regarded as worthless any philosophic position that was not vouched for by the philosopher himself, even at the risk of his entire personal existence.

While Nietzsche intended a break with the past and its standards of value, his will to the future still throve on the spiritual and moral substance of the western tradition. His entire work is saturated with the greatness of the European past, and even his most violent condemnations vibrate with his secret admiration for the objects of his wrath. "How much has already been accomplished," says Zarathustra, "how rich is this earth in . . . good and perfect things, things well made and deeds well done!"

Aware of the crisis of Western civilization, and himself unafraid of the dangerous abyss which he had opened up with his thinking, Nietzsche plunged into that very abyss and demonstrated to his age with his own tragic fate the inescapable alternatives which lay before modern man. An *existential* thinker in the manner of Kierkegaard, Nietzsche valued more highly the "how" than the "what"; more highly the subjectivity of the thinker than the objectivity of the "system," more highly the growth of human personality than the conceptual integrity of abstract thought. In Nietzsche's view, it is the test of every genuine philosophy "that it be capable of forming a human being."

Nietzsche no more than Kierkegaard could accept J. J. Rousseau's theory of the natural goodness of man, the view that "all is good in nature" (*tout bien dans la nature*). Looking at man's historical reality, they both found something fundamentally wrong with human nature. "Man is something which must be overcome," says Nietzsche's Zarathustra. But while Kierkegaard, the Christian, called for a restoration of the religious integrity of human existence, Nietzsche, the neopagan, demanded that man be de-Christianized, because he thought that it was Christianity which had brought about the corruption of human existence. In the advent of *European Nihilism* Nietzsche sees a major symptom of the progressive disintegration of the Christian type of man. The impact of Nihilism, he contends, has created a unique historical situation, making it possible to prepare the way for the "higher man" or the "Super-Man" of the future. But the emergence of this "new man" he expects not from supernature, but from nature; more precisely, from man's preying instincts and urges and thus ultimately from the "Will to Power." This Will to Power manifests itself in two phases or stages: in the first it appears as Nihilism, while in the second it is "sublimated" into the will to create the "higher man."

The common element in the anthropological views of Nietzsche and Kierkegaard is their conviction that modern philosophy has shown itself unable to resolve the problems of human existence. The "systems" of pure thought, such as Hegel's dialectic idealism, do not correspond to reality and therefore cannot express reality. The two thinkers are thus in search of a philosophy which will affect and transform human existence decisively. Although they almost totally disagree in their ideas as to what constitutes authentic human existence, they are both existential thinkers in the sense that their thinking aims at arousing and creatively forming the human self. Both stand in uncompromising opposition to their age, and it is this opposition which animates and invigorates their philosophy.

While Kierkegaard mercilessly dissects and unmasks a "Christendom" that has become a mere external façade, a mere tradition or a mere habit, without vital actualization in the human individual, Nietzsche proclaims the definitive failure of Christianity on the historical proving and testing ground of European life and civilization. Both find the "paradox" of human existence in the mysterious union of the temporal and eternal, of nature and spirit, of the subhuman and the suprahuman, but whereas Kierkegaard calls upon the power of the Absolute Divine Spirit to raise man into his suprahuman dimension, Nietzsche calls upon the forces of the earth and of a purely this-worldly nature to restore wholeness and haleness to human existence. Thus Nietzsche's "new man" is the divine beast of prey, "the blond beast" whose untamed power and beauty he sees enhanced by the admixture of spirit. For Nietzsche the "Absolute Spirit" is identical with Hegel's *Weltgeist,* and like Kierkegaard he turns against this supreme abstraction of the Hegelian dialectic. He never relinquishes his intense interest in the life of the spirit and its evolution in history and civilization, but for him this evolution must proceed in the movement of *life* rather than in a sphere of abstract ideas; it must have its place in *existence* rather than in a realm of conceptualized essences.

Nietzsche's archenemy is the theorist whose thinking remains unrelated to his existence and thus becomes in the end hostile and harmful to life. The prototype of such a theorist is for him as for Kierkegaard the philosopher Hegel who in his metaphysics of abstract idealism established what Karl Löwith calls "an ambiguous unity of theology and philosophy, of religion and atheism, of Christianity and paganism." It seems to Nietzsche that Hegel thereby merely "procrastinated the advent of honest atheism." In Nietzsche this "honest atheism" becomes fully articulate. His "Zarathustra" voices both the praise and lament of the human soul that has abandoned God and has been abandoned by God. Zarathustra's songs are the lyrics of rebellious man who has taken it upon himself to evade the reality of God and who suffers ultimate shipwreck in the attempt to put the Man-God in the place of the God-Man. But, Nietzsche asks himself when he nears the end of his tragic odyssey, has his attack really harmed the cause of God and Christianity? His answer is in the negative: "For thus it has always been and thus it will always be: one cannot aid a cause more effectively than by persecuting it, by hunting it with all hounds. . . . This — I have done."

II

Friedrich Nietzsche was born at Röcken, a small village in the Prussian province of Saxony, as the descendant of two families whose heads had been Lutheran pastors for many generations. His sister Elisabeth, two years younger than Friedrich, became the philosopher's close companion, later on (during the final years of his insanity) his guardian, and his first (though not overly reliable) biographer. The father died of a brain hemorrhage when Friedrich was five years old, and the family moved to the city of Naumburg shortly afterward.

Friedrich grew up in the belief that, like his father and his male ancestors, he was destined for a life of intimacy with God as a Lutheran pastor. At the age of ten he entered the *Gymnasium* (humanistic secondary school) at Naumburg, and his mother was soon told that her son's superior intelligence made it advisable to send him to an institution of higher scholastic standing. Thus, at the age of fourteen, he was placed in the renowned *Fürstenschule* (princely school) of Pforta, a boarding school located near Naumburg which, in pre-Reformation days, had been a Cistercian monastery (*Monasterium sanctae Mariae de Porta,* 1132–1543). Schulpforta had preserved some of its ancient monastic austerity, combined with a spirit of humanism, strict moralism, and Prussian discipline.

During the years at Schulpforta, Nietzsche prepared himself conscientiously for the pastorate. His program of study included classical languages and natural, technical, and military sciences. "And, above all," he writes in his notebook, "religion, the foundation of all human knowledge. Great is the domain of knowledge, everlasting the search for truth." At the age of seventeen, meditating on the relationship of knowledge to life, he quotes Byron's verses,

> Sorrow is knowledge: They who know the most
> Most mourn the deepest over the fatal truth,
> The tree of knowledge is not that of life.

And though Nietzsche accumulates a surprising amount of knowledge, his mind remains restless and dissatisfied. Is there perhaps, he asks himself, a *tertium quid,* a higher synthesis beyond knowledge and faith? And he believes he has found that *tertium quid,* an escape and a refuge, in the realm of art and especially in music. He tells his horrified mother of his plan to devote himself to a musical career. But her violent protestations finally make him relinquish this idea.

The very thought, however, of choosing music in place of theology resulted from a gradually developing religious crisis which was never to be resolved as long as Nietzsche retained his sanity, and which even extended into the darkness of his mental night. The fact that he felt his religious faith slipping away filled him with growing apprehension, because he dimly realized the dangers that were lying ahead. "Ah, it is easy to destroy," he writes, "but to rebuild, to reconstruct, that is another matter!"

Nietzsche was still a student at Schulpforta when, with the advent of the summer heat, he experienced for the first time those violent headaches and visual disturbances which henceforth were to recur with increasing frequency and which periodically incapacitated him for his work as a writer and teacher. Meanwhile, the thought of his professional future continued to perplex and worry him. "It is a question," he wrote, "of finding that precise field in which I may hope to give my all."

At about the time Nietzsche departed from Schulpforta he wrote in the solitude of his study some verses which he addressed "To the Unknown God" and which gave striking expression to the questions which he pondered in his doubting and searching mind:

> Once more, before I part from here
> And turn my glance toward the future,
> I raise my hands in solitude
> To Thee, to whom I flee,
> To whom, in the depth of my heart,
> I have solemnly dedicated altars. . . .

I am His, even though to this hour
I have remained in the impious crowd.
I am His — and I feel the snares
Which drag me down, fighting,
And, whithersoever I flee,
Force me into His service. . . .

I wish to know Thee, God unknown,
Thou, who seizest my innermost soul,
Thou, who roarest through my life like a storm. . . .

And a second poem of the same period reveals a similar mood:

Unspeakably terrible Thou art!
Thou, huntsman behind the clouds! . . .
Thou — God unknown! . . .

Speak, at last!
What dost Thou ask of me, Thou thief of the great highways? . . .
Thou wantest me — all of me?

In mid-October, 1862, Nietzsche entered the University of Bonn on the Rhine. Out of filial respect for the wishes of his mother he matriculated in the faculty of theology, but he devoted considerably more time to the study of classical philology, which was taught at Bonn by two of its then most brilliant representatives, Otto Jahn and F. W. Ritschl. The latter, to whom Friedrich occasionally refers as "Papa Ritschl," became his first guide and adviser.

A sizable number of Nietzsche's fellow students pursued philosophic studies. Some were enthused with the idealism of Fichte, Schelling, and Hegel, while others were more interested in the materialism of Vogt, Büchner, and Feuerbach.[1] But neither of these fashionable trends could hold Nietzsche's interest. Many of the younger generation, following the lead of Auguste Comte and Feuerbach, believed they had discovered a substitute for Christianity in these thinkers' man-centered "humanism" and humanitarianism. Nietzsche would have none of that. For him "the happiness of the greatest number" and a minimum of suffering were not worthy goals of youthful aspiration. In a conversation with his friend Paul Deussen, who was a disciple of Schopenhauer, Nietzsche took exception to the theological "liberalism" advocated by David Friedrich Strauss in his *Life of Jesus* (1836): "The question is an important one; if you give up Jesus, you must also give up God."

Nietzsche seemed to be willing to accept his own advice with all

---

[1] Cf. the author's *Germany: 2000 Years* (Milwaukee: The Bruce Publishing Company, 1950), pp. 500–507 and p. 594 f.

its tragic implications. Evidence of his turning away from the religious beliefs of his family is contained in an essay written in 1862, two years before he left Schulpforta, and entitled *Fate and History*. Here he questions for the first time the traditional contents of Christian doctrine. Recalling the domestic influences in his religious upbringing, he violently turns against them.

"I departed from Bonn like a fugitive," Nietzsche wrote to his sister. He came to look upon this first year of his academic studies as the emptiest period of his life. After a brief stay in Berlin he followed Ritschl to the University of Leipzig, where the latter had accepted a chair in classical philology. Quite by accident he became acquainted with Arthur Schopenhauer's masterpiece, *The World as Will and Idea,* and from its perusal his life and thought received a new inspiration and direction. Even in Schopenhauer's negation of life and "the will to live" Nietzsche felt the dynamic force of life, a vitality which corresponded to his own thirst for life. He there and then adopted Schopenhauer as his teacher and spiritual "father."

What Nietzsche really sought and found in Schopenhauer's writings was not so much a rigorous philosophic and logical argumentation as inspiration and edification. Moreover, he thought he had discovered in Schopenhauer's doctrine a possibility of salvation without the necessity of a savior. In the Christian dispensation man cannot save himself. He is saved by divine grace through the mediatorship of Christ. According to Schopenhauer, on the other hand, man can save himself by his own unaided effort. By virtue of his own inner worth he can raise himself above the nullity and absurdity of existence. By the exercise of his own intellectual, moral, and aesthetic powers he can attain to truth, goodness, and beauty. These were intoxicating ideas for Nietzsche, the young scholar, who had become conscious of a strong driving force within his own self and who proudly felt that he could dispense with any divine aid. You are strong and noble in your aspirations, he told himself. The time is out of joint, but you may be able to set it and yourself right if only you remain true to the call of your innermost being. "What led me to Schopenhauer, was his atheism," he confessed. Christianity, he felt, "was lying on its death-bed." It had been transformed into a gentle moralism: "What remains is not 'God, Freedom, and Immortality,' but benevolence, a feeling of decency, and the belief that throughout the universe, too, benevolence and feelings of decency will become prevalent. We are witnessing the euthanasia of Christianity."

The same dynamic force which had fascinated him in Schopenhauer attracted Nietzsche to Bismarck, the Prussian *Junker:* "Unchained power, without moral restraint. How happy they are, how strong they are, these pure wills which are untroubled by the spirit!" And he was more than anxious to contribute his share to Bismarck's edifice of a new Prussia and a united Germany. Despite his deficient eye-sight he enlisted in an artillery unit of the Prussian army and relished the ascetic discipline of Prussian militarism. In the military service he found "an antidote to that paralyzing skepticism the effects of which we have only too deeply experienced."

This enthusiasm was, however, of short duration. Nietzsche soon bemoans the fact that an artillery soldier with literary tastes and interests is a very unfortunate creature. An injury incurred in a fall from his horse put an early end to his military exploits. In a letter to Ritschl he deplores the frailty of human beings "which is never as obvious as at the moment one gets a glimpse of a fragment of one's skeleton." After his recovery Nietzsche resumed his studies at the University of Leipzig.

The same spirit of action which Nietzsche admired in Bismarck he found, coupled with a strong aesthetic component, in Richard Wagner. He had heard of Wagner's stormy life as a composer, poet, publicist, and revolutionary, and he had read some of his works and listened to some of his music. At Leipzig, in 1868, he was personally introduced to the maestro. Their common high esteem of Schopenhauer became the starting point of their friendship.

Before the year was ended Ritschl one day surprised his pupil with the question, "Would you be interested in a professorship at the University of Basel?" Nietzsche had just completed his twenty-fourth year and had not yet obtained his doctoral degree. After some hesitation he accepted the offer. In view of his brilliant record the University of Leipzig conferred upon him the degree of doctor of philosophy without the usual examination.

Not far from Basel (in Switzerland), at Tribschen near Lucerne, lived Richard Wagner in his sumptuous "Villa." The main reason for Wagner's retirement to the idyllic solitude at Lake Lucerne was the scandal that had been caused by his *liaison* with Cosima, the daughter of Franz Liszt and the Countess d'Agoult, the wife of the famous pianist and conductor Hans von Bülow. Wagner and Cosima were married in 1870, after several children had been born out of wedlock.

For some years Tribschen became the center of Nietzsche's life. To his friend Erwin Rohde, the classical philologist, who had invited him to join him on a sojourn in Rome, the young Wagner enthusiast replied, "I too have my Italy; its name is Tribschen. . . . Believe me: Schopenhauer and Goethe, Pindar and Aeschylus are still alive." But back in Basel, separated from Wagner, he was immediately seized by a feeling of loneliness and by that gnawing anguish and spiritual unrest which were to haunt him for the rest of his life.

The gathering political clouds that heralded the approaching Franco-Prussian War (1870-1871) filled Nietzsche with dire apprehensions. His admiration for Bismarck turned out to be short-lived, after all. "There must not be war," he wrote shortly before the outbreak of hostilities, "the Prussian State would become too powerful." He was fearful of the threatening hegemony of Berlin, that detested metropolis, that "citadel of bureaucrats and bankers, journalists and Jews."

When Nietzsche had accepted the professorship at Basel, he had been required to renounce his German citizenship. But when he read of the heavy losses incurred by the German armies in their first victorious battles, he solicited and obtained from the Swiss authorities the permission to join the German ambulance corps. And in the ambulance service he visited the battlefields in France, displaying great courage and a singular devotion in aiding and comforting the wounded and the dying. His only regret was to be barred from active military service. "All my military passions are aroused, and I cannot satisfy them: the Swiss neutrality ties my hands," he jotted down in his notebook while the battle of Sedan was raging.

With the hospital train of the sick and wounded Nietzsche returned to Karlsruhe, the capital of Baden, himself a victim of dysentery and diphtheria. He eventually found refuge and shelter in the home of his mother and sister at Naumburg. The experiences of the war had made a proud German out of the "loyal Swiss." War, it seemed to him, exerts an ennobling influence on human beings. It makes them aspire to an ideal order of duty and responsibility. The Romanic nations of Europe, he argues, have been enfeebled by their utilitarianism. To Germany, the land of poets and soldiers, he assigns the task of assuming that leadership which the "decadent" nations have lost by default.

But even while Nietzsche thus indulged in wishful patriotic fancies, he was not blind to the fragility of his idol. Much that he observed in the new Germany was "human and all-too-human." He soon grew suspicious of the "patriotic delirium," of the brazen display of national boasting and pride, and he inveighed against the crude and stupid bureaucracy which he saw at the helm in his native Prussia. "Confidentially speaking," he wrote to his friend Gersdorff, "I am of the opinion that this modern Prussia constitutes a powerful and dangerous threat to human culture."

In February, 1871, Nietzsche's strength suddenly gave way: he was plagued by neuralgia, the usual visual disturbances, persistent vomiting, and sporadic attacks of jaundice. Upon his urgent appeal Elisabeth arrived from Naumburg. Together they journeyed to Lugano in the Swiss Ticino. In the mail coach in which they crossed the St. Gotthard Pass, Nietzsche made the chance acquaintance of Mazzini, the champion of Italian liberalism and of a united Italy, who quoted to him some lines of Goethe which remained strongly engraved in his mind: "We must wean ourselves away from all half-heartedness, to live resolutely in wholeness, fulness, and beauty."

Nietzsche recovered rapidly at Lugano and spent two happy months in the Italian part of Switzerland. Spring came, the war was over, and in April the young classical scholar returned to Basel to continue his research on the tragedies of the ancient Greeks, in which he believed he recognized the prototypes of the Wagnerian music-drama.

Nietzsche held the chair of classical philology at the University of Basel from 1869 to 1879. In 1870, as has been pointed out, his academic work was interrupted by his participation in the Franco-Prussian War, and later on, especially in 1875, he had to take leaves on account of his poor health, until he was finally forced to resign from his position for the same reason.

Toward the end of 1870 Wagner had begun pondering the plan of a novel theater or *Festspielhaus* at Bayreuth in Bavaria. When these ideas were taking concrete shape, the composer had to leave Tribschen for Bayreuth. When Nietzsche arrived at Tribschen in April, 1872, Wagner was already on the move. The "idyl of Tribschen" was ended.

III

The Birth of Tragedy from the Spirit of Music (1871), Nietzsche's first major work, grew out of some preliminary sketches on Greek philosophy and civilization. It was in the first place an attempt to trace the development of Greek tragedy from the ritualistic choral dances of the Dionysos cult to its classical height in Aeschylus and

Sophocles and, further on, to its decline in Euripides, and to demonstrate that in Greek tragedy two different and even antagonistic concepts of life and art fused. Beyond this immediate purpose the book
presented a new interpretation and evaluation of Greek antiquity.
Third, it was an attack on the "Socratic spirit" in its ancient and
modern manifestations and contained a highly original exposition of
the "Dionysian" philosophy of life. Last but not least, it was a
propagandistic manifesto in favor of Wagner, whom it pictured as the
savior and renovator of modern civilization.

Nietzsche's presentation dealt not primarily with the historical
aspects of the evolution of Greek tragedy. He adopted from Schopenhauer the distinction between the plastic arts (architecture, sculpture,
painting) and music, and he derived from these two types of art two
fundamentally different vital human experiences and attitudes, which
he designated as "Apollonian" and "Dionysian." These resemble each
other in only one point: they both lift man above the level and the
concerns of everyday life. The plastic arts, according to Nietzsche, owe
their existence to human imagination. They correspond to the "Apollonian" experience, in which man seeks an escape from the harshness
of reality in a realm of beautiful forms. The objects of reality are
changeable and transitory, but the Apollonian artist transforms and
transfigures these objects by liberating them from their limitations
and their contingency, thus raising them above the flux of time into
a realm of lasting validity. The Dionysian artist, on the other hand,
is possessed of an intoxicating enthusiasm which in its turn defies
and transcends the finiteness and narrowness of external reality. He
loses his own individuality and becomes one with all mankind and
with the vital forces of the universe. "Dionysian art" is not subject to
the principles of beauty and therefore not concerned with the creation
of pleasing and agreeable forms. It is an art which in its violent
expressiveness manifests both human pain and irresistible passion.

It was Nietzsche's conviction that these two basic human experiences
were reflected and embodied in early Greek culture and that they
finally blended in the art form of Greek tragedy, in which the Dionysian *ecstasis* appears solidified and sublimated in Apollonian form.

Nietzsche accordingly finds the origin of Greek tragedy in the
Dionysian chorus. The ecstatic choral dance gave birth to the tragic
"mythos," and the tragic *mythos* in turn assumed on the stage the
form of a tragic play. But while the speakers or actors expressed themselves in Apollonian language, there remained beneath the smooth

surface of the spoken dialogue the dark and irrational sentiments expressed by the chorus, the irrationality of Dionysian intoxication.

At the very moment, however, when Greek tragedy and Greek civilization had achieved their towering height, the spirit of Greek "rationalism" emerged, a spirit of skeptical doubt which no longer understood the Dionysian experience, which no longer had any organ for the mysterious and tragic horrors of human existence. Incapable of recognizing any truth behind and beyond soberly observed facts, this new rationalism and skepticism destroyed both Greek mythology and Greek tragedy. The "moralism" of Socrates and the "rationalism" of Euripides were incapable of that enthusiasm and that sympathy which more sensitive Greek minds had experienced in viewing the undeserved and unjust suffering and death of the tragic hero.

Modern opera, like ancient Greek tragedy, was born, according to Nietzsche, out of a Dionysian experience of life. The modern listener completely misunderstands the nature of operatic music when he demands that its artistic form be clearly intelligible and that the music be subordinated to the text. The exact reverse was true in early Greek tragedy: music was the dominant, vital element, and the words and action served only as media to convey the musical mood.

But the most dangerous embodiments of the destructive "Socratic spirit" Nietzsche finds in pure rational knowledge and pure empirical science. Schopenhauer, says Nietzsche, had already pointed out the limitations of both rational and scientific knowledge and had shown that neither can lead to the comprehension of the ultimate ground of Reality. As soon as the conviction of these limitations of knowledge will have become more general, a new evaluation of life will ensue: life will then be viewed and understood *artistically*. The tragic *mythos* will be revived, and out of the spirit of *music* a new form of tragedy will be born. Liberated from rationalistic and scientific complacency, *culture* will perhaps once more reach true greatness and reveal new insights into the mysteries of Reality.

The basic premise of Nietzsche's argument was his thesis of the prevalence of pain, suffering, and evil in human life, a thesis which both Schopenhauer and Martin Luther had taught him. Luther in particular had asserted that human nature was hopelessly perverted and corrupted by the consequences of original sin. But while Nietzsche no longer accepted the Lutheran view on original sin, he still retained the conviction of the actual depraved condition of human nature. Familiar through personal experience with the pain and suffering of a "fallen" state of existence, his philosophy set out to answer the ancient outcry of man for redemption and salvation.

The Christian answer to the human call for redemption was no longer acceptable to Nietzsche. The answer of Schopenhauer, on the other hand, he still accepted, though with qualifications. According to Schopenhauer, the purpose of tragedy was "the presentation of the horrible aspects of life. . . . It presents on the stage the nameless pain and grief of mankind, the triumph of iniquity, the mocking dominion of chance, and the irretrievable fall of the just and the innocent. And in this lies a significant hint as to the actual condition of the world and of existence. Tragedy reveals the inner conflict of the will with itself, a conflict which here, on the highest level of its objectivation, manifests itself in the most frightful way."[2] Tragedy depicts, as it were, the sadness and meaninglessness of human existence, and in his own destruction the hero overcomes the "will to live" and reaches that timeless Reality which lies outside and beyond life's contingencies. Some tragedies, Schopenhauer admits, do not go that far. The hero sometimes refuses to be intimidated: he clings to the "will to live" and dies without remorse. It is only in the greatest tragedies that the hero attains to a complete detachment from the "will to live." Tragedy thus represents for Schopenhauer the sublime possibility of art to illustrate the absurdity of existence. If man has not attained as yet to that knowledge by his personal suffering, he will attain to it by his compassion with the suffering tragic hero.

But Schopenhauer's way of "self-redemption" by an escape from the "will to live" no longer held much attraction for Nietzsche. He resented in particular the idea of complete detachment, of ascetic renunciation and resignation. The Greeks, he argued, were in an extraordinary way capable of suffering, but as soon as they found themselves face to face with the extreme cruelty of life they were in danger "of submitting to a yearning for a sort of Buddhistic negation of the will. They were saved, however, from this danger by art: through the medium of their art they made life triumph over death."

Finally, Nietzsche offered a radically new interpretation of Schopenhauer's concept of the "Thing-in-itself." For Schopenhauer the Thing-in-itself is in a permanent state of quiescence, unmoved by desire and untouched by the tempests of existence. Nietzsche, on the other hand, placed the root of life's unrest and suffering in the Thing-in-

---

[2] Arthur Schopenhauer, *The World as Will and Idea*, I, § 51.

itself. For Schopenhauer suffering attached only to the world of phenomena, and man could escape suffering by turning either to the world of Ideas or to the realm of the Thing-in-itself, by either seeking a temporary refuge in the contemplation of art and beauty or a permanent release from the "will to live" in the eternal silence and tranquillity of "Nirvana." For Nietzsche it is the Thing-in-itself that suffers from an intolerable "tension," and this tension can only be resolved and overcome in the world of phenomena, in a restless creative activity which transforms itself into ecstatic rapture. In "Dionysian rapture" man becomes one with ultimate Reality: "For short moments we actually *are* ourselves that aboriginal Being and share in its boundless desire and lust of life." Dionysos is thus the creative spirit of the world, the artist-god, and human beings, like the rest of creation, are only the pictures or images he paints, appearances he calls into existence to destroy them again at will. But this process of perpetual creation and destruction is also the perpetual healing process of the festering wounds in the innermost recesses of existence. The world and human life have their sanction and justification not in any moral norms, but in Dionysos, who creates and destroys for his own pleasure and enjoyment. The world and human existence are justified no more and no less than the playing of a child. To such a play the criteria of "good" and "evil" do not apply.

Dionysos became thus for Nietzsche a substitute for the discarded God of his childhood, and *art* had to fill the vacated place of a lost paradise of heavenly bliss. *The Birth of Tragedy* presented a philosophy of life that was inspired and transfigured by that ancient artist-god of Thracian-Phrygian origin in whose cult the powerless and lonely individual might experience the raptures of the "Will to Power."

The Birth of Tragedy was received enthusiastically by Nietzsche's friends, especially by Wagner. But the author waited anxiously for the reaction of his fellow philologists. It finally came in the form of a polemic pamphlet, written by Ulrich von Wilamowitz-Moellendorff, a young scholar who, like Nietzsche, was an alumnus of Schulpforta and who was destined to become one of the most prominent classical philologists of Europe. He answered Nietzsche's challenging book with an indignant protest. "Here," Wilamowitz wrote, "I find the negation of the long tradition of western knowledge and science. Here the truths of philosophy and religion are wiped out, so that a wishy-washy pessimism could in self-created solitude exhibit its bittersweet face. . . . And all this in order to make us kneel in the dust before the idol of Richard Wagner." Nietzsche, the author of the pamphlet asserted, had shown himself unfamiliar with the work of some of the greatest classical philologists; he had shown no regard for historical facts: "What nest of nonsense is your book, Herr Nietzsche! ... Do you realize how you have disgraced Schulpforta, your intellectual mother? ... Let him step down from his academic chair; let him gather at his knees tigers and panthers, but not the younger generation of German philologists!"[3]

Nietzsche showed himself unwilling to accept the criticism of Wilamowitz at its face value and immediately imputed personal motives to the author. But the majority of classical philologists sided with Wilamowitz, and the controversy destroyed Nietzsche's reputation as a philologist once and for all.

In the winter semester of 1869–1870, and again in the summer of 1872, Nietzsche had lectured on the Pre-Socratic philosophers. In preparing these lectures for publication he wrote two prefaces in which he expressed the conviction that "in every philosophic system, no matter how false and transitory it may be, there is always something imperishable: it is part of the unique personality of the philosopher." It is from this personalistic (or "existential") point of view, he explained, that the history of Greek philosophy ought to be written. In this manner he had himself studied the works of the early Greek philosophers.

Nietzsche claimed that the study of Heraclitus had confirmed him in his view that war was the father of all things; that change, tension, and strife reveal the secret of Reality. Heraclitus saw in Fire the original substance of the world (cf. p. 19 ff.), the permanent reality which underlies all the changes of visible existence, the *One* which is the substrate of all multiplicity, the Being which underlies all becoming. This aboriginal Fire, which Heraclitus calls the divine Principle, is dynamic, not static: it moves in opposite directions, and in its dynamic movement it creates those tensions and conflicts which find their visible expression in the phenomena of change and evolution. As Nietzsche sees and interprets this Heraclitean idea, it means "a becoming and passing away, a building and tearing down, without any moral responsibility, in eternal innocence. ... As the child and the artist play, so plays the eternally living Fire; it innocently builds and destroys."

---

[3] Ulrich von Wilamowitz-Moellendorff, *Zukunftsphilosophie,* pp. 23 and 32.

Parmenides of Elea, in diametrical opposition to Heraclitus, had described Reality as a huge, homogeneous, immutable sphere; as pure being, from which all becoming is excluded. By degrading and belying the data of sense perception, argued Nietzsche, Parmenides had destroyed the integrity of the intellect itself and encouraged the fallacious dualism of spirit and matter, mind and body: a radical division which, especially through Plato's fault, became "the curse of philosophy. Truth from then on was supposed to reside only in the most colorless and abstract generalities. . . . And by the side of such a lifeless truth was seated the philosopher, himself bloodless like an abstraction and enveloped in the webs of empty formulas."

On the whole it may be said that though there is much profound insight in Nietzsche's interpretation of Greek thought and life, it represents above all a projection of the needs and wants of his own discordant mind into the objects of his research.

IV

Toward the end of the year 1872 the problems of his own age and in particular the problem of contemporary culture began to weigh more and more heavily on Nietzsche's thinking. He saw a Europe drunk with its plenitude of material goods; he saw a Germany delirious with her recent total victory over France. But underneath this glittering surface he believed he could discern the symptoms of an approaching new barbarism. And he felt that it had become necessary to restore to this modern age a sense of culture, of virtue, and of passion. What higher mission and vocation could there be for a genuine philosopher? He felt the call to become for his age, as it were, an anti-Socratic Socrates.

Suffering from severe headaches as well as from eye and stomach trouble, Nietzsche found writing more and more difficult, but his mind worked feverishly, and his notes accumulated. In a short dramatic fragment, entitled *Oedipus,* he faces life as Oedipus faced the Sphinx. "My heart cannot believe that love is dead," Oedipus-Nietzsche exclaims; "it is incapable of sustaining the horror of this most solitary of solitudes."

At Easter, 1873, Nietzsche took a two weeks' vacation and departed for Bayreuth. There he learned that things were going badly for Richard Wagner. Lack of funds threatened to force the suspension of the construction of the *Festspielhaus.* Nietzsche finally decided to aid Wagner's cause with the publication of a pamphlet.

A few weeks before his visit to Bayreuth, Cosima had called Nietzsche's attention to a new book by the liberal Protestant theologian David Friedrich Strauss, entitled *The Old and the New Faith*. Wagner himself had referred to it and condemned it as a symbol of the evil times. Strauss seemed to be just the kind of adversary Nietzsche desired. He was a popular writer who enjoyed a high reputation among the members of the German bourgeoisie. In his youth he had written a *Life of Jesus* (1836), in which he had tried to prove that the Gospels were nothing but a chance accumulation of contradictory and questionable data. That book had established Strauss's fame, and he had soon assumed pontifical airs. The new book, written at the age of sixty-four, was a further exposition of his liberal-rationalistic creed.

In *The Old and the New Faith* Strauss asked four questions: (1) Are we still Christians? He answered with an unequivocal "No." (2) Do we still have a religion? This question was answered in the affirmative. (3) How do we understand and interpret the world? The answer was given on the basis of Strauss's shallow optimism and was couched in the terms of the scientific theories of the age. (4) How can we restore "order" to our lives? The answer was that of a respectable, moderately conservative and patriotic bourgeois philosopher, who had lost faith in the traditional moral and spiritual values of the Western world, but who hesitated to renounce them *in toto* and therefore merely diluted and rationalized them.

Nietzsche saw in Strauss the prototype of a "bourgeois philistine." In former times, he stated, the philistine was at best tolerated, but in the nineteenth century he has at last come into his own. His triumph has gone to his head: he has become a fanatic, the founder of a "new religion," and Strauss is the prophet of this new religion of Philistinism.

Nietzsche's pamphlet appeared in 1873 under the title *Thoughts out of Season*. Strauss died a few months after its publication, and Nietzsche was disconsolate because he remained convinced that his essay was the major contributing cause of Strauss's death.

The anti-Strauss and pro-Wagner essay began with an attack on the culture of the "new Germany," a prelude to the personal attack on Strauss, who appeared to Nietzsche as the typical representative of this new type of *"Kultur."* On the basis of his own Dionysian, antirational, and antimoralistic philosophy, Nietzsche indicted Strauss's complacently optimistic belief in progress and generally condemned the moralistic and rationalistic tendencies of modern European "humanism."

Referring specifically to Germany's recent victory over France, Nietzsche asserted that a great victory is always a great danger, because human nature is so constituted that it finds it harder to retain its integrity in triumph than in defeat. He claimed that the illusory belief in the superiority of German *Kultur* threatened to convert the German victory into a total defeat; it threatened to extirpate the "German mind" for the greater glory of the "German Empire."

The book of Strauss, Nietzsche contends, is the confession of a cynical philistine, and "to the philistine, even a Straussian metaphysics is preferable to that of Christianity." He calls the Straussian "pocket-oracle" a combination "of impudence and weakness, of daring words and cowardly concessions," and its great success seems to him symptomatic of the general decline of scholarship. The "scientific man" with his frantic haste and his total disregard for the ultimate problems of human existence (the questions, "Wherefore?", "Whither?", and "Whence?") appears to him as a strange and monstrous paradox. Our scholars, he asserts, have become totally forgetful "of the most vital question of all — the 'Wherefore' of their own work . . . and their painful ecstasies." And the essay concludes with the accusation that the German "culture-philistine" has altogether lost the healthy and manly instinct for what is real and what is right. "And yet," Nietzsche exclaims pathetically, "what can one lonely individual do against a whole world, even supposing his voice were heard everywhere?"

Nietzsche's work on a continuation of his *Thoughts out of Season* was interrupted by a call of distress from Bayreuth. Things were moving toward a crisis there, and Wagner thought that only an appeal to the German public could avert the complete failure of the Bayreuth enterprise. He wanted Nietzsche to draft such an appeal, and the philosopher accepted the assignment. At the end of October, 1873, he read his *Appeal to the Germans* to the assembled chairmen of the German Wagner *Vereine*. But Nietzsche's listeners considered his language too undiplomatic and provocative. Some called his draft a "monkish sermon." The author thereupon withdrew his text and abandoned the idea.

The second part of *Thoughts out of Season,* entitled *On the Usefulness and Harmfulness of History in Relation to Life,* was published in February, 1874. Nietzsche's main thesis stated that an excess of historical knowledge endangers and maims the spontaneity of life. He distinguishes three types of historiography or historical method: the *monumental,* the *antiquarian,* and the *critical.* Each of these can serve life or stifle life; each of them can be useful or harmful. *Monumental historiography* is interested primarily in the great men of the past, those heroic characters who are as beacon lights to future generations. By presenting exemplars of courage and valor it stimulates human hope and aspiration. *Antiquarian historiography* satisfies the needs of people of a conservative and reverent nature. It comforts and enriches human beings, enlarges their horizons, filling the void of the present with the opulence of the past. In understanding the history of their native lands, cities, and towns they learn to understand their own selves. They identify themselves with the spirit of the houses, the families, the manners and customs of their ancestors. In their lives they find inspiration and meaning for their own.

In meditating thus on the past Nietzsche may have thought of the traditional family life and the devout Christian spirit of his own Saxon forebears. Though he had left the land and abandoned the faith of his fathers, he still felt the ancient ties. He knew only too well that what real substance there was in his own life had its wellsprings in that venerable past. But he was equally sure that for him there was no possibility of turning back: he had to go forward. And thus he envisaged a *third* kind of historical understanding which was to justify this refusal to turn back: a *critical historiography,* of which he hoped that it would liberate him from those revered and dreaded bonds of the past.

Antiquarian historiography, Nietzsche felt, might easily degenerate, once the springs of piety and reverence were dried up. The learned habit might then turn the scholar into a "mad collector," who knows of no higher ambition than the scraping together of the fragments of the past. And thus the *critical* approach to history might become mandatory: the sifting and evaluating judgment of the past. But who is to sit in judgment and pronounce sentence? No other than Life itself, Nietzsche answers his own question, "that dark, driving force that insatiably desires only itself" and whose judgment is always unmerciful and unjust.

But the *critical* method, too, is beset with specific dangers of its own, for the knowledge of the extent to which we ourselves are heirs of the past, of its glories as well as of its errors, perversions, and crimes, may have a paralyzing effect on our own vital efforts. This danger, Nietzsche argues, can only be avoided by those who succeed in liberating themselves from the constraints of the past by developing, as it were, a strong, self-reliant "second nature."

No matter, concludes Nietzsche, to which of the three methods of historiography we give preference, one thing is certain: We cannot do without historical knowledge, even though it harms us at times and may threaten to destroy our intellectual substance and moral spontaneity. But this need of historical knowledge should not make us blind to the dangers inherent in an oversaturation with history. And, it seems to Nietzsche, modern scholarship and research has largely succumbed to these very dangers: "Modern man carries within himself an enormous heap of indigestible rocks of knowledge which occasionally rattle in his body. . . . And the rattle reveals the most striking characteristic of modern man, the presence of something inside to which nothing external corresponds; and vice versa." Knowledge, in short, has lost its power of transforming and elevating human lives, and real culture has been replaced by some vague knowledge *about* culture: "We moderns have nothing of our own. We are only noteworthy for filling ourselves with foreign customs, arts, philosophies, religions, and sciences; we are wandering encyclopedias."

A purely encyclopedic knowledge of historical and scientific facts represents, according to Nietzsche, a mortal threat to the integrity of human existence and human culture because it leads to an attitude of irony and cynicism in regard to everything that has a claim to greatness and nobility. To counteract this tendency, he demands that historical knowledge be subordinated to life and that the individual be taught to live "unhistorically." Only in this way, he believes, can the modern scholar again learn to distinguish between essential and nonessential truths; only thus will he cease to be "a cold demon of knowledge" and acquire again a strong sense of justice and a vital desire for truth. Historical "objectivity," Nietzsche claims, is often merely a disguise for that cold detachment which remains supinely indifferent to all values. Genuine historical knowledge requires nobility of character and a profound understanding of the ultimate problems of human existence: "Only he who is building the future has a right to judge the past. And a hundred such men — educated against the fashions of today — would suffice to give an eternal quietus to all the noisy sham education of this age." As man is creative only in love, in an unconditional faith in what is perfect and what is right, everything which falls short of such a love and such a faith "cuts at the very root of man's strength: he must wither away."

There is good reason for the modern boasting about the triumphs of science, says Nietzsche. But would a life ruled by science be of

much value? And can the "scientific" study of history be conducive
to "historical culture?" It rather seems that the "scientific" approach
merely makes the student lose every feeling of admiration and wonderment. Since he has learned that things were different in every age,
he grows skeptical regarding all ideas and all moral values, and he
pays less and less heed to the status and stature of his own self. He
is filled to the brim with historical and scientific "facts": "You need
only shake him, and wisdom will rattle down into your lap; but the
wisdom is rotten, and every apple has its worm." And thus "solid
mediocrity becomes more and more mediocre; science becomes more
and more 'useful.' . . . True enough, the progress of science has
been amazingly rapid during the past few decades; but look at the
savants, those exhausted hens. They are anything but 'harmonious'
natures: they merely cackle more than ever before, because they lay
eggs oftener. The eggs, however, are getting smaller and smaller,
although their books get bigger and bigger."

The modern "historical man," says Nietzsche, is a strange phenomenon: he has renounced all power in heaven and on earth merely to
become an idolatrous worshiper of *power as such*. Thus he is prepared to kneel in the dust before the "power of history" and nod
"yes" in the end, like a Chinese doll, to the power of government,
of public opinion, or of a mere numerical majority. It is only the
"virtuous man" who even in this modern age will rise against "the
blind force of facts, against the tyranny of the actual. . . . He always
swims against the waves of history, whether it be by fighting his
passions (the nearest brute facts of his existence) or by pledging
himself to honesty amidst the glittering nets spun round him by
falsehood."[4]

And who is the real power behind the throne of all "historical
power," asks Nietzsche? It is "the prince of this world," the great
master of "success" and "progress." The modern world has become
very skillful in giving new names to things, and it has even tried to
baptize the devil. Is this not truly an hour of great danger? "O you
proud European," Nietzsche exclaims, "are you not mad? Your
knowledge does not complete nature: it only kills your own nature.
. . . On the sunbeams of your knowledge you climb toward heaven —
but also down toward chaos. . . . The ground slips under your feet

---

[4] Nietzsche, *The Use and Abuse of History*, translated by Adrian Collins (New York:
The Little Library of Liberal Arts, No. 11, 1949), p. 61.

into incertitude; your life has no longer any stay but spiders' webs which every new stroke of your knowledge tears asunder."

In his conclusion Nietzsche frankly admits that his own treatise exhibits and illustrates the maladies of the modern age and of modern man. It is the work of a "weak personality"; it is immature and full of critical exaggerations; it wavers between irony and cynicism, between pride and skepticism. And it can hardly be otherwise, he contends, since a young modern scholar is to a large extent the product of the kind of education he has received. The goal of modern education is, however, no longer the liberally educated man, but the "scientific man," who takes his stand apart from life. The young scholar thus develops into a precocious and sophisticated "babbler on Church, State, and Art; the sensorium that receives a thousand impressions; the insatiable belly that yet knows not what real hunger and thirst is. An education with such an aim and such a result is against nature." It is thus no wonder, according to Nietzsche, that modern man "crumbles and falls asunder," that "his whole being is divided," and that he is "sown with abstract concepts as with dragon's teeth." He has become a lifeless and yet uncannily agile manufacturing plant of concepts, a "thinking substance" who may justly apply to himself the Cartesian *Cogito, ergo sum* but who has long forgotten what it means to say, *Vivo, ergo cogito:* I live, I am — therefore I think.

The antidote against the "historicist" disease is for Nietzsche the "unhistorical" and "suprahistorical" attitude. He calls *Art* and *Religion* "suprahistorical powers" because they turn the eye away from the process of becoming and impart to existence the character of the permanent and the eternal. *Science,* on the other hand, must of necessity feel antagonism to art and religion because the "scientific" attitude sees everywhere only the historically actual and nowhere the everlasting permanence of Being.

Nietzsche's essay ends on a hopeful note. He sees in the youth of Europe the vanguard of a happier and sounder humanity of the future. Though the younger generation may be raw and intemperate, it calls its own a brave, unreflecting honesty and the consolation of a great hope. True, these young people "will be more ignorant than the 'educated' men of the present age: for they will have unlearned much . . . ; but at the end of the cure they will be *human beings* again."

To reach this goal, modern youth must follow the exhortation of the Delphian oracle, "Know thyself!" This hard saying demands that each individual "organize the chaos within himself and that he rally all the honesty, sturdiness, and truthfulness of his character to rebel against secondhand thinking, secondhand learning, secondhand action." For "everything that makes for greater truthfulness is a step toward true culture, even if such truthfulness may harm the fashionable educational ideals of the day, even if it may lead to the overthrow of an entire system of merely decorative culture."

In spring and summer, 1874, Nietzsche wrote the third part of *Thoughts out of Season,* in which he tried to sketch the strong and integrated personality that would be capable of pointing the way to a new integrated *Kultur.* This essay bears the title, *Schopenhauer as an Educator.*

Observing realistically that most human beings never become actually what they are potentially, Nietzsche propounds a dynamic ethics of self-realization. Man, if he wants to escape mass-stupor and become a personal self, must follow the call of his conscience which constantly exhorts him, "Be yourself! You are not actually all that which you do, think, and desire."

In the process of self-realization the human person may succeed in closing that gap which separates his presently given nature from his "true nature." Most men, Nietzsche avers, are loath to heed this call of conscience, either because they are afraid of being themselves or because they are too lazy to rouse themselves from their comfortable everyday routines. And their inertia is fostered and fathered by the State and by Society which are both inimical to human selfhood and which lure man into a listless conformism. "True existence," therefore, means emancipation from such collective beguilements and pressures.

One sure way for man to discover his "true self" is, according to Nietzsche, to fashion his existence in conformity with those exemplars of the species whom he has lovingly and discriminatingly singled out as his "educators." In the context of the essay this means for Nietzsche to mold himself in the image of the best features he has been able to discern in the personality and work of Arthur Schopenhauer. And in trying to do this he is convinced that he follows the precise directives which he had himself outlined in the second part of *Thoughts out of Season,* especially in the discussion of the benefits deriving from both the "monumental" and "critical" types of historiography.

Schopenhauer thus becomes for Nietzsche a symbol of the "existential" educational significance of the great historic personality whose exalted function it is to be culturally creative by "promoting . . . the generation of the philosopher, the artist, and the saint, and in this way working at the perfection of nature." By becoming culturally creative, Nietzsche implies, the great personality not only works at the perfection of nature but also (as a teacher and educator) aids his fellow men in perfecting themselves. "The men with whom we live," he writes, "resemble a field of ruins . . . , and everything shouts at us: come, help, perfect . . . , for we yearn with infinite longing to become whole."

But it may be asked: how does Nietzsche justify his contention that the philosopher, the artist, and the saint are the supreme specimens of man's "true nature" or of his natural perfection? As Walter A. Kaufmann points out, Nietzsche "accepted Darwin's doctrine concerning the lack of any cardinal distinction between man and animals as incontrovertible empirical fact," but he "tried to counter this 'deadly' gospel with the new, Nietzschean, assertion that man *can* rise above the beasts. . . . There are certain pursuits which are super-animalic, and the man who engages in them is a truly *human* being and has a unique worth. The artist, saint, and philosopher are representatives of true humanity and culture."[5]

In a recent Nietzsche biography, Schopenhauer, the hero of Nietzche's essay, is described as "a half-wild, feline-creature . . . , at first thin, starved, and neglected, with no settled home; then, as he grew stronger, vociferous, inharmonious, and combative on the rooftops, and finally a sour old tom-cat, settling warily into a selfishly guarded comfort."[6] Yet, in Nietzsche's opinion, Schopenhauer "was great through and through, and in every respect." He mentions in particular three qualities which he believed he had discovered in the great pessimist and which for him became henceforth the distinctive marks of any authentic philosopher: *Redlichkeit* (intellectual integrity), *Heiterkeit* (serenity), and *Beständigkeit* (steadfast consistency).

V

Even before he had completed the essay on Schopenhauer, Nie-

[5] Walter A. Kaufmann, *Nietzsche: Philosopher, Psychologist, Antichrist* (Princeton: Princeton University Press, 1950), p. 149.

[6] H. A. Reyburn, H. E. Hinderks, J. G. Taylor, *Nietzsche. The Story of a Human Philosopher* (London: Macmillan, 1948), p. 205 f.

tzsche's views had begun to change. This change was at first slow, but later on more radical, leading in the end not only to a break with his own Dionysian philosophy of life, but to a growing estrangement with most of his friends, especially with Wagner. His new outlook eventually uprooted his professional career and deprived him of his metaphysical anchorage, so that he became a restless wanderer without a definite goal and burdened with sickness and suffering.

In his search for stability Nietzsche had found a temporary support in the music of Richard Wagner. And yet, his love for Wagner was from the outset a kind of love-hatred, a love which was soon poisoned by disappointment and doubt and which in the end turned into open hostility. The more Wagner, in his struggle for recognition, displayed the marks of the clever propagandist, the more he appeared to Nietzsche as a mere showman and actor. As early as 1873 he characterized Wagner's art in his notes as "a monstrous effort for self-affirmation and self-control in an antiartistic age. But the antidote it offers is merely another poison."

In March, 1875, Wagner's ill fortunes took a sudden turn for the better: King Louis II of Bavaria intervened in his behalf and saved the Bayreuth venture by a gift of one million marks. Nietzsche did not see Wagner again until July, 1876, when he attended the festivities at Bayreuth. In the meantime he had written an essay entitled *Wagner in Bayreuth,* which was still meant as a defense and eulogy of Wagnerian art. Section IV portrays Wagner as a great personality, destined to restore the unity and integrity of human existence. Section VII represents an attempt to determine Nietzsche's personal relationship to the great composer, and after having spoken at length of the magical force of attraction that issues from Wagner's personality, the author abruptly comments in Section VIII on the fact that Plato had banished the dramatic artist from his ideal State. But, he adds, one would have to be a Plato to dare expel such a swindler from the national community. The very fact that contemporary society still needs Wagner is an indication that it is not in a healthy state of mind. There will perhaps arise a society of the future in which artists of the Wagnerian type will have become superfluous.

Nietzsche evidently believed that he himself had progressed beyond Wagner, that he had the call to point the way to a world of the future that would be more natural and more honest than the one in which he lived. To the question as to what Wagner can possibly mean to those who really understand him, he answers that he can be at best an interpreter of an idealized past but not a prophet of the future.

After a week's stay at Bayreuth a new spell of sickness caused Nietzsche to depart for a near-by mountain retreat, but he returned on the eve of the first performance of the *Ring of the Nibelungs* and stayed through the entire period of the Wagner festival. The French religious philosopher Edouard Schuré, one of the thousands present at this epoch-making international musical event, recorded the impression he received of Nietzsche in a remarkably penetrating description: "Conversing with Nietzsche," he relates, "I was struck by the superiority of his mind and the strangeness of his physiognomy. A large forehead, short hair, projecting Slavic cheek-bones. His big, drooping moustache, his sturdy profile, would have given him the appearance of a cavalry officer if it had not been for a certain mixture of timidity and haughtiness in his bearing. The melodious voice and his slow speech revealed an artistic temper; his pensive and meditative expression betrayed the thinker. But nothing could be more deceptive than the outward calm of his features. The fixed stare of his eye spoke of the painful labor of his thought. It was at once the eye of a fanatic, a keen observer, and a visionary. During the performance of the tetralogy he seemed sad and depressed."

In October Nietzsche accepted an invitation from Malwida von Meysenbug, his motherly friend and the author of the then widely read *Memoirs of an Idealist*. Malwida had rented a *villa* at Sorrento near Naples. The second houseguest was Paul Rée, a German Jewish thinker, whom Nietzsche had first met at Basel and whose mind had been formed by such French and British philosophers as La Rochefoucauld, Chamfort, and John Stuart Mill. Malwida's house overlooked the Mediterranean and was surrounded by olive and lemon orchards, cypress groves, and vineyards. "Of what kindness and benevolence," she wrote in her *Memoirs,* "was Nietzsche animated at that time. His amiable and good nature counterbalanced his destructive intellect."

In the beginning Nietzsche felt very much at home and at ease at Sorrento. "I do not have sufficient strength for the North," he wrote in November, 1876; "up there life is dominated by clumsy and artificial souls; among them I have spent my entire youth. . . . I shudder and I pity myself when I become aware that I began my life as an old man; and I shed tears of gratitude that I was saved at the last moment. I am spirited enough for the South." But the early Italian summer caused a recurrence of his ailments, and in

May he returned to Switzerland. Dreading, however, the approaching winter semester in Basel, he pondered the idea of resigning from his position at the university but was finally persuaded by his sister to continue in his academic office.

Among Nietzsche's new friends was, aside from Paul Rée, the young musician Heinrich Köselitz, better known by his adopted name, Peter Gast. He had come to Basel to make Nietzsche's acquaintance and was so deeply impressed that he decided to stay. He remained Nietzsche's most understanding and faithful friend to the end. He was exceptionally talented as a musician and composer and made himself indispensable as a kind of secretary who could take dictation and copy the manuscripts before they were sent to the printer.

In 1876, on account of his poor health, Nietzsche had been granted a year's leave of absence with full pay. He resumed his academic work in fall, 1877, but suffered a serious relapse early in 1878. In spring, 1879, he broke down completely. All the ailments from which he had been suffering for the past four years seemed to have been only the preliminary symptoms of that total disease which now invaded his body and his mind. He felt certain that the end was near. His sister was summoned, and upon her arrival she found Friedrich in the most pitiful condition. There was little hope that he would ever be able to resume his academic duties. He gave up his position, and the university and city of Basel granted him an annual pension of 4,000 Swiss Francs.

Elisabeth suggested a change of climate and environment, and a trip to St. Moritz in the beautiful lake country of the mountainous Swiss Engadine brought relief and respite. But even there Nietzsche suffered from depressive moods. Shortly before his departure from the Engadine in September he wrote a letter to Peter Gast which was filled with brooding reflections and several allusions to religious problems — to Dante, the mediaeval church, Martin Luther, the Psalms, and to Christ: "I have reached the end of my thirty-fifth year. . . . So now I stand in 'the middle of life,' but surrounded by death, which may seize me at any moment. . . . Renunciation of everything: a small room with a bed, the food of an ascetic. . . . Renunciation up to one point: I have clung to my thought — what else could I have done! But this precisely is for my mind the most pernicious thing of all."

In this mental state of painful resignation Nietzsche's memories of his early youth and of his parental home forcefully reasserted themselves, and he yearned for the peace and security of those years. On September 20, 1879, he departed for Naumburg, the town where his mother lived and where he had spent his happy childhood days. He wanted to return to the simple things of life, to forget for a while the many problems which tortured his mind. He took a lease on a piece of land near the mediaeval city wall and intended to plant fruit trees and raise vegetables and flowers. But soon his interest in gardening faded, and he found himself again alone with his unsolved problems.

In a letter to his sister, Nietzsche calls this year the most horrible of his life and he bemoans his return to "the gloomy North." But he is willing to accept his suffering like a supreme test, like a spiritual exercise. A letter of January 14, 1880, addressed to Malwida, speaks of "the terrible and almost incessant martyrdom" of his life and of his "thirst for death." "I have suffered so much," he writes, "I have renounced so many things that there is no religious ascetic with whose life my own could not justly be compared. . . . But I also know that many have been guided by me to a more elevated, a more serene existence. . . . We both, you and I, are brave, and neither distress nor contempt can turn us from the path which we have once recognized as good and right. . . . We still have hopes for the human race and, without much noise, we offer ourselves as a sacrifice. . . . Receive, dear friend, who are as a sister to me, the greetings of a young old man to whom life after all has not been too cruel, although it has nurtured in him the desire for death."

In February, 1880, Nietzsche left Naumburg for Venice. Despite all handicaps he had been writing almost without interruption, from the time of his visit at Bayreuth, in 1876, to his arrival at Naumburg, in 1879. The bulk of his notes he gathered into a single volume which, after it had been carefully rewritten by Peter Gast, was handed to the publisher and came off the press under the title, *Human, All-too-Human. A Book for Free Spirits* (1878, 1879). The book was dedicated to Voltaire. A second volume was added to the third edition of 1886.

Nietzsche was by nature inclined toward optimism. Even at the time he was most strongly influenced by Schopenhauer, he had always found refuge in a self-created inner world which to some extent restored meaning to that external world in which he had lost confidence. But his optimism grew out of a profound experience of the tragic aspects of human existence. With the ebbing of his youthful energy the Dionysian intoxication subsided, and he longed for peace, harmony, and simple human happiness. This change is, as always, reflected in his works. "I have," he said, "composed all my writings with my whole body and soul. I do not know of any purely intellectual problems."

Human, All-too-Human was written for those "free spirits" who agreed with Nietzsche that there existed no supernatural or suprasensible world, no reality behind the surface phenomena of experience, no eternal lawgiver, and no life beyond. The world simply *is,* but it has no meaning. It is the human being who creates all values, and he is not responsible to anyone but himself for his choice of the values of his own making.

Nietzsche wrote his book in a pointed, glittering, and sophisticated style, following the model of those French "moralists" and skeptics who had inspired his writing, such as Montaigne, Voltaire, Chamfort, and Stendhal. Much of it is autobiographical, and a significant theme is the nostalgia for the great thoughts and accomplishments of the past. "The best things in us," he writes, "are perhaps the heritage of the experiences of earlier times to which we have no longer direct access; the sun has already set, but the horizon of our lives still gleams and glows in its light, although we have long lost sight of it."

The final section of Part Two of the work bears the title, *Man alone with Himself.* It contains a profound self-analysis of great beauty and force. The motif of "the Wanderer" reappears. He who has attained to freedom of thought, Nietzsche muses, is as a forlorn wanderer on this earth. He looks at the world with open eyes but must take care never to attach his heart too strongly to the things of this world. "To be sure, such a man will have his bad nights when he comes home tired and finds the city-gate locked, the gate of the city in which he had hoped to find rest. . . . Then the terrible night descends upon him like a desert in a desert, and his heart feels tired of wandering. And when at last the morning sun rises, glowing like a god of wrath, and when the city-gate is opened, then he may discover in the faces of the city-dwellers an even greater desert, more filth, fraud, and insecurity than outside the gate — and the day will perhaps be worse than the night. . . . But then there are compensations: there are the blessed mornings . . . when in the dawn of day the dancing muses swarm about him in the mountain haze; and, later on, when he walks silently among the trees in the harmonies of the awakening day, and from the tree tops and the foliage all those good and bright things are showered upon him, the gifts of all those free spirits who are at home in mountain, forest, and solitude and who, like himself, are in their gay and thoughtful ways sages, wanderers, and philosophers. . . . They are in search of the *philosophy of the early day.*"

The sentiments expressed in this passage are indicative of the inner conflicts and contradictions that run through the entire work. Nietzsche preaches a gospel for "free spirits," but almost in the same breath he denies that there is any real freedom. He demands liberation from all illusions and superstitions, but at the same time he insists that life cannot be lived without illusions. He says a melancholy farewell to art but concludes with a hymnic praise of beauty. The work thus gives voice to the conflict between Nietzsche's passionate desire for absolute freedom and his religious need for dependence on some unconditional absolute.

A second major theme is the conflict with Wagner. The publication of Nietzsche's book coincided with the appearance of Wagner's *Parsifal.* As a Christian music drama of redemption it aroused Nietzsche's violent antagonism. But although he called its psychology fantastic he admired the dramatic dynamism of the opera and praised its great poetic beauty.

Nietzsche had destroyed the simple faith of his early youth. With the aid of philosophic reasoning he had endeavored to create a synthesis of Dionysian rapture and an artistic transfiguration of life. But this wished-for synthesis, too, crumbled under the impact of his corrosive intellect. His skepticism forged weapons against both his Dionysian faith and his artistic vision, weapons which eventually struck at the roots of his own existence. What remained in the end was his passionate desire for freedom, the hope that he might succeed in transfiguring all existence by means of beauty, and, above all, the longing for the divinization of all life, including his own self.

VI

After the break with Wagner, Nietzsche for a while deprived himself of all music. But "to live without music, what absurdity," he wrote in inner revolt. This self-imposed abstention from music ended with his arrival in Venice, in the spring of 1880. Peter Gast helped him to find a composer to his liking. It was Chopin, whom the friend interpreted for Nietzsche on the piano.

With the advent of the humid summer heat Nietzsche fled from

Venice, first to Marienbad in Bohemia and then to Genoa, where he spent the winter of 1880–1881 in the small attic room of a house located on top of a hill overlooking the bay, living "simply, exacting toward myself, but tolerant with others. A light sleep, a brisk, quiet walk, no princes nor other celebrities, no women, no newspapers, no honors. . . ."

In 1880 Nietzsche became acquainted with a recently published book by Hermann Oldenberg, dealing with Buddhism and the life of the Buddha. He was deeply impressed with the similarity he believed he discovered between Buddha and himself. Buddha too had devoted his life to the search for truth and, like Nietzsche, he had been called an atheist and a nihilist. But actually, Nietzsche concluded, Buddha was a God-seeker, and the Buddhistic Nirvana was not "the nought"; it was pure, unfettered, ecstatic Being. At Genoa, in his simple lodgings, in his ascetic living habits, the ideal of the Buddha shone all the more brightly. The simple people of the neighborhood referred to Nietzsche as their *piccolo santo* (little saint). The things nearest and dearest to him were the people, the sea, and the sky, and in their proximity he acquired a new taste of that Reality the loss of which had been his great misfortune.

While Nietzsche was thus enjoying another respite, he was working on a new book to which he gave the title, *Aurora or the Dawn of Day* (1881). He had hardly finished this work when his health again broke down. He fled to the Engadine and discovered to his delight the small village of Sils-Maria, where from then on he spent his summers. In the winter he would return to Genoa or its vicinity.

The scenery of Sils-Maria admirably suited the mood of the ailing thinker. Located at a lake of the same name, the village is surrounded on one side by an austere chain of rugged mountains capped with eternal snow, while on the other side spreads the glistening white beauty of the Fex-Glacier. In summer the landscape is a symphony of color: the vast meadows are covered with a carpet of the red, blue, and yellow of the alpine flora, extending far up into the mountain slopes; a panorama of mountains, hills, forest, and water.

Nietzsche rented an inexpensive room in one of the small shingle-roofed farmhouses, a room protected from the brightness of the sun. There he lived in complete solitude, elated over the freedom he had at last won, and filled with nostalgia for the personal and spiritual ties he had lost. "Sometimes, my friend," he wrote to Peter Gast in August, 1881, "I have a distinct feeling that I really live a very dangerous kind of life, for I am one of those machines that burst easily! The intensity of my emotions makes me shudder and laugh. A few times I felt unable to leave my room for the ridiculous reason that my eyes were inflamed. And why? I had wept too much on my wanderings the day before; not sentimental tears, but tears of jubilation, tears mingled with song and nonsensical chatter; my soul was filled with a new vision."

The new vision which so exulted and transported Nietzsche's entire being was the idea of *Eternal Recurrence*. Only a short time ago, he had written, "Doubt devours me. I have killed the Law, and now it haunts me as a cadaver haunts a living person. If I am not *more* than the Law, then I am among the damned souls the most damned." From this haunting experience the idea of Eternal Recurrence seemed to offer an escape. Nietzsche believed he had found this doctrine anticipated not only in the speculation of modern positivists, such as Spencer and Vogt, but in the thought of Heraclitus and Buddha. The idea that everything that is happening now must have happened innumerable times before and will happen innumerable times in the future, had become a metaphysical and moral necessity for Nietzsche.

At noontime, near Sils-Maria, on the road to neighboring Silvaplana, Nietzsche experienced the Eternal Recurrence in an ecstatic vision: he saw the cosmos animated by an endless cyclical movement, composed of a finite number of eternally recurring elements. "That everything returns eternally, this is the closest possible rapprochement of the world of becoming and the world of being," he wrote. The ancients, who had been unfamiliar with the idea of eternity, had merely asserted that everything returns. For Nietzsche, on the other hand, the meaning of being and existence lay in the newly gained assurance that everything returns *eternally*. When he was a child he had known eternity by faith. When he was a young man and a disciple of Schopenhauer and Wagner, he had tried to satisfy his thirst for eternity in aesthetic contemplation and in Dionysian rapture. In the vision of Sils-Maria he experienced eternity not as residing in an intangible beyond, but in every fulfilled instant of existence, so that even the harshest and most cruel aspects of reality appeared exalted and transfigured by the sheen of eternity. Therefore, no matter how hard and burdensome life be, it calls for total affirmation on the part of man. *"Lux, mea crux; crux, mea lux!"* (Light, thou art my cross; Cross, thou art my light), Nietzsche jotted down in his notebook.

With the idea of Eternal Recurrence Nietzsche gained access to a new concept of *immortality*. He found in it a substitute for his lost Christian faith. It thus represents the fulfillment of his this-worldly optimism. Above all, it served to express some basic "existential" needs of Nietzsche: the eternal recurrence of all things seemed to place the highest stress and strain on personal existence and personal action, for every action of the individual must now make manifest the eternal quality of his existence. Eternal recurrence, furthermore, means that all things are co-present in the idea of Being: as there is nowhere a beginning and nowhere an end, the world is always whole and perfect. Eternity, which is present in each fulfilled moment, clothes every such moment with perfection and thus redeems all things.

Faith in Eternal Recurrence means, according to Nietzsche, "that you love life in the very form in which it has confronted you and has made you what you are — and that you crave eternity for just this kind of life. . . . Let us then impress upon our lives the image of Eternity." This faith then becomes for Nietzsche a moral imperative which demands that man live in such a way that he must desire to live again and again.

Still entranced with his "vision," Nietzsche began work on two other books, one of which was to be a continuation of *Aurora,* while the second was to be a song of praise and triumph. The first, entitled *The Joyful Wisdom (la gaya scienza),* was written at Genoa during the winter months of 1881–1882; the second, entitled *Thus Spake Zarathustra,* followed in 1883. Zarathustra, the founder of the ancient Persian religion (eighth century, B.C.), the prophet and mystagogue, was to occupy the center of the latter work.

Nietzsche was placing himself more and more in radical opposition to the spirit of his age, and he began to feel more and more isolated. *Aurora* was ignored by the critics and received with great coolness even by the author's few remaining friends. Materialism in nineteenth-century philosophy seemed to have run its course, and the younger generation of thinkers, following the lead of Henri Bergson, was groping for a new spiritual anchorage. What Nietzsche had to offer was a kind of cryptomaterialism. Politically and socially, Europe was moving toward democracy, dreaming of universal peace and security. The future which Nietzsche envisaged looked somewhat different. "We may," he wrote, "expect some centuries of war and revolution the like of which the world has never seen before. . . . We are entering upon the classical age of war, the age of scientific and universal warfare on the largest scale. . . . The twentieth century will fight for the domination of the globe." In his own age and environment Nietzsche discerned the signs of a decisive historical change: the end of one historical sequence and the beginning of another. And as the most conspicuous features of this radical break he cites the "leveling process" and the rapid growth of the "spirit of the herd." The revolt of the slaves, he avers, began as a reaction against the power politics of the ancient Roman Empire; it continued during the centuries of the Christian era, and it has reached its culminating point in the age of "democratic socialism." Both bourgeois and socialists have divorced themselves from religion, and it is for this reason that they both lead a phantomlike existence.

Democratic socialism disregards the actual inequalities among men; it makes the average and the mediocrity the standard of measurement and thus leads to the tyranny of morons and to the sham morality of the herd. The result will be "a flock without a shepherd, a flock in which all the sheep are equal. . . . The democratic-socialist ideal is nothing but a stupid misunderstanding of the Christian idea of morality." Nietzsche then contrasts the featureless "masses" with "the people" and asks "to create a people again out of the masses." A people (*Volk*) is for him something noble, while the masses are "the sand" of humanity: "all alike, all very puny, very round, very sociable, and very boring." Where the masses prevail, the individuals no longer dare to assert themselves. The masses think only of prosperity, comfort, the gratification of sensual desires, and as a consequence "this social-democratic world is headed for a type of intellectual and moral slavery unsurpassed in all history."

The growing domination of nature by modern science, which Nietzsche foresees for the twentieth century, fills him with grave apprehensions. He does not rule out the possibility that modern civilization may perish by its own technical devices. The religious forces, though greatly enfeebled, "might still be strong enough to produce a religion of atheism."

The much-vaunted "democratization of Europe" means for Nietzsche "an involuntary arrangement for the breeding of tyrants." And the steady growth of general insecurity and uncertainty will cause men "to kiss the dust before any will power that commands." The "Lords of the World" will then serve as substitutes for God. Does the remedy for the ills of the modern age then perhaps lie in the establishment of a constitutional world government? If mankind does not want to destroy itself by world government, it must, in Nietzsche's opinion, first of all acquire a thorough knowledge of those conditions which make true civilization possible: "In the discovery of the standards and criteria for world government consists the monumental task of the great minds of the twentieth century."

VII

In November, 1881, at the time he was working on the manuscript of *The Joyful Wisdom,* Nietzsche wrote to his sister from Genoa: "As I did in the Engadine, I wander over the mountains with jubilant gladness and with a vision of the future as no one before me has ever dared. . . . Perhaps a time will come when the eagles will timidly look up to me, as they do on that picture of St. John the Evangelist of which we were so fond when we were children." In January, 1882, he completed the fourth book of *The Joyful Wisdom.* It began with words of calm confidence: "I shall try more and more to see the beauty of things in the fact that they are necessary. . . . *Amor fati:* that shall be my love from now on. . . . In a word, I want to be nothing but a great Yea-Sayer [*Ja-sager*]."

During the same winter at Genoa Nietzsche had discovered in Bizet's opera *Carmen* a type of music that fully compensated him for the loss of Wagner. In Bizet's passionate Mediterranean melodiousness Nietzsche experienced a liberation from the seductive charms of northern romanticism. Nevertheless, it remained his avowed ambition to perpetuate and surpass what was best in the work of Wagner. The new hero who is to triumph over the somber clouds of the "Twilight of the Gods" is not Parsifal, the errant knight, poor in spirit, but *Zarathustra,* mighty in mind and heart.

The last paragraph (342) of *The Joyful Wisdom* bears the significant title, *"Incipit tragoedia."* It introduces Zarathustra who, when he was thirty years of age, went forth into the mountains to live in solitude for a period of ten years. But at last he became "weary of his wisdom, like the bee that has gathered too much honey." Like the liberated slave in Plato's famous parable of the Cave, Zarathustra feels the urge to descend again to the valleys of men "to bestow and distribute," so that "the wise may once more become joyous in their folly, and the poor happy in their riches. . . . Thus began Zarathustra's down-going."

At the end of the winter of 1881–1882 Nietzsche followed one of his sudden impulses and went to Messina in Sicily. He felt so happy there that he decided to stay for the writing of his *Zarathustra*. But early in April the hot sirocco wind drove him away from this newly found haven. Letters from Malwida and Paul Rée urged him to join them in Rome on his way north. Malwida was anxious to have him meet Lou-Salomé, a young girl of great charm and an avid reader of Nietzsche's books. He accepted the invitation and, shortly after his arrival in Rome, Lou was introduced to him on the occasion of a visit to St. Peter's Basilica. She was the daughter of a Russian general and at that time in her early twenties.

Lou-Salomé's book, entitled *Friedrich Nietzsche in his Works,* contains a vivid description of the philosopher. "Loneliness," she writes, "that was the first strong impression which Nietzsche's appearance conveyed. . . . This man of medium height . . . had nothing spectacular about him. . . . The fine and very expressive lines of his lips were almost completely concealed by a large, drooping moustache. He had a soft laugh, a way of talking almost inaudibly, and a cautious, pensive gait. . . . His hands were nobly shaped and incomparably beautiful. . . . Truly revealing were his eyes. Half blinded, they nevertheless had nothing of the spying, blinking, involuntarily obtrusive expression of many near-sighted people; they rather looked like the guardians of hidden treasures, of mute secrets that must not be disturbed by intruders. . . . He showed great politeness and an almost womanly tenderness, a steady, benevolent equanimity." In his distinguished formality "there was also the enjoyment of wearing a mask, a mask that covered his never revealed inner life."

Nietzsche and Paul Rée accompanied Lou and her mother to Lucerne in Switzerland, where Nietzsche showed her Wagner's former residence at Tribschen and talked to her of his relationship to the composer. He told her of his childhood, his early doubts, and of the new inspiration he had received from Schopenhauer and Wagner. But Schopenhauer, he confided, was too much steeped in negation, and Wagner's world was built on illusions. "Yes," he concluded this confession, "thus the cycle began, and it goes on, but where will it end? After having run the full course, whither are we to turn? . . . Perhaps we will have to make a new start with faith? Perhaps a Catholic faith?"

Nietzsche believed, or at least tried to make himself believe, that he had found in Lou a worthy partner for his life. He loved this young girl who had shown so much sympathy and understanding, but he lacked the courage to speak for himself. So he asked Paul Rée to speak in his behalf, while he himself fled to Basel. There he finally got Lou's answer: she gently but firmly rejected the idea of marriage. All she could promise Nietzsche was the enduring friendship of a faithful disciple.

The first performance of Wagner's *Parsifal* was scheduled for July 27, and Nietzsche could not resist the temptation to be at least in the vicinity of Bayreuth, especially as he knew that Lou had planned to be there. So he journeyed to Tautenburg in the Thuringian Forest, located a short distance only from Bayreuth.

Parsifal, enthusiastically received by the international audience, became Wagner's greatest triumph. "The old sorcerer has scored a tremendous success," Nietzsche wrote to Peter Gast. After the end of the Wagner Festival Lou-Salomé, accompanied by Elisabeth, visited Nietzsche at Tautenburg. "The hours," wrote Lou of this meeting, "in which he revealed to me his thoughts are unforgettable. . . . He spoke with a low voice and with all the appearances of the deepest horror. And indeed, life was for him such a profound suffering that the certitude of an Eternal Recurrence must of necessity have struck him as a frightful idea."

"Lou Salomé was never sincere," Elisabeth commented on these days of Tautenburg; "she was eager and curious to listen, contented with being idolized, but her passion and enthusiasm were feigned." As a matter of fact, Elisabeth had grown more and more jealous of the young Russian girl. She regarded her brother as a kind of precious and exclusive possession of hers, and she felt that he was slipping away from her tutelage. Brother and sister exchanged harsh words and, filled with deep resentment, Friedrich departed for Leipzig.

But Nietzsche's relationship with Lou also deteriorated. Evidently the young girl was unwilling and unable to give that total and unconditional assent to Nietzsche's ideas which he demanded. She left Tautenburg in accordance with her previous plans and, although Nietzsche continued writing and confiding to her his ideas and projects, his faith in the possibility of this idyl was shattered. He fled to Basel, and from there to Genoa and Rapallo, where he spent a solitary winter, plagued by insomnia and depressed by melancholy.

By the middle of January, 1883, the philosopher had sufficiently subdued his somber mood to begin the writing of the first part of *Thus Spake Zarathustra.* Yet it was but a flicker of light: ten days later darkness descended again. During a severe attack of influenza he wrote in reply to a letter he had received from Elisabeth, "I am glad to learn that you no longer intend to wage war against your brother. . . . This has been my hardest and most miserable winter, aside from *ten days* which, however, have made it possible for me to create something that makes my entire painful and troublesome existence seem worthwhile."

Early in May Nietzsche joined Elisabeth in Rome and stayed with her to the middle of June. During this time she partially regained her domineering influence over him. From Rome Friedrich went to the solitude of Sils-Maria to work on the second part of *Zarathustra*. But the quarrels with and about Lou followed him to his alpine retreat. Elisabeth made matters worse and precipitated a complete and definitive break by writing an offensive letter to her young Russian rival. When Lou complained to Nietzsche about this provocation, he stood up for his sister and in his farewell letter gave Lou a severe and genuinely Nietzschean scolding. Lou Salomé later on became the wife of Professor Andreas, a famous Iranist of the University of Göttingen, and the friend of several prominent personalities in the realm of arts and letters, among them the German poet Rainer Maria Rilke.

It was in the midst of this emotional turbulence that the first two parts of *Zarathustra* were written. The third part was composed at Nice, in February, 1883, and the fourth (and last) part in Zurich, Mentone, and Nice, in the autumn and winter of 1884–1885.

VIII

The first part of *Thus Spake Zarathustra* contains no arguments and attempts no demonstration. It is simply the outpouring of a soul's inner experiences. "All that I have thought, suffered, and hoped is in it, and in such a way that my entire life appears now somehow vindicated," Nietzsche wrote from Rome, in May, 1883. And to Gersdorff, in June: "Behind all these simple and strange words stands my deadly seriousness and *my entire philosophy*. It is a beginning of my self-revelation — no more." Later on, in *Ecce Homo* (1888), Nietzsche analyzes the ecstatic experience which inspired his writing: "Has anyone at the end of the nineteenth century," he asks, "an idea of what the poets of manly ages called inspiration? . . . If there were even a minimum of superstition left in us, we should hardly be able to deny that in such moments we are nothing but the incarnation, the mouthpiece, the medium of supernatural powers. What actually happens in such a state is best described by the term 'revelation,' in the sense that suddenly, with ineffable certainty and subtlety, something becomes visible and audible, something that shakes and overwhelms us in our innermost depths. One hears — one does not seek; one receives without asking who is the giver; an idea blazes like a flash of lightning, with a necessity that allows no hesitation — I have never had a choice. There is a rapture whose tremendous tension is sometimes released by a stream of tears . . . a complete *ecstasis* . . . a profound bliss in which even the most somber experiences appear not as a contrast, but as a complement, as a necessary nuance of a superabundance of light. . . . Everything happens in the highest degree involuntarily, but in a storm of freedom, of power, of God-likeness."

Part One of *Zarathustra* comprises twenty-three songs of hymnic prose. The two ideas which had been predominant in Nietzsche's mind when he first broached the subject in 1881 were the idea of *Eternal Recurrence* and the idea of the *Super-Man,* but in the completed manuscript the Eternal Recurrence was hardly mentioned. Zarathustra's message expresses Nietzsche's desire to wrest from actual life a lasting meaning and value, whereas the idea of Eternal Recurrence was to give voice to the longing for a greater and higher reality above and beyond actual existence.

It is the mission of the Super-Man to overcome the philosophy of pessimism. "Man is something that must be overcome"; that is, only a new, a higher and better creature can impart once again meaning to this earthly human existence. And so Zarathustra leaves his mountains and begins his descent to the big city. He meets the crowds and prepares those individuals who are willing to listen for the acceptance of his doctrine. He warns them to beware of those who wish to entice them by promising them the bliss of another world, and he tells them that man's salvation is in his own hands.

Zarathustra wants to arouse the people from their complacency and self-satisfaction, so that they may learn again to know themselves and to appreciate the breadth and depth of human nature: "Man is a rope stretched between the animal and the Super-Man — a rope over an abyss." Man is not an end in himself, but a bridge to an end higher than himself. But, alas, Zarathustra laments, the time of the most despicable man is close at hand — the man who can no longer despise himself. When this time arrives, there will be only a huge herd without a shepherd: all will be equal, all will have the same desires, and "he who feels differently will go voluntarily to the madhouse." But Zarathustra's message falls on deaf ears. "They understand me not," he says to his heart, "I am not the mouth for these ears."

From an attack on those philosophers who demand that man adjust himself to the actual situations and conditions of life, Zarathustra proceeds to a castigation of the modern concepts of State and Society. He calls the State "the new idol, the coldest of all cold monsters." This modern State "is false through and through." It claims for itself absolute power: "And this lie also creepeth from its mouth: 'I, the State, am the people! . . . There is nothing on earth greater than I; it is I who am the regulating finger of God' — thus roareth this monster." And all the people fall on their knees to worship this new idol. They lose their own selves and become mere cogs in the gigantic mechanism of a collective pseudo-absolute: "Just look at all these superfluous ones! . . . They vomit their bile, and call it a newspaper. . . . They acquire wealth, and they become poorer thereby. They seek power and, above all, much money, the lever of power. . . . Badly smelleth their idol to me . . . badly they all smell to me, these idolaters. My brethren, will ye suffocate in the fumes of their mouths and their lusts? . . . Flee from the steam of these human sacrifices! Open still remaineth the earth for great souls. . . . Verily, he who possesses little is so much less possessed: blessed be poverty!"[7]

But if the State is a false god and if all supernatural concepts are illusory, where is man to find that "absolute" that will rescue him from absurdity and that will redirect his existence? "Dead are all the gods," Zarathustra proclaims; "now do we desire the Super-Man to live." Thus the divinized heroic man, the *Man-God,* is to take the place of God; and the future domain of the Super-Man is to supersede the Kingdom of God.

Most of Part Two of the work was written at Sils-Maria, in the midsummer of 1883, with the exception of the *Night-Song,* which had been composed in Rome during the spring of the preceding year. This particular chapter (31) gave vent to a mood of deep melancholy. From the *loggia* of his boardinghouse on the Piazza Barberini, Nietzsche could overlook the Eternal City as the twilight of the evening descended upon it and as from down below sounded the soft murmur of the fountains. In the dark night Zarathustra's soul joins in the

---

[7] Nietzsche, *Thus Spake Zarathustra* (translated by Thomas Common; New York: The Modern Library, reprinted by arrangement with Macmillan), p. 64 f.

awakening songs of all the loving ones. There is within him something unappeased and unappeasable that clamors for expression: it is a craving for love. In the dark night he alone is Light, and it is his utter lonesomeness that condemns him to live in his own light: "I drink into myself the flames that break forth from me. . . . Ah, there is ice around me. . . . Ah, there is thirst within me. . . . Thus sang Zarathustra." And while Nietzsche listened to the murmuring of the fountains, he vaguely realized that his melancholy and his lonesomeness had their ultimate cause in his own stubborn and self-centered will. While his soul was full to overflowing, emptiness was spreading, fastening its deadening grip on his mind.

Zarathustra sings his *Dance-Song* to a group of girls, who are dancing on a meadow. It, too, ends on a note of sadness and doubt. He asks himself whether it is not folly to go on living, since there seems to be no answer to the questions "Why?" "Wherefore?" "Whither?" "How?" — In the *Grave-Song* the sage mourns his lost past, the death of all the visions and consolations of his youth. If he still clings to that past it is because from there emanates a sheen of love, a love which died too soon but for which the heart of "the lone seafarer" feels an unspeakable longing.

In some of the concluding chapters of Part Two Zarathustra takes issue with the founders and servants of religion and with the dispensers of knowledge and science — prisoners all, tied down by false values. His soul, he confesses, sat hungry at their tables. These "scholars" like nothing better than to "sit cool in the cool shade; they want in everything to be mere spectators, and they carefully avoid sitting in the burning sun."[8] They fill themselves with the thoughts which others have thought, and if one lays hands on them they give forth a dust like flour sacks. "But who would ever guess that their dust came from corn and from the yellow delight of the summer fields? . . . In their wisdom there is often an odor as if it came from the swamp." But "they are good clockworks; only be careful to wind them up properly! Then they will indicate the hour without mistake, and make a modest noise thereby."[9]

Gradually the reader is initiated into the secret of the *Eternal Recurrence*: life, as it is actually lived, is miserable, fragmentary, imperfect. How can it be perfected? How can it be redeemed? Above all, how can the past be redeemed, and how can man's dissipated existence

---

[8] *Ibid.*, p. 136.   [9] *Ibid.*

be made whole again? Zarathustra hints at the answer, but he is not prepared as yet to reveal it fully. The will can accept the past and, in affirming itself, affirm also the past; then the past will return and become present and future. Thus the will can break the yoke of time. But, evidently, Zarathustra-Nietzsche is appalled by the thought that in this case all the horrors of the past will also have to be lived through again and again.

In Part Three Nietzsche's visionary power reaches its greatest height. Zarathustra's message is centered in the idea of the *Eternal Recurrence*. He preaches the new *religion of atheism,* and he implements this new gospel with Nietzsche's own early religious experiences, with his reminiscences of Christianity, and with elements of the ecstatic cult of Dionysos. The chapter entitled *The Vision and the Enigma* elucidates the main idea. An obnoxious dwarf, the personification of the spirit of gravity and inertia, has cast a gloom on Zarathustra's soul and has paralyzed his action. But his courage overcomes his dejection, "for courage is the best slayer. . . . It slayeth also dizziness at abysses: and where doth man not stand at abysses! . . . Courage slayeth even death itself; for it saith: *'Was that* life? Well then! Once more!'"[10]

The dwarf's previous remark, "Time is a circle," had indicated that the Eternal Recurrence was not entirely unfamiliar to him. Now they have both stopped in front of a gateway at which two roads meet: one running backward and the other forward, but both continuing into eternity. The gateway itself is named "This Moment." Behind man and ahead of man stretches an eternity, so that all things "must already have happened, run their course and gone by." And what about the gateway, "This Moment"? What about you and me? "Must not we also have already existed? And must we not return and run on in that other road out there ahead of us . . . must we not eternally return?"

The idea of Eternal Recurrence is an intoxicating and a nauseating thought. How can the eternal repetition of the sufferings and terrors of existence be made tolerable? By freely accepting life in its totality, with all its joyful and frightful implications, answers Zarathustra-Nietzsche, and by learning simultaneously that the present human race represents a transitional phase in the flux of evolution, that it must give way to a superior race of the future, a higher kind of

---

[10] *Ibid.,* p. 165 f.

existence, in which all human aspirations to love, beauty, and truth will be fulfilled. Only in the vision of such a divinized future existence, present-day man in his pettiness and seeming futility is also justified as a steppingstone on the road to the Super-Man. Thus the idea of Eternal Recurrence and the idea of the Super-Man fuse.

The religious overtones in these philosophic-poetic dreams of Zarathustra are unmistakable. They are inspired by the dominant theme of all religion, the yearning for redemption from human finiteness and insufficiency, the desire for a wholeness and security which are to be found in a Reality that is both timeless and infinite.

In Part Two Zarathustra had made the astounding statement, "If there were gods, how could I bear it not to be a god? *Therefore,* there are no gods." In Part Three he goes one step farther: Dionysos and all the other gods of the past are dead. Their thrones are vacant, and Zarathustra finds himself alone beneath the starry sky, the abandoned abode of the defunct gods. After having groped so long in the dark, on errant ways and rocky paths, he now feels himself worthy of partaking of the glowing splendor of the highest heavens. He has risen above fear and guilt, above law and duty, and he looks down upon human life and blesses it: "A blesser have I become and a Yea-Sayer. And therefore strove I so long and was a wrestler that one day I might get my hands free for blessing. . . . And blessed is he who thus blesseth. For all things are baptized at the font of Eternity, and beyond good and evil. . . ."[11] In the rapture of self-deification Zarathustra experiences life as a divine bliss, in the fruition of which the Eternal Recurrence becomes the source of redemption and of lasting happiness.

But for Nietzsche himself the experience of Zarathustra provided no guarantee for this kind of happiness. He knew in his innermost heart that for mortal man the greatest height always harbors the possibility of the deepest fall. And even Zarathustra, in the hour of his greatest triumph, experiences the inevitability of suffering: the enraptured Dionysian god seems to assume the agonized features of the suffering God-Man of the Gospels, who died on the cross, so that man might live and live more abundantly.

As Christ suffered death because of the new gospel he preached, so also Zarathustra's downfall begins with the revelation of his great secret: "I have spoken my word, I am broken by my word: so willeth

---

[11] *Ibid.,* p. 174.

it my eternal fate — as a prophet do I perish!" Zarathustra's knowledge of the smallness of man makes him shudder at the thought of Eternal Recurrence: "Alas, man returneth eternally! The small man returneth eternally. Naked had I once seen them both, the greatest man and the smallest man! All too like one another — all too human, even the greatest man! All too small, even the greatest man! That was my disgust at man! And the eternal return also of the smallest man — that was my disgust at all existence!"[12]

The concluding chapter of Part Three bears the title *The Seven Seals* and the subtitle *The Yea and Amen Song*. It reaffirms the doctrine of Eternal Recurrence and proclaims its wholehearted acceptance. Each paragraph ends with the refrain, "Oh, how could I not lust for Eternity and for the bridal ring of rings — the ring of the Return? Never yet have I found the woman by whom I should want to have children, unless it be this woman whom I love: for I love thee, O Eternity!"[13]

Contrary to his original intention, Nietzsche soon began to think of a continuation of *Zarathustra* — a fourth part which was to be more systematic than the preceding ones. He even contemplated writing a fifth and sixth part: Zarathustra was to leave his mountain cave to wander again to the big city. There he was to preach to his disciples, prior to his final departure. Nietzsche had evidently planned to paraphrase the Gospel narrative of Christ's entrance into Jerusalem. But only Part Four, comprising twenty chapters, was actually completed.

For many years the prophet has been living in the solitude of his mountains. He has grown old and white haired. He knows, however, that some day he will become the founder of a great realm that is to last for a thousand years. But the time is not yet. Man must come and seek him, and patiently he waits for this sign and signal.

One day a visitor arrives, "the soothsayer," who tells Zarathustra of the sad state of the world. The hermit's heart momentarily wells up with pity, but he overcomes this "weakness" and refuses his help. The present human race, he knows, is beyond redemption.

The first visitor is soon followed by a group of several men, among them two kings. They all represent the "higher" type of human existence. From them Zarathustra learns anew of the human outcry for help. He finally yields to persuasion, and together they start out

---

[12] *Ibid.*, p. 225 f.   [13] *Ibid.*, p. 234.

on a search for further exemplars of the "higher man." On their way they meet an anonymous retired old pope who has gone forth in search of "the last pious man, a saint and a hermit who, alone in his forest, had not yet heard . . . that the old God no longer liveth." The old pope had loyally served that old God "until his last hour." Thus the last remaining Christian meets Zarathustra, the atheist. "Is it not thy very piety," the pope finally asks Zarathustra, "which no longer letteth thee believe in God? . . . Nigh unto thee, though thou professest to be the most god-less of all, I sense the fragrance of long benedictions." And the forlorn wanderer is shown the way to the shelter of Zarathustra's cave.

Next Zarathustra meets "the ugliest man," the man who "has murdered God." How can this horrible deed be justified? *"He had to die,"* the ugliest man tells Zarathustra, "he looked with eyes that saw *everything* — he saw man's depths and abysses, all his concealed shame and ugliness. . . . He always looked at *me.* . . . Man cannot *endure* it that such a witness should live." Thereupon Zarathustra "got up and prepared to go on: for he felt frozen to his very bowels." He pursues his way more thoughtfully and slowly than before, "for he asked himself many things and knew no easy answer." In this striking scene Nietzsche, the God-killer, meets Nietzsche, the God-seeker.

Meanwhile in Zarathustra's cave are gathered together those nine men who represent the highest types of the presently existing human race. They are "the last remnants of God among men: that is to say, the men of great longing, of great disgust, of great satiety — all those who do not want to live unless they learn again to *hope.*" But when Zarathustra returns to his cave in the late afternoon, he sternly tells his guests that, though they be "higher men," they are not high and strong enough. They are not the stuff out of which the Super-Man can be formed. They are not the disciples for whom he has been waiting in his mountains: "Nay! Three times Nay! For *others* do I wait. . . . Such as are squarely built in body and soul: *laughing lions* must come!"

The final two chapters of Part Four bear the titles *The Drunken Song* and *The Sign.* Mood and language are serious and somber. Late in the evening Zarathustra and his guests leave the cave and contemplate the moonlit landscape. From the distant valley is heard the tolling of a bell announcing the approaching midnight. Then follows the second *Night-Song,* a hymnic and almost humble praise of life. Once more the theme is the Eternal Recurrence: Zarathustra has finally come to realize that he is no god, after all, but only a sensitive soul, condemned to suffering. But he also knows that there are ineffable joys and raptures above and beyond the agonies of temporal existence. The sheen of Eternity illumines beauty and ugliness, good and evil. "For, although woe be deep, joy is deeper still than grief can ever be. . . . Joy wanteth itself: it wanteth Eternity, it wanteth Recurrence, it wanteth everything eternally-like-unto-itself."

In the brief concluding chapter of the entire work, Zarathustra is shown in exultant expectation of the "great noontide." He finds himself surrounded by a swarm of doves as by "a cloud of love," and at his feet rests a mighty yellow lion — signs and symbols of the disciples, who cannot be far away. "The lion hath come," he exclaims, "my children are nigh. . . . My hour hath come . . . arise now, arise, thou great noontide!" With these words Zarathustra leaves his cave, "glowing and strong, like a morning sun coming out of gloomy mountains."

IX

Thus Spake Zarathustra bore the subtitle, "A Book for All and None." For the time being and for some time to come it remained a book for "none": Nietzsche's literary masterpiece and personal confession aroused no one's interest. Very few read it; no one was either provoked or enthused by it. For Part Four the author could not even find a publisher, so that Nietzsche finally decided to have forty copies printed at his own expense. But the number forty exceeded the demand: Nietzsche had not that many friends and readers. Thus the hoped-for disciples had failed to arrive. Looking out from his lofty mountain retreat for kindred minds and hearts, what was Zarathustra-Nietzsche to do if no one was willing to listen? The author did not know the answer.

The enthusiasm which had inspired the writing of *Zarathustra* gave way to a mood of melancholy depression after the completion of the work in February, 1885. One of the external reasons for Nietzsche's dejection was the marriage of his sister to Dr. Bernhard Förster, a teacher in one of the secondary schools of Berlin, who had been forced to resign because of his rabid anti-Semitism and who was planning the establishment of a "racially pure" German settlement in Paraguay. But though both her mother and her brother were strongly opposed to her association with Förster — Nietzsche had nothing but loathing for the anti-Semitic movement and its representatives —

Elisabeth had proved stubborn and had gone ahead with her marriage plans. Friedrich's opposition gradually weakened, but he refused to be present at the wedding ceremony. Early in 1886 the German colonists departed for Paraguay. "I have now lived for forty-three years," Nietzsche wrote to Erwin Rohde at this time, "and I am still just as lonely as I was in the years of my childhood."

After the completion of Part Three of *Zarathustra,* Nietzsche had written to Peter Gast, "The next six years will be devoted to the elaboration of . . . 'my philosophy'!" And as these years passed, the notes and aphorisms accumulated, but the promised systematic outline was never written. In 1885, Nietzsche made another start, but he found himself unable to concentrate his mind on the task. He thereupon decided to publish a kind of prelude to the great undertaking, to which he gave the title *Beyond Good and Evil.* In 1888, he began to revise his earlier writings and to provide them with new prefaces, in which he traced his intellectual development and evaluated the relative merits of these earlier publications. Two years before, he had written to his sister, "In the course of the next four years a major work in four volumes may be expected. Its very title is frightening: *The Will to Power. An Attempt at the Transvaluation of all Values."* In the spring and summer of 1887 he again interrupted the work on his major project to compose another preliminary study, entitled *The Genealogy of Morals.* Then, in the spring of 1888, there followed in rapid succession two more small works, *The Case of Wagner* and *The Twilight of the Idols.* Finally, likewise in 1888, he added another fragment containing his most bitter attack on Christianity, which bore the title *The Anti-Christ.*

These successive publications used up a substantial part of Nietzsche's collected notes, so that there was really not sufficient material left for the execution of the original monumental plan of *The Will to Power.* Nevertheless, the main theme emerges clearly enough: Nietzsche recognized that modern Europe was in the midst of a "moral crisis," and it seemed to him that this crisis had its roots in the hitherto accepted system of values. He saw the minds of his contemporaries in turmoil, uprooted and shaken by forces and experiences unknown to previous generations. The question was whether by a "transvaluation" of the established values the substance of the European tradition could be regenerated and saved. "The inhabitants of hell are more consistent than you," Nietzsche had told his contemporaries through the mouth of Zarathustra. "You are the living

refutation of faith itself. . . . But he who has the call for creation is
the possessor of dreams and of stars — and he has faith in faith!"

In 1885 Nietzsche had underlined in his own copy of Pascal's
works the words, "Without the Christian faith . . . you will be to
yourself a monster and a chaos." Nietzsche's intellectual development
had by no means extinguished his profound religious needs and instincts. But, since the Christian God was "dead" and Dionysos, too,
had disappeared, Nietzsche now became submissive to a new deity
which he called "chance." He was hoping against hope that "chance"
might be powerful enough to raise his individuality to the heights of
infinite power and glory. Nietzsche's final self-apotheosis is his final
and desperate attempt to break out of the vicious circle of his endless
search for a new "god," a god whom he needed and desired, but
whom he had to destroy again and again in his thirst for limitless
power.

During the last meeting with his sister before her departure for
Paraguay, Nietzsche had talked to her about the difficult problems
which occupied his mind: "All alone with myself," he had said, "I
am . . . in danger of losing myself in a forest. . . . I need help. I need
disciples; I also need a teacher, a master. I should find it sweet to
obey. . . . If only I could find someone capable of clarifying for me
the value of our moral ideas. . . . But I find no one; no disciples, to
say nothing of teachers."

Nietzsche had experienced the impact of his ideas on his own ego,
and at times he felt concern for equally sensitive minds and souls who
might be exposed to the destructive force of his thinking. One Sunday
at Nice a young girl of the neighborhood asked him whether he
had been to church. "Today," he replied, "I was unable to go." And
to a friend who had witnessed the scene he explained afterward, "Not
every truth is for everyone; if I had troubled the heart of this young
girl, I should have felt disconsolate." In the observatory of Arcestri,
on the heights of San Miniato al Monte near Florence, the philosopher
made the acquaintance of a distinguished astronomer. "I wish," he
observed to his companion on this visit, "this man had not read my
books. He is too good. My influence on him could be very disastrous."

"Every profound spirit needs a mask," Nietzsche wrote in *Beyond
Good and Evil*. Wearing a mask became a necessity for Nietzsche, and
this theme recurs again and again in his later works. What the
thinker was hiding behind his several masks was his heart-rending
knowledge of the agony of Western civilization. Most of his con-

temporaries seemed to be entirely unaware of the approaching crisis. Nietzsche alone was clairvoyant enough to realize that Europe was menaced by disruptive forces which worked as yet underground, but which might erupt at any moment, especially since the guiding and binding power of God was no longer alive in human hearts and minds. In Nietzsche's opinion, Christianity was ultimately to blame for the emergence of European "nihilism" because, he charged, it had transposed the highest values of mankind from this world to a world beyond. The "death of God" consequently deprived human existence and the generally accepted human values of their meaning and foundation. Everything remained suspended in the void of nothingness. Laboring vainly in this void, Nietzsche observed a multitude of hands, engaged in the manufacture of tools and of arms, a greedy acquisitiveness, a perpetual motion without an ultimate aim and end: "Strong passions whirling around objects which are of no value. Even the greatest energy no longer knows *why* it is active. All the means are still there, but no ends." These then were the dark forebodings that burned and consumed Nietzsche's soul.

Before returning from Venice to the Engadine, Nietzsche paid a visit to his mother. When he mentioned the fate of his books, she told him that she detested them and that they deserved being disregarded and forgotten. From Naumburg the philosopher traveled on to the Engadine, but instead of the hoped-for sunshine he found those winterly mists which always deeply depressed him. "Horrible," he wrote in his notebook, "is this being alone with the judge and avenger of one's own law. Thus a star is flung into empty space and into the icy breath of solitude."

X

Nietzsche's philosophy represents the most extreme and perhaps also the most consistent form of that branch of Western thought which is usually referred to as *idealism*. It began with Descartes and proceeded through several stages in the speculation of Spinoza, Malebranche, and Leibniz, to achieve its most systematic formulation in the works of Kant, Fichte, and Hegel. In nineteenth-century *German* idealism man is conceived as the epistemological center of the world which as such is regarded as a mere product or artifact of the innate faculties of the human mind. This kind of idealism imprisons man in the fortress of his own thought, and man in turn imposes the structure of his mind on whatever there is admitted as extramental reality. Man is no longer confidingly opened toward Being and Reality, but he is filled with distrust and doubt as to anything which is not in the mind, of the mind, or the mind itself. It is this "prison of the mind" that later on became the object of the attacks launched by "realists," "phenomenologists," and "existentialists," from Kierkegaard, Feuerbach, and Marx to Bergson and Husserl, and from Husserl to Heidegger, Jaspers, Sartre, and Marcel.

Nietzsche, in following the premises of German idealism to their extreme conclusions, strips extramental reality of the last vestiges of independence and truth. Man, he argues, does not *discover* laws and values: he *creates* all values and then projects them into a chaotic conglomerate of phenomena. The supposed object of knowledge is for Nietzsche nothing but an artifact arbitrarily created by the human mind and will. Ideas are nothing but arbitrarily chosen signs and symbols without any objective validity. And it is this extreme epistemological subjectivism that leads Nietzsche to the denial of any objective laws of nature and in nature. The human mind constructs its own world by transforming, uniting, ordering, and simplifying a meaningless mass of phenomena. Both the world of sense experience and the supposed ontological or metaphysical realm behind sense experience are equally unreal. There is no "real" world at all. There is only a multitude of subjective, private worlds which Nietzsche calls "human perspectives." And thus, having started out from an idealistic and subjectivistic premise, Nietzsche proceeds to the complete annihilation of objective reality.

But the history of philosophy (Berkeley — Hume — Watson — Dewey — Carnap) shows that with the dissolution of the objective world and of objective truth the individual subject too is threatened with annihilation. Nietzsche was not unaware of this fact. "There is neither 'mind,' nor reason, nor thought, nor consciousness, nor soul, nor will, nor truth," he wrote in *The Will to Power*. "All these are fictions and quite useless." Beyond the illusory "perspectives" of the animal species called "man," there is —*nothing*.

"Nihilism," Nietzsche wrote early in 1888, "is an attitude of strong minds and wills. Negation in both thought and action is part of their nature." But what happens when this philosophy of "nihilism" meets with the idea of "Eternal Recurrence"? "Let us consider this thought in its most frightful form: existence, such as it is, without any meaning and goal, but inevitably recurring, inevitably moving in nothingness.

... That is the extreme form of nihilism: nothingness, meaninglessness eternalized!"

It is hardly surprising that Nietzsche found it impossible to maintain or endorse this kind of nihilism for any length of time. He soon came to see "Nihilism" and *"décadence"* as parallel phenomena. Modern Europe, he thought, was decadent and, aside from brief interludes, such as the Renaissance and the era of the Napoleonic Empire, it had been decadent since the fall of ancient Rome. Like Edward Gibbon, Nietzsche blamed Christianity (which he regarded as a late and hybrid form of Judaism) for having destroyed the strong and healthy paganism of the Roman Empire. Once the masses had triumphed in the French Revolution of 1789, they began to tyrannize the great individuals and, depriving them of their self-respect, drove them into nihilistic despair. Nihilism was thus seen as a consequence of individual and social *décadence*. But while the masses were sinking deeper and deeper into the void, the exceptional few might still succeed in saving themselves from the nihilistic snare.

Salvation from nihilism, Nietzsche tries to persuade himself, lies in the Will to Power. While all ideas, including the idea of the Will to Power, are fictions, some fictions may at times prove very useful. In fact, argues Nietzsche, we accept ideas not because they are true, but because they are useful. He thus pragmatically identifies "truth" with anything that strengthens and perpetuates Life. In other words, man's ideas are true to the extent that they beget practical results or serve to increase human power. The Will to Power is then conceived by Nietzsche as both the source and the criterion of all values, of all value judgments, and of human existence as such. All goals, purposes, ideals, and ends are expressions, derivations, instruments, or at best sublimations of the Will to Power.

All values fall a prey to Nihilism, all except the value judgment itself. Thus the only certainty which remains is the certitude of the judgment that every so-called value is false and fictitious. The weak ones, Nietzsche claims, are crushed by this "truth"; the stronger ones aid in the destruction of everything that has not already been broken; the strongest ones alone are able to overcome Nihilism and to survive the annihilation of all established "values." But to do that they must first have learned to stand alone and forsaken in a meaningless world. Aware of the fact that the so-called objective world harbors no genuine values, they will then feel free to engage creatively in value projects of their own making, and in this way they will eventually learn how to dominate the world: the world will serve them as an instrumental means for their own personal aggrandizement. Thus the breeding of great, heroic individuals, that is, of genuine representatives of the Will to Power, becomes for Nietzsche at this stage both the *raison d'être* and the most important goal of human society. Being sovereign masters of their free choice, this higher breed of men will be their own lawgivers. They will be "beyond good and evil," but the consciousness of their responsibility for their choices will raise them far above the brutes.

But these future "Lords of the World" must also be capable of enduring the greatest pain and suffering. "To such men," Nietzsche writes in *The Will to Power,* "I wish suffering, abandonment, sickness, maltreatment, humiliation; I wish that they may not be spared deep self-contempt, the torture of distrusting themselves, the misery of defeat: I have no pity on them because I wish for them the only thing which today can demonstrate a man's value or disvalue — *perseverance."* The brutal conqueror, the "tropical beast of prey," turns in the end away from all external triumphs, to the conquest of his own self. It hardly need be pointed out that Nietzsche's concept of the highest type of human existence comprises some contradictory elements.

Europe, says Nietzsche, has been infected with the leveling spirit of mediocrity — a spirit which, according to his way of thinking, was fostered by Christianity. The "spirit of the herd" has invaded science and manifests itself in varying degrees in democracy, socialism, and anarchism. The "higher men" must fight against all these tendencies and movements: they "must declare war on the masses." And hand in hand with the checking of the influence of "the herd" must go the breeding of a new aristocracy. The philosopher, the educator of the future, is to become the companion, guide, and counselor of the new rulers.

There is only one thing which holds the modern world back from undertaking its remaining task, the breeding of the "Lords of the Earth": those inherited values and valuations which all derive ultimately from one source — Christianity! For this reason *Christianity* now becomes for Nietzsche the mortal enemy; that Christianity which in its Lutheran version he knew from his parental home and whose heavy residue he still felt as a cumbersome burden on his soul. This enemy must be destroyed!

In September, 1888, Nietzsche began writing *The Anti-Christ.* The only new element in this "manifesto" is the intensity of passionate hatred. It is interesting, however, that Nietzsche exempts Christ from his general attack on everything Christian. Jesus, according to Nietzsche, taught "a new way of life" that was to bring peace and harmony to the human soul, so that the pacified soul might then effect the total transfiguration of all things. Such a unity and harmony of soul, though contrary to Nietzsche's own teaching, was by no means foreign to his innermost longing. And while his doctrine forced him to reject such a concept of life and of the world, he rejects it hesitatingly, gently, and almost reverently.

Christ died on the cross, says Nietzsche, and with Him died the essence of Christianity; for Christ was and has remained "the only Christian." His glad tidings was followed by "the *worst* tidings: the tidings of Paul . . . that genius of hate." Most of Nietzsche's accusations against Christianity have a feverish and hysterical ring: "I call Christianity the One great Curse, the one great inward corruption . . . the one immortal mark of shame of the human race." And yet, only a short time prior to this emotional outburst he had written to Peter Gast, "I hope I shall never show myself ungrateful to Christianity, for I owe to it the best experiences of my childhood."

In 1887 Nietzsche had written to Peter Gast from Sils-Maria: "I live . . . constantly in the vicinity of danger — without an answer to the question, 'Whither?'" For the past ten years he had tried desperately to meet this question with his answer of the Eternal Recurrence. But in Part One of *The Genealogy of Morals* another answer seemed to have suggested itself: "Can anyone," Nietzsche had asked there, "imagine anything that equals in miraculously enchanting force the symbol of the 'Holy Cross'? Nothing equals in impressive strength that paradox of a 'Crucified God' . . . of a God crucifying Himself for the salvation of men. In this sign and symbol at least Israel triumphs eternally over any other ideal."

In the autumn of 1888 Nietzsche told his sister in a letter from Italy that he was writing a review of his life. The reference is to *Ecce Homo,* perhaps the strangest autobiography and the most glowing self-apotheosis ever written. The title relates to a passage in the Gospel of St. John (19:4-6): "And now Pilate went out again, and said to them: See, I am bringing him out to you, to show that I cannot find any fault in him. Then, as Jesus came out, still wearing the crown of thorns and the scarlet cloak, Pilate said to them: *Ecce Homo* (see, here is *the Man*)." It seems clear that Nietzsche wanted to have these words applied to himself, who was also wearing "a crown of thorns."

Ecce Homo consists of four parts, the titles of which are self-explanatory: (1) "Why I am so wise"; (2) "Why I am so prudent"; (3) "Why I am writing such excellent books"; (4) "Why I am a Fate." On the whole this work is less bitter and polemic than *The Anti-Christ.* Nietzsche seems so certain of his victory that he can afford to forgive his enemies. But he remembers with pride that he has always been a warrior, and he enumerates the principles of his "war strategy": to attack only matters that are victorious; to attack only where he stands alone, without any allies; never to attack persons, but to use persons only "as a kind of huge magnifying glass" in order to make visible some creeping but as yet intangible *crisis.* In the final section of the book Nietzsche sees himself as the man of destiny who, though he has contradicted "as no one has ever dared to contradict," is nevertheless "the opposite of a spirit of negation." On the contrary, he is "the bearer of glad tidings," a Yea-Sayer with whom "the hope of the human race has been restored: *Ecrasez l'infame!* — Have I made myself clear? — Dionysos against the Crucified. . . ." With these words this bizarre autobiography ends.

XI

On November 13, 1888, Nietzsche wrote to Peter Gast from Turin, begging his friend to come and see him. This appeal was repeated more urgently in a second letter, written five days later. Comparatively little is known as to what happened during Nietzsche's last days at Turin, between Christmas, 1888, and early January, 1889. We have, however, his own testimony for the fact that he was beginning to have hallucinations of the dual presence of Christ and Dionysos. He was writing many letters during these days which reveal, among other things, that he was gradually losing the consciousness of his identity. Each of them was carefully inscribed on costly paper, and each bore a different signature. Thus he wrote, for example, to the Swedish playwright August Strindberg (signed: Nietzsche Caesar), to the Pope and the Papal Secretary of State, and to the King of Italy (signed: The Crucified). Other letters bore the signature "Dionysos." Nietzsche, in the progressive delusion of his mind, began to identify himself with the suffering god in the two forms in which the Deity had haunted his life and his thought. But he also identified himself with two criminals whose crimes had been publicized in the Paris press; or with Lesseps, the builder of the Suez Canal.

On January 9, Jacob Burckhardt, the famous historian and author of *The Culture of the Renaissance in Italy* — one of Nietzsche's oldest friends and a former colleague — went to see Franz Overbeck, the liberal Protestant theologian of the University of Basel. The two men were only casually acquainted, and Overbeck sensed immediately that Burckhardt had come to discuss the fate of Nietzsche, their common friend. After a consultation with Professor Wille, the director of the psychiatric clinic, Overbeck immediately departed for Turin. He found Nietzsche in a most pitiful condition. From the landlord he learned about the most recent events: on January 3, on leaving his living quarters, Nietzsche had witnessed a cab driver brutally mistreating his horse. With tears and sobs he had thrown his arms about the animal's neck and had threatened anyone who tried to come near him. Then he had collapsed in the street. After he had been carried to his room and had regained consciousness, he believed himself transformed into the dual deity of Christ and Dionysos. A physician was called in, and the police and the German consul were notified.

Overbeck was enthusiastically welcomed by Nietzsche, who soon began to improvise on the piano and to sing "sublime, wonderfully visionary and unspeakably horrible things about himself as the successor of the defunct God." Overbeck then enlisted the aid of a German dentist to transport Nietzsche to Professor Wille's clinic in Basel. His mother arrived on January 13, and she accompanied her son from Basel to an asylum in the German city of Jena. There, under the care of Dr. Binswanger, Nietzsche grew gradually calmer, although the mental derangement (usually diagnosed as progressive paralysis) advanced steadily.

Early in 1890 Nietzsche's mother moved from Naumburg to Jena. And when her son, at the end of March, was permitted to leave the asylum, she took him into her home. After her death, in 1897, Elisabeth, whose husband had died and who had thereupon returned from Paraguay, cared for her brother during the last years of his life.

Nietzsche became famous almost overnight, and the royalties on his works began to be pouring in. Elisabeth bought an estate at Weimar, not far from the Goethe house, and there she assembled all of her brother's books, manuscripts, and notes. And here Nietzsche, the author of *The Will to Power,* resided, entirely passive and absolutely powerless, unaware of his growing fame. He died on August 25, 1900, and was buried in the little churchyard at Röcken, next to his father's resting place.

XII

The modern *philosophy of existence* wants to call man back to himself. José Ortega y Gasset expresses a conviction common to all the thinkers of this school when he asserts that modern man, afraid of the lonesomeness of his existence, has been trying to steal himself into the anonymity of the social collective. Miguel de Unamuno saw in modern man a sort of Don Quixote engaged in a restless search of his own substance and to that end embarking on the adventures of an incalculable existence. "Man," he said, "must be thrown into the ocean, deprived of every anchorage, so that he may learn again what it means to live as a human being."

While the ancient Greek thinkers were primarily concerned with the problem of the intellectual penetration of the "cosmos," the Fathers of the Church and the mediaeval schoolmen discerned in this cosmos a divinely created order of Being, an order in which and through which man was to find his way to God, the supreme Being (*Ipsum esse subsistens*) and the Author of the entire order of beings or existents. The way of Christian ethics was described by St. Thomas Aquinas as "the movement of the rational creature toward God" (*motus rationalis creaturae in Deum*). And, as the action of every creature flows from its "being" (*operari sequitur esse*), the action of man, the rational creature, must correspond to his rational nature which as such has the capacity of knowing the hierarchical order of Being. In trying to conform his existence to his essence (or nature), man may expect to realize the meaning of his life in the created universe: in obedient reverence for the order of Being, for his own self, and for God, the Creator of all essences and existences, in whose Being essence and existence are self-identical or one.

The cosmo-centered view of pagan antiquity and the God-centered view of Christianity gave way in the secularized modern world to a man-centered view of reality. In Hegel's metaphysics all beings are still situated "in God," but only as dialectically determined entities, as "phases" of the historical movement of the self-realization of the absolute "World Spirit." God Himself is drawn into the evolutionary process and is ultimately identified with this process. When this Hegelian metaphysics is radically dissolved in the thinking of Feuerbach, Marx, Stirner, and Nietzsche (the "Young Hegelians"), man finds himself without God, confronted with the Promethean task of becoming the sole "creator" of all truth and of all values. From then on human existence begins to sway back and forth between the desire for self-deification and the experience of failure and shipwreck. And in this hour of "crisis," man, who by his very nature is both a questioning and a questionable, problematic being, begins in anguish to probe into the meaning of his self, of the world, and of his "being-in-the-world."

Both Kierkegaard and Nietzsche are opposed to the bourgeois complacency of Hegel's synthetic "system" of philosophic idealism; both are opposed to the dissolution of the individual in the historico-logical processes of thought as well as to any and all forms of State-idolatry. On the other hand, both experience profoundly the growing homelessness of the individual in the "objective" and collective modern world. This forlornness begets existential despair, but despair may beget salvation if, face to face with "nothingness," the individual can be reawakened to an "authentic" existence. Both Kierkegaard and Nietzsche confront man with the nightmare of an "unauthentic" existence in a meaningless world and, by doing so, they mean to warn him of that abyss and to call him back to his true self. But while Kierkegaard, the Christian, knows that man's true selfhood is grounded in God, that man is "nothing" without God — Nietzsche, the apostate, solemnly proclaims the "death of God" and thereby destroys not only man's individual self but simultaneously all the selves or "thous" in the communal order with whom the individual shares his human essence or nature.

Nietzsche's saying, "God is dead," appears for the first time in Book Three of *The Joyful Wisdom,* but already in *The Birth of Tragedy,* his first major work, he had written, "I believe in the ancient Germanic saying: all the gods must die." Section 125 of *The Joyful Wisdom* contains the following passage: "Have you not heard as yet of that mad-man who on one bright forenoon lit a lantern, ran out into the market-place and cried out again and again, 'I seek God! I seek God!' — Because there were standing about just at that time many who did not believe in God, the mad-man was the occasion of great merriment. Has God been lost?, said one of them. Has He lost His way like a child?, asked another. Or is He hiding Himself? Is He afraid of us? Has He boarded a ship? Has He emigrated? Thus they cried and laughed. But the mad-man pierced them with his glance: 'Whither has God gone?,' he cried; 'I am going to tell you. *We have killed Him* — you and I! We all are His murderers. But how have we accomplished this? How have we been able to empty the sea? Who gave us the sponge with which to wipe off the entire horizon? What were we doing when we unchained this earth from its sun? Whither does the earth now move? Whither do we ourselves move? Away from every sun? Are we not constantly falling? . . . Are we not groping our way in an infinite nothingness? Do we not feel the breath of the empty spaces? Has it not become colder? Is there not night and ever more night? . . . How do we manage to console ourselves, we master-assassins? The most holy and the most mighty being that the world possessed — it has bled to death under our knives. Who is going to wipe this blood off our hands? Where is the water with which to purify ourselves? What feasts of atonement, what sacred rites shall we have to invent? . . . Must not we ourselves become gods to make ourselves worthy of such a deed?'"

The saying, "God is dead," means that nothingness is spreading. *Nihilism,* "the uncanniest of all guests," stands at the door. An ultimate goal is lacking, and there is no longer an answer to the question, "Why?" "Never again will you be able to pray, to adore, to rest in an infinite trust . . . there is no longer any reason in whatever happens and no love in whatever will happen to *you* — no longer any resting place for your heart. . . . Man of the great renunciation, all this you are willing to renounce? Who will give you the power to do this? No one has yet had such power!"

The new valueless world and existence demand the creation of new values or, in Nietzsche's words, a "transvaluation of all values." An incomplete or halfhearted Nihilism merely attempts to fill the vacuum created by "the death of God" with such paltry substitutes as humanitarianism, utilitarianism, or socialism, while a complete or total Nihilism courageously proceeds to the "transvaluation" of all traditional values. In this way it may yet generate a "superabundance of Life." Thus Nietzsche, who in the frailty of his physical constitution felt himself cruelly cheated by nature, believed he had discovered a means of self-exaltation in the divinization of Nature and Life. He knew perfectly well that man cannot live a meaningless life and that therefore any *absolute* Nihilism remains an impossibility.

In this as in other respects Nietzsche's position became in the end self-contradictory. To make possible the proposed "transvaluation of all values," Nietzsche had to proclaim a strict relativism of all values. The Super-Man, who is "beyond good and evil," becomes the sovereign and arbitrary "creator" of the new values of his choice. But does he not thereby become himself the absolute norm and measure and the archenemy of relativism?

Nietzsche, furthermore, advocates the moral self-determination of man: he demands that man should live in such a way that he can and must desire the "Eternal Recurrence," that is, the eternal repetition of the cycle of his earthly existence. And yet, under the influence of Darwinism, Nietzsche preaches an *amor fati,* that is, a rigid deterministic fatalism.

Again, Nietzsche mournfully announces "the death of God," but he gives the lie to his avowed atheism by his never ending seeking and longing for "the unknown God," by his thirst for the eternal and the divine: "All the streams of my tears flow toward thee! And the flame of my heart burns for thee! Oh, come back to me, my unknown God! My sorrow and my ultimate happiness!"

Nietzsche's final self-deification bears witness to the truth of Martin Luther's saying that "man worships either God or an idol." In other words, Nietzsche cannot evade the fact that man is essentially a "worshiping being" (*ens adorans*) and as such always pays homage to some "highest good" (*summum bonum*), either to God, the true "absolute," or to some pseudo-absolute, such as money, fame, power, "the race," "the state," "the nation," "society." In the case of Nietzsche his own ego usurps in the end the vacated throne of God.

As Johannes B. Lotz points out, the objects of Nietzsche's attack are in the main three: *Christianity, God,* and *Spirit* (or Intellect).[14] "At the age of twelve," Nietzsche writes in retrospect, "I saw God in His splendor." The German critic suggests that this terse sentence perhaps refers to the one unique hour in which Nietzsche answered God's demand for a total self-surrender with a rebellious *"non serviam,"* so that henceforth the lonely thinker was destined to circle round the living flame of Divine Love like one of the fallen angels.

Contrary to historical truth Nietzsche began to see *Christianity* in the discoloration of Schopenhauer's pessimism. It was presented to him as a religion that demanded hatred and contempt of life, and thus he came to oppose to it his own eulogy of earthly existence. The spirit of the age and the conventionalized "bourgeois" religion of many of Nietzsche's contemporaries seemed to demonstrate furthermore that *God* had lost His power over men's minds and hearts. God was

---

[14] Cf. Johannes B. Lotz, S.J., *Das christliche Menschenbild im Ringen der Zeit* (Heidelberg, 1947), *passim.*

"dead," and man had to rebuild his existence without God and against God. Following Ludwig Feuerbach's line of reasoning, Nietzsche began to regard God as an illusory phantom into which man had projected his fears and hopes. Once the illusory nature of this god was recognized, man remained as the sole creator, and he had to safeguard his creative freedom from any future "divine" infringements.

The consequences of the loss of God which Nietzsche experienced so strongly and disastrously in his own existence, he visualized in magnified proportions in the large context of contemporary Western civilization: "The greatest of recent events," he wrote in *The Joyful Wisdom,* "that 'God is dead' — begins to cast its shadows over Europe. . . . We may expect a long sequence of breakdowns, destructions, revolutions . . . an eclipse the like of which this earth has perhaps never seen before."

Nietzsche's *anti-intellectualism,* finally, wants to confine human existence to man's bodily and earthly life. Man's salvation must come from "below," from the telluric forces of instincts and urges. Nietzsche's "new man" must reclaim these forces from an illusory "beyond" and must then utilize them for the construction of his this-worldly realm. The *Man-God* or *Super-Man* is an *Ersatz-Gott* functioning as the primary cause of a "new world" which in the eternal recurrence of its constitutive elements will manifest the superabundance of "Life." This is the new form of "eternity" that is born simultaneously with the new "Lord of the World."

Nietzsche's concepts of *Christianity, God,* and *Intellect* represent merely the final phase of a historical evolution which took its start from the declaration of absolute human autonomy in the age of the Renaissance, an evolution which is carried to its logical conclusion in the self-deification of the Super-Man, the *Man-God,* who in his attempt to dethrone God strikes at the roots of his own self.

When Nietzsche designates Christianity as the greatest antihuman force in the history of mankind, his distorted view evidently derives not only from Schopenhauer's atheism but also from his early indoctrination with Martin Luther's doctrine of nature and grace. Orthodox Lutheranism had so radically divorced nature from supernature that everything natural, temporal, and human had been emptied of any eternal and metaphysical meaning. Man had been judged incapable of co-operating with divine grace and consequently incapable of "good works." But in the Gospels, Christ actually refers to Himself as "the Life" (John 14:6), stating that He has come "that they may have

Life, and have it more abundantly" (John 10:10). Reborn in Christ, the *God-Man,* man is said to have become "a partaker of the divine nature" (2 Pet. 1:4) and a "son of God" (1 John 3:1). This means that the life of grace does not destroy or mutilate human life and human nature but, on the contrary, saves them and preserves them. The Christian cross is thus, as Johannes Lotz points out, not the negation of *life,* but the negation of *death:* it signifies the restoration of life in its integrity and plenitude.

The "God" whose "death" Nietzsche announces bears no resemblance to the God of the Judaic-Christian tradition. This "God" is the same scurrilous specter that is satirized by Kierkegaard and Ibsen, that "good old uncle," the "God" of a complacent bourgeois society, who has been divested of all power and majesty: the guarantor of the safety and satiety of man's "everydayness," the conniving helper of man in the attainment of his selfish desires. Nietzsche's love of greatness and heroism rose in revolt against such a "God."

The Christian God is neither man's "chum" nor is He (as in the theology of Luther and Calvin) a total stranger to all human affairs and concerns. He is Personal Life in the highest degree and in infinite plenitude; a superabundant Life whose sheen is reflected in different shades of brightness in the being of all creatures. Because He is man's origin, ground, and end, He is also the guarantor of man's ultimate perfection and happiness. He is man's highest good and end so exclusively that no earthly, temporal, finite good is ever capable of fully satisfying the human heart which, in the words of St. Augustine, is restless until it finds rest in Him. Without God, therefore, human existence shrinks and withers away in meaninglessness and absurdity. Man's self-surrender to God, which for Nietzsche signifies abject self-enslavement, is for a Christian the highest form of self-affirmation and self-realization. In God he truly finds himself and acquires his authentic freedom, strength, and greatness.

The *Intellect,* finally, is not, as Nietzsche contends, inimical to life but, according to St. Thomas Aquinas, "the highest degree of life" (*supremus gradus vitae*). It opens up for man the totally new perspectives of the infinite, the eternal, and the divine. And it is in virtue of his intellect that man may be said to be *"capax Dei,"* that is, capable of embracing God by sharing in some measure in the Light of the Divine Intellect.

But if Christianity values the human intellect so highly, does it do so perhaps at the expense and to the detriment of the human *physis,* man's bodily, "fleshly" existence? St. Augustine, in turning against the gloomy view which the Manichaean sect (and, later on, the "Reformers" and the "Puritans") took of human nature and the life of the body, emphasizes again and again that all natural and physical life is metaphysically good because it is a creation of the "good God," whose goodness and glory it reflects. Catholic theology and philosophy insist in opposition to Lutheranism and Calvinism that even original sin could not completely corrupt human nature, a nature which has forever been redeemed, healed, and consecrated by the *God-Man,* who in His Incarnation assumed the physical nature of man. Thus in the integrally Christian view even the final and eternal status of man is not that of a pure spirit, but that of human nature in its totality: the renewed substantial union of soul *and* body. The fully or authentically *human* existence is therefore, as Kierkegaard's insight had unwaveringly proclaimed, the totally *Christian* existence.

CHAPTER FOUR

THE CALL OF TRUTH AND BEING:
HUSSERL AND HEIDEGGER

I

THE contemporary Philosophy of Existence in all its branches is inspired by the thinking of Kierkegaard and Nietzsche. As has been shown in some of the preceding chapters, this does not mean that the problem of existence was not faced and subjected to philosophic analysis long before the advent of the nineteenth century. Heraclitus, Socrates, St. Augustine, and Pascal as well as many of the great Christian mystics were undoubtedly genuine existential thinkers. What is new in contemporary existentialism is the visualization of human existence within the general frame and the specific conditions of the present age.

In an almost completely secularized and disenchanted world the ancient questions concerning the nature of man and the meaning of life are being asked with a new urgency. The loss of God in the widely disseminated philosophies of atheism, materialism, and naturalistic "humanism" has thrust modern man into a situation of spiritual abandonment and homelessness in which everything, including his own existence, has become questionable. Thus the problem of "to be or not to be" is once more forced upon him as an alternative involving self-preservation or self-annihilation.

While the contemporary Philosophy of Existence presents in most of its discussions modern variations of the major themes of the existential thinking of the past, the orchestration of these themes as well as the technical nomenclature used in their elaboration stems to a large extent from the German philosopher Martin Heidegger. This in spite of the fact that Heidegger himself has repeatedly disavowed his association with "existentialism," insisting that his philosophy is primarily concerned with "being" rather than with "existence."

The existentialist themes, discussed by various authors in the terminology coined by Heidegger, include, among others: the contingency, insecurity, self-estrangement, and dereliction of human existence (*Dasein*); its ultimate meaning; its "temporality," "historicity," and "authenticity"; its "care," its "dread," and its encounter with the abyss of "nothingness"; its "being-toward-death" (*Sein zum Tode*) and "freedom-toward-death"; the interrelation of "being" and "existence," "being" and "truth," "being" and "nothing," "being" and "transcendence." The connotations implied in these philosophical and anthropological concepts and the conclusions educed from them vary according to the theological and metaphysical convictions of individual authors, but the questions and problems to which they refer are essentially the same.

The method which is adopted by most of the contemporary existentialist thinkers for the analysis and elucidation of these basic problems is similarly uniform: it is the "phenomenological method" which was first developed by Edmund Husserl (1859–1938), the founder of the school of Phenomenology. A native of the Bohemian province of Moravia, Husserl began his academic career as a mathematician. Having turned to philosophy under the influence of the German philosopher Friedrich Paulsen, it became the great ambition of Husserl's life and work to transform philosophy into an exact and absolutely trustworthy science.[1] From 1916 until 1929 he held the chair of philosophy at the University of Freiburg in Baden. He died in exile in Paris, and his last work, the *Méditations Cartésiennes,* was written and published in the French language. In 1929, Martin Heidegger, Husserl's most promising and prominent pupil, became his successor in the University of Freiburg.

Husserl acknowledged his indebtedness to the *Wissenschaftslehre* of Bernhard Bolzano (1781–1848), and to the neo-Aristotelian "descriptive psychology" of Franz Brentano (1838–1917). Bolzano was a native of Bohemia and achieved international fame not only as a Catholic theologian but as an astute philosopher and mathematician. Brentano was a Catholic priest and at one time a distinguished member of the theological faculty in the University of Würzburg in Lower Franconia. He came, however, into conflict with the ecclesiastical authorities and was suspended from his priestly office and relieved of his academic duties. From 1874 to 1895 he was a lecturer at the University of

---

[1] Cf. especially *Ideas: General Introduction to Pure Phenomenology* (London: Allen and Unwin, 1931).

Vienna, and the final years of his life were spent in retirement in Italy and Switzerland.

With his distinguished teachers Husserl shared the conviction that in the present age more than ever philosophy must be able to present a doctrine and a truth of universal validity. What kind of truth is it, he asked, which can claim to provide an unshakable foundation for a universal science? It must be a truth, he answered his own question, that is absolutely univocal and immutable in its universality. Husserl thus showed himself strictly opposed to any kind of relativism. There must be, he argued, an essence of truth as there is an essence of every other idea, and this essence is reflected in all particular truths. Without this essential principle of truth the existence of the world would be impossible. Though truth in its essence transcends every contingent existent, it is the "intentional object" of every true judgment of the human mind. This essence of truth, Husserl asserted, is revealed in a mental act of "intuition" (*Wesensschau*). His philosophic position thus entails a realism of essences, that is, a form of epistemological realism as extreme and radical as that of Plato and Descartes.

What is meant by Husserl's "intuition of essences" may be illustrated by referring to the artistic or poetic experience as distinguished from scientific knowledge. In the natural sciences an object is understood and explained in terms of its visible and tangible elements, qualities, and functions. An aesthetic apperception of the object, on the other hand, is, according to the testimony of both creative artists and aesthetic theorists, of a more immediate and, at the same time, a more fundamental and comprehensive nature. The French novelist Flaubert, for example, speaks in one of his letters of his "entering into the particular thing" — be it rock, plant, animal, or human being — that he depicts in his writings. An artist who is interested in the essential nature of the world of objects — a painter with the penetrating vision of a Michelangelo, a Greco, a Van Gogh — starts, to be sure, from sense perception, but he goes far beyond it in rendering the essences of things and beings. There are then, it would seem, aspects of reality which are hidden from sense perception and inaccessible to it, but open to a different kind of mental or intellectual apperception. This is obviously what both Plato and Husserl have in mind when they speak of the knowledge of "Ideas" or "Essences," respectively.

In both kinds of perception — sense knowledge and "eidetic" knowledge (or "ideation") — something "real" is directly given and perceived. Husserl therefore repeatedly emphasizes that there is nothing "mystical" in such an "intuition of essences," even if the objects thus perceived are above and beyond sense perception. All "ideation," he insists, is rooted in sense objects and sense perceptions and can never dispense with them. The philosopher has to rely as much on the perceptive faculties of his senses as the painter has to rely on his optical vision, the composer on his sense of hearing, and the poet on both his eyes and his ears. What makes the artist is, however, not his faculties of visual, auditory, and tactual perception, but precisely his capacity to erect on the foundation of his sensory perceptions a new world and reality of higher validity and truth. And the reality and truth with which the philosopher is concerned are of a similar nature. Philosophy, according to Husserl, is thus not so much a science of facts as a science of essences (*Wesenswissenschaft*), and philosophic knowledge is not a knowledge of facts but a knowledge of essences.

Husserl calls the world of philosophic truths a world of *ideal phenomena*. They have, he says, no "real" existence in the sense in which existence is attributed to a rock or a tree or a dog, but neither do they have a purely "ideal" existence in the manner of Plato's "Ideas" or Kant's "things-in-themselves" (*noumena*). The Kantian *Ding an sich* remains unknowable: the human mind knows only its phenomenal manifestations as they "appear" in human consciousness. Husserl professes no interest in this central problem of the Kantian theory of knowledge. His own interest is centered in the elaboration of a science of the "pure phenomena" or "pure essences" of consciousness. Such "eidetic sciences" are, for example, pure geometry or pure arithmetic: they are sciences in which concepts are formed, judgments passed, and conclusions arrived at, independent of sense experience (*a priori*). Such purely mathematical concepts as number, triangle, and circle, Husserl calls pure essences, and he claims that such pure essences can also be encountered in a purified intellectual and philosophic intuition. He therefore proposes to analyze and describe such intellectual experiences in analogy with the mathematician's analysis and description of the objects and contents of physics. He thus develops his "phenomenological method" as an instrument to be used in the radical analysis of "pure consciousness."

The phenomenological method in its application to the analysis of the contents of human consciousness demands the simple and unprejudiced observation and description of those phenomena which are actually encountered either in sense perception or in "eidetic" perception. As his starting point Husserl chooses the point of view of everyday life with its experience of a surrounding external world. In this familiar environment I perceive certain real and definite objects. But I may decide to shift my attention from such directly observed objects — this desk, this inkstand, this bookshelf — to any number of things which I know to be there, even if I do not observe them visually at the moment: the pictures on the wall behind my back, the lecture rooms and students in the building in which my office is located, the neighboring buildings, the gardens and playgrounds, and so on. All these things I know to be integral parts of my surrounding world, and the shifting of my attention to them makes them the more or less clearly co-perceived contents of my consciousness.

Into this natural experience of my everyday surroundings Husserl now proposes to introduce a radically different point of view. What would happen, he asks in effect, if I were to apply to these everyday experiences the principle of the Cartesian doubt? I might tell myself: it is possible that I am being deceived. I have the illusion that there is a desk with its utensils in front of me, and I merely imagine the existence of all those other things which, on the basis of previous observations, I had taken for granted. What, then, will remain if I call in question the existence of these supposedly "real" implements of my surrounding world? Nothing will remain but the experienced contents of my consciousness; for, no matter whether the objects of my experience are real or imagined, there can be no doubt that they are genuine experiences as contents of my consciousness.

And what has happened to the "real" world in the process of Husserl's "phenomenological reduction"? The external world of natural and normal everyday experience has simply been "disconnected," "bracketed," "put out of play," together with all my preconceived beliefs, opinions, prejudices, and convictions in regard to existing objects. There remains nothing but the sphere of "pure consciousness" with its indubitable contents. If rigorously applied, Husserl claims, this "phenomenological method" will ultimately answer the epistemological question, "How is it possible to gain access to transcendent reality?"

In all the transformations which a thing may undergo, there persists, according to Husserl, an identity and unity of certain essential features which remain unchanged. And phenomenological description is the description of these essential features. There are several degrees of evidence, and the final goal of phenomenological description is the attainment of an adequate evidence of the transcendent reality of the phenomenon. As a "science of essences" phenomenology thus aims at the recognition of the essential predicables that belong to individual objects.

Attention has been called to the fact that Husserl acknowledged his indebtedness to the teachings of both Bolzano and Brentano. The question therefore suggests itself to what extent his Phenomenology shares in the philosophic heritage of the *philosophia perennis,* that is, that broad and vital stream of philosophic thought which reached its crest in the synthetic digest of Greek and Christian speculation embodied in the works of the leading mediaeval scholastics, especially those of the Thomistic school.[2]

Both Husserl and St. Thomas Aquinas teach that truth exists objectively, independent of the seeker and knower. They disagree, however, in their interpretation of the nature of Truth as such. For St. Thomas the object of the "first philosophy" (*prima philosophia,* i.e., metaphysics) is God. After having discussed the idea of God and the modes of His being and knowledge, he proceeds to a definition and description of the relationship which exists between the essence, existence, and knowledge of created beings and the essence, existence, and knowledge of God. In this connection St. Thomas also inquires into the capacity of human beings for knowing God, knowing themselves, and knowing other created beings. Each being, he asserts, has received the mode and essence of its existence from God and, correspondingly, also its specific measure and manner of striving, feeling, and knowing, its specific grade and type of truth and perfection.

As against this God-centered view of the world and of every created being in it, Husserl's Phenomenology presents a radical shift of accent and viewpoint. Taking its start from the human subject and his consciousness, Phenomenology remains ego-centered throughout; at no point does it achieve a genuine transcendence of the sphere of immanence. St. Thomas, on the other hand, knows of an order of intelligibility which not only transcends every created being but is prior to it, an order of which every created being partakes analogically. Intellectual knowledge, according to St. Thomas, is only possible in proportion to the range of intelligibility that is comprised in the object of knowledge. And while things and beings are thus known to some extent in their relation to the transcendent universal order

---

[2] Cf. the author's *A Realistic Philosophy* (Milwaukee: The Bruce Publishing Company, 1944), pp. 18–21.

of intelligibility, the range and mode of such knowledge is strictly proportionate to the capacity of the human intellect.

"The human soul knows all things in the light of their eternal reasons," says St. Thomas.[3] He agrees with Husserl that the perceived objects or phenomena are the material cause of human knowledge, but he denies that they are its ultimate term. In St. Thomas' view this ultimate term and object of human knowledge is God and the Divine Intellect. The human intellect is described by him as *"capax Dei,"* that is, as capable of being assimilated to some extent to the Divine Intellect in intellectual knowledge.

The potentialities of the human intellect with regard to the plenitude of the intelligible order may, however, never be fully realized in *statu viae* (i.e., in this earthly life), and for this reason every philosophy will ultimately remain fragmentary. St. Thomas points out that even material objects are known by man only imperfectly and not with the richness and fullness of perfectly comprehensive knowledge. And this more or less perfect knowledge comes to the human mind directly through created things but indirectly through the Divine Intellect, the infinite and eternal source, cause, and measure of all truth and all being. In the words of St. Augustine, "If we both recognize that truth is contained in what you say and in what I say: whence then comes our knowledge or vision of it? Neither do I see it in you, nor do you see it in me, but we both see it in that immutable Truth which is superior to our minds."[4] In short, the *philosophia perennis* holds that truth cannot be properly defined without referring it to God and the Divine Intellect. For if there were no absolute norm of things, prior to them and prior to finite minds, then every judgment regarding things would remain arbitrary, and any objectively certain articulation and evaluation of both essences and existences would become impossible.

Husserl, then, deviates from some of the basic tenets of the *philosophia perennis* when he assumes that the capacities of the human mind and the reaches of human knowledge are well-nigh unlimited. The fullness of truth exists, says St. Thomas with Husserl, but, he adds, only Divine knowledge and the Divine Mind can ever comprehend and comprise it in its plenitude. Husserl's ideal goal, in other words, is realized only in Divine knowledge where being and knowing are one, whereas for the finite mind they are distinct and apart.

---

[3] St. Thomas Aquinas, *Summa Theologica,* Ia, qu. 84, a. 5.
[4] St. Augustine, *Confessions,* XII, 25.

Again, for St. Thomas all human knowledge is gained by way of the rational analytic and synthetic treatment of the data furnished by sense perception. Husserl, on the other hand, insists that philosophic evidence results from an "intuition of essences." The implied meaning seems to be, however, that the philosopher need not compare a number of objects before he proceeds to abstract from them their essential qualities, but that a single "intuitive" illumination reveals the essence in the individual object. Phenomenological "reduction" or abstraction means "looking away" ("bracketing") from all accidental qualities in order to concentrate on the essence of the object. St. Thomas, who assigns to the intellect the function of *"intus-legere,"* that is, of reading and disclosing the essential natures *("rationes")* of things, would in all probability have no quarrel with such an "intuition of essences." Husserl's conviction that this kind of "intuition" penetrates deeper into the world of existence than the traditional logical syllogism is shared by some leading Thomists.

Husserl and St. Thomas, furthermore, seem united in their opposition to any integral idealism and rationalism that regards the objects of knowledge as constructs or creations of the human mind and its innate categories. But whereas St. Thomas conceives of the analytical activity of reason as both active and passive, devoting considerable effort to the elucidation of the abstractive function of the "active intellect" *(intellectus agens)*, Husserl asserts the primarily passive nature of rational intuitions.

Husserl claims for his "intuition of essences" the same kind and degree of "immediacy" or self-evident truth that St. Thomas restricts to "first principles."[5] Phenomenological intuitions, in other words, are regarded by Husserl as *a priori* truths and thus beyond the jurisdiction of experience. Only in two other instances (aside from "first principles") did St. Thomas admit such an immediate and *a priori* certitude of knowledge: one is the general knowledge of "the Good" (as distinguished from what is good in this or that particular instance or situation), which he describes as an *a priori* of practical reason; the other is the immediate experience and evidence which man has of his own existence. This latter is an *a priori* knowledge in the sense that it does not depend on any kind of demonstration.

It had been Husserl's original endeavor to break down Kant's dogma of the rational inaccessibility of "things-in-themselves." His

---

[5] Cf. the author's *A Realistic Philosophy*, p. 32 ff.

own realm of intuitively known essences was to replace Kant's *Ding an sich*. Husserl's philosophic interest, in other words, turned from the subject to that object which for Kant had remained an *"ignotum X."* In this original effort Husserl did, however, not persist: he never succeeded in actually reaching the sphere of transsubjective reality. St. Thomas succeeded where Husserl failed because he included in his approach to reality not only sense experience and intellectual experience but, in addition, the contents of revealed truth. While the focus of Husserl's Phenomenology is a purified transcendental consciousness, the focus of Thomistic philosophy is the creative and uncreated Being of God and His relationship to the various gradations of created being.

II

It had been Husserl's original intention to turn from the subjectivism of Kantianism to the objects themselves and to free the realm of essences from its lifeless rigidity in order to reveal its interrelation with concrete historical existences. This objective, which Husserl himself later on relinquished in favor of a Cartesian immanence of consciousness, reappears in the speculation of Martin Heidegger. For him as for Husserl, philosophy is primarily a reading of phenomena, but beyond that it is for Heidegger "a universal ontology, starting out from a hermeneutics (i.e., an ontological analysis and interpretation) of man."[6] On the basis of sense experience and side by side with it, Husserl's philosophy aspired to a supra-empirical "intuition of essences" (*Wesensschau*). Heidegger applies Phenomenology and its methodological devices to a Philosophy of Existence which he wants to anchor, however, in a new "fundamental ontology." The central question, therefore, of Heidegger's philosophy concerns not "existence" but "Being." It reads: "What is Being and why is it?" or, in the phrasing which Leibniz had given to the same question, "Why is there something rather than nothing?"[7]

Martin Heidegger was born in 1889 in the little town of Messkirch in the German province of Baden, and he lives at present in seclusion at Todtnauberg in the Black Forest. "There on top of a mountain," writes Stefan Schimanski, "with the valley deep down below, with nothing but space and wilderness all around, in that small skiing hut, I spoke to the philosopher. . . . His living conditions were primitive; his books were few, and his only relationship to

---

[6] Heidegger, *Sein und Zeit* (1927); 6th edition (Tübingen: Neomarius Verlag, 1949), p. 37 f.

[7] Cf. Leibniz, *Principes de la nature et de la grâce fondées en raison.*

the world was a stack of writing paper. . . . The atmosphere of
silence all around provided a faithful setting for Heidegger's philosophy. . . . The external world faithfully reflected the world of the
mind . . . , the spirit of overwhelming solitude."[8]

Born and raised as a Roman Catholic, Heidegger shows himself
well acquainted with the scholastic tradition in its Thomistic and
Scotistic branches. His academic training proceeded at first under the
influence of the Neo-Kantian school of Wilhelm Windelband and
Heinrich Rickert and then brought him into contact with Husserl
and his Phenomenology. He taught at the University of Marburg and,
in 1929, succeeded Husserl at the University of Freiburg. In 1933, as
rector of the latter institution, he delivered an address in which he
expressed qualified approval of the National Socialist revolution. In
1935, he declined Adolf Hitler's invitation to accept the rectorate of
the University of Berlin. After the defeat of Germany and the occupation of southern Baden by the French, Heidegger, for political
reasons, was not permitted to resume his teaching.[9]

Heidegger's first published work was his inaugural dissertation
(for the university lectureship), dealing with Duns Scotus' doctrine
of Categories.[10] Part One of his masterpiece, *Sein und Zeit* (Being and
Time), representing two of the originally planned six sections of the
work, appeared in 1927. Part Two is still unpublished. The essays
Kant and the Problem of Metaphysics, On the Essence of Cause (or
"Ground"), and *What is Metaphysics?,* were published in 1929. The
first was a reinterpretation of Kant's *Critique of Pure Reason,* the
second (dedicated to Husserl on the occasion of his seventieth birth-
day) a discussion of the problem of "transcendence," and the third
a new and critical approach to the problem of metaphysics.[11] Three

---

[8] Cf. *Existence and Being,* with an introduction by Werner Brock (Chicago: Henry
Regnery Company, 1949), p. 10 f. This work represents the first English paraphrase,
translation, and interpretation of some of Heidegger's major writings. Compiled by
the co-operative effort of Werner Brock, Stefan Schimanski, Douglas Scott, R. F. C.
Hull, and Alan Crick (all of England), it contains a summary account of *Sein und
Zeit* and both outlines' and translations of the essays *Hölderlins Gedicht: Andenken*
(1943), *Hölderlin und das Wesen der Dichtung* (1936), *Über das Wesen der Wahrheit*
(1943), and *Was ist Metaphysik? Mit einem Nachwort* (1929, 1943).

[9] Officially Professor Emeritus, he has, in the meantime, been given a *Lehrauftrag,*
i.e., he is conducting seminars and offering a few specified lecture courses.

[10] *Die Kategorien- und Bedeutungslehre des Duns Scotus* (1916).

[11] *Kant und das Problem der Metaphysik; Über das Wesen des Grundes; Was ist
Metaphysik?* (1929); the latter was republished with a *Postscript* (1943).

studies dealing with the German poet Friedrich Hölderlin were published in 1936, 1941, and 1942.[12] Two additional works appeared in the postwar period: an analysis of *Plato's Doctrine of Truth,* with an appended *Letter on Humanism,* addressed to M. Jean Beaufret of Paris, and a volume entitled *Holzwege,* containing essays on Anaximander, Hegel, Nietzsche, Rainer Maria Rilke, and on several other subjects related to philosophy, art, and literature.[13]

Heidegger is "a peasant by birth and tradition," says Schimanski, and this is precisely the way the author of this book remembers his onetime teacher: stocky, sturdy, and stubborn, rooted in the maternal earth of his homeland, wrapped up in his search for truth and scarcely interested in enticing others to follow him on his lonely path. That Heidegger has found many such followers nevertheless and that the influence of his thought extends today far beyond the boundaries of Germany is not at all attributable to his own efforts; he has, on the contrary, done everything possible to render difficult the access to his philosophy. First of all, he has created a philosophic language and terminology all his own, frequently either reverting to the long-forgotten root meanings of words and concepts, or coining new ones to satisfy his groping quest for an adequate verbal expression of his ideas. He has, furthermore, abandoned time-honored ways of thinking to an extent that makes it almost impossible to fit his philosophic concepts into any established categories. It is thus hardly surprising, and at least partly his own fault, that he has been so often misunderstood and misinterpreted, especially by non-German thinkers who must of necessity find his modes of thinking puzzling and disconcerting. The fact, finally, that Heidegger's terminology and principal concepts have experienced an almost complete perversion of their original meaning at the hands of Jean-Paul Sartre (cf. Chapter Seven) has added to the confusion and has multiplied the difficulties of interpretation.

Heidegger's philosophy is usually associated with the contemporary movement of "existentialism," although the philosopher has himself repeatedly disavowed any such association. He has been accused of atheism, immoralism, antihumanism, and outright nihilism, notwithstanding the fact that Heidegger has at various times convincingly

---

[12] *Hölderlin und das Wesen der Dichtung; Hölderlins Hymne: Wie wenn am Feiertag. . . ; Hölderlins Gedicht: Andenken.*

[13] *Platons Lehre von der Wahrheit. Mit einem Brief über den "Humanismus"* (Bern: A. Francke, 1947). *Holzwege* (Frankfurt am Main: V. Klostermann, 1950).

refuted all these charges, most recently in his revealing *Letter on Humanism* (cf. p. 144 ff.).While the Belgian Thomist A. de Waehlens, in his comprehensive monograph,[14] concurs in the negative evaluation of Heidegger's philosophy, the Catholic philosopher Max Müller, who at present occupies Heidegger's former chair in the University of Freiburg, as well as the German Jesuit, Johannes B. Lotz, who at one time was one of Heidegger's pupils, suggest a much more positive approach and arrive at the conclusion that Heidegger's thinking is informed by deeply Christian impulses.[15] Friend and foe, however, are in agreement as to the highly original and provocative nature of the German thinker's basic ideas. It is also interesting to recall that at the Philosophic Congress held at the University of Cuyo in the city of Mendoza in Argentina in 1949, a large number of the papers presented dealt with the major problems thrust into the limelight by Heidegger's speculation, and that among those who followed Müller and Lotz in their constructive critical appraisal were several leading Spanish Thomists.[16]

"I am not primarily concerned with existence," Heidegger told Stefan Schimanski on the occasion of the latter's visit with the recluse of the Black Forest. "My book bears the title *Being and Time,* not 'Existence and Time.' For me the haunting question is and has been, not man's existence, but 'being-in-totality' and 'being as such.'" In other words, Heidegger is primarily interested in ontology, not in anthropology.

It is true nevertheless that the central concept in the published part of *Being and Time* is "existence," not "being," and it is this fact, among others, that has led to the adoption of the term "existentialism" to designate certain trends in contemporary philosophy that show the influence of Heidegger's major work. Why then Heidegger's protestation that he has no affiliation with "existentialism"? Because for him "existence" and "man in existence" or "existence in man" is merely a starting point and a means for the illumination of *Being as such,* that is, for the elaboration of a *universal and fundamental ontology.* Schimanski states quite correctly that Heidegger's philosophy begins where that of Sartre ends.

---

[14] Cf. A. de Waehlens, *La Philosophie de Martin Heidegger* (Louvain, 1942).

[15] Cf. Max Müller, *Existenzphilosophie im geistigen Leben der Gegenwart* (Heidelberg: F. H. Kerle, 1949); and Johannes B. Lotz, S.J., *Das christliche Menschenbild im Ringen der Zeit* (Heidelberg: F. H. Kerle, 1947).

[16] Cf. Oswaldo Robles, *En torno al primer Congreso Argentino de Filosofía* (Mexico: Ábside, XIII, 4, 1949), p. 435 ff.

It is Heidegger's contention that the inquiry into the meaning of "Being" was the central problem of occidental philosophy, from the Pre-Socratics down to Hegel, but that after Hegel the problem fell almost completely into oblivion. "Being" was, as it were, henceforth taken for granted; it was treated as if it were something self-evident, and it is being made use of in an extremely vague manner in all human knowledge, in all statements and judgments, in all human behavior. Kierkegaard profoundly speculated on the problem of human existence, but owing to the fact that his own thinking was negatively determined by Hegel's essentialism, the problem of "Being" and the interpenetration of existence and "Being" escaped him almost completely. He criticized Hegel for having omitted or suppressed the actual existence of the individual, and he offered his own "existentialism" as a means to aid himself and others in the practical ethical and religious conduct of life. True existential thinking, however, is, according to Heidegger, intimately related to both theoretical insight and practical conduct.

In his attempt to inquire anew into the meaning of "Being," Heidegger's first objective is the ontological analysis of human existence. What does it mean when I say: "I am?" Is the meaning the same as when I say: "a stone is," "a tree is," "a dog is"? And if the meaning is not the same, what is the difference? In short, what is the meaning of "is" in each of these statements? Heidegger answers that, while stones, plants, and brutes certainly exist, they lack the means to illuminate the meaning of their existence. Human life, however, differs ontologically from the life of all other existents in that it alone is and must of necessity be concerned about its Being and its potentialities. And human life alone is capable of piercing the mystery of its own existence. It alone makes genuine choices and decisions. It may gain full possession of itself and thus exist authentically, or it may lose itself and disintegrate into an unauthentic form of existence.

To carry on his ontological analysis Heidegger makes use of Husserl's "phenomenological method." To describe the way man exists, in contradistinction to other beings, he uses the term *Dasein* ("being-there"). Human *Dasein* "ex-sists" rather than "in-sists," that is, it does not "stand in itself" like things or plants or brutes, but it "stands out" comprehendingly into that boundless realm of "being" from which it receives its own meaning and which imparts to it the understanding of its own self as well as the understanding of the being of every other existent. In its "existentialistic" structure human *Dasein* thus differs ontologically from all other existents. While these latter are either simply *"vorhanden"* (present, at hand) or *"zuhanden"* (at man's disposal, e.g., man-made tools, such as a saw or a hammer), man alone can learn to know by insight into his own existence the absolute ontological ground of everything that is and can thus prepare himself for the humble and obedient acceptance of the mandates of "Being."

Human *Dasein* is, furthermore, "being-in-the-world," and in this respect too man's mode of being differs essentially from the ways in which other existents (trees, stars, animals) are in the world. Man, as existing, is actively related to the objects and beings which surround him, and without his active insertion into the world, knowledge would be impossible. If man tries to withdraw himself from the world in detached observation, he perceives only the external aspects of things but fails to penetrate into their essential meaning. To seize reality, man must live and act. The external world, in turn, has no complete existential autonomy: it is rather a constitutive element of human *Dasein,* the subject matter and term of human action, a potential means for the realization of human existence. The world is the "space" which in the sum total of its implements is related to man and the indispensable condition of his *Dasein*.

In his ontological analysis of the structure of human *Dasein,* Heidegger distinguishes several modes or *"existentialia."* The most important among these are *"Befindlichkeit"* (the way in which man is "placed" in life and in the world), *"Verstehen"* (the understanding of the dominant purpose or end for the sake of which man exists, and the understanding of the potentialities of his being), and *"Rede"* (the faculty of speech, including listening and silence).

In order to point out the difference between authentic and unauthentic existence, Heidegger proceeds from an analysis of the banality of everyday life (*"Alltäglichkeit"*) and refers to a potentiality of human *Dasein* which he terms *"das Verfallen"* (the "falling away," disintegration). Who is this, he asks, who in "everydayness" exists in the world and with others? It is not the individual, private ego, he answers, with its genuine intentions, endeavors, and possibilities, but an anonymous and featureless public ego (*"das Man"*), the "one-like-many," shirking personal responsibility and taking its cues from the conventions of those who live *en masse.*

Das Man thinks, believes, speaks, behaves as "one does" and thus expresses the conformist leveling which characterizes the average human life. *Das Man* has fallen a prey to the things in the world and has become alienated from authentic human purposes and possibilities. It expresses itself and communicates with others not in genuine speech (*Rede*) but in conventional, superficial chatter (*Gerede*). The atmosphere of publicity in which *das Man* moves begets either a satiety which rests on the pretense that everything is in the best of order and that the momentum of a stale inertia must under no circumstances be disturbed, or it generates a restless activity that leaps from distraction to distraction, in its craving for ever new surface impressions and sensations (*Neugier*), in its indifference to any essential insight and understanding. In either case the result is a "self-estrangement" (*Selbstentfremdung*) of human existence, leading eventually to the blotting out of its potentialities and to its disintegration in the irrelevancy of everyday life.

To exist authentically does not mean, however, that one has to disown or discard all the attitudes of everyday life. Such a demand would be impossible of fulfillment, since man exists and must continue to exist in the world and with others. Authentic existence is something decisively different from everyday life nevertheless, because it makes man capable of seeing his everyday life in an entirely new perspective. Heidegger follows at this point a line of thought which seems to have been suggested by Kierkegaard's category of "repetition": Kierkegaard's "knight of infinite resignation," having arrived at the highest religious level of existence, makes an act of absolute and unconditional renunciation, but he is rewarded in the end by receiving back in a richer and fuller measure everything he has surrendered. This is true as much of Abraham, the "knight of faith," as of Job, the "knight of infinite resignation." Having surrendered all things to God, their total detachment actually restores all things to them: they now really possess them rather than being possessed by them. With Kierkegaard or with St. John of the Cross this perfect sacrificial offering carries, of course, a strictly religious significance, but the religious undertones are still audible in Heidegger's philosophic argument.

Human *Dasein*, as has been stated, differs from other modes of existence in that it is always concerned about its Being and its possibilities. It is permeated and saturated by "care" (*Sorge*). As a preliminary for the analysis of "care" Heidegger first inquires into the ontological character of "dread" (*Angst*). And again Kierkegaard's "concept of dread" provides the psychological setting for Heidegger's ontological analysis.

Both Kierkegaard and Heidegger distinguish between "dread" and "fear": while the object of fear is always something definite of which man is afraid, the object of dread is "that indefinite something which is nothing" (i.e., no thing). What threatens is found nowhere in particular, and yet, it is everywhere. What is dreaded is the world as such and one's "being-in-the-world." The struggle with "dread" and its outcome ultimately determines whether man finds himself in the ground of "Being" or whether he is swallowed up and annihilated in "nothingness."

Man discovers and discloses the world in which he exists by way of those objects among which he moves, about which he is concerned and cares, and to which he attends. And to illustrate the all-pervasiveness of "care" in human *Dasein,* Heidegger alludes to an ancient Roman fable which also inspired some of the scenes in the second part of Goethe's *Faust:* "One day," the story reads, "when Care was crossing a river, she noticed some clay on the river bank. She took up a piece and began to fashion it. While she was still reflecting on what she had fashioned, Jupiter arrived on the scene. Care asked him to give this form of clay a soul, which Jupiter promptly did. But then a dispute arose between Care and Jupiter: each wanted to give his own name to the new creature. And while they were still arguing, Earth came along and insisted that her name be given to the creature, since it was she who had provided it with a body. The three of them thereupon called in Saturn to judge their dispute. 'Jupiter,' said Saturn, 'since you have given this thing a soul, you shall receive this creature after its death; you Earth, shall in the end receive its body; but since Care first shaped this creature, she shall possess it as long as it lives. And as for the quarrel over the creature's name — let it be called man (*homo*), since it has been fashioned out of earth (*humo*).'"[17] Human *Dasein,* says Heidegger, is "thrown" into a world not of its own making, and it is left there in its "thrownness" (*Geworfenheit*) to "care," to engage itself and concern itself, using its own devices and acting under its own responsibility.

III

Section Two of *Being and Time* discusses the "temporality" (*Zeitlichkeit*) and "historicity" (*Geschichtlichkeit*) of human *Dasein.* From

---

[17] Cf. William Barrett, *What is Existentialism?* (New York: Partisan Review Series, No. 2, 1947), p. 32.

its very beginning, Heidegger asserts, philosophic thought intimately linked the meaning of "Being" with the phenomenon of "Time." And the understanding of the "temporality" of *Dasein,* in its relations to the dimensions of past, present, and future, opens up the "horizon" for a new interpretation of "Being."

Heidegger begins this second major part of his investigation with two fundamental questions: (1) in what way can *Dasein* be approached and analyzed as a "whole" (*im Ganzen*), in its totality? And (2) in what way can *Dasein* be established as "authentic"? The first question is answered by the statement that to envisage *Dasein* as a whole it is necessary to understand it as "being-toward-death" (*Sein zum Tode*). For death, being the "end" of *Dasein,* completes and integrates it. Death — *my own death,* viewed as an ever present possibility — is part of the *Being* of *Dasein.* As soon as *Dasein* exists, it is "thrown" into this possibility, and this "being thrown" reveals itself in "dread."

According to an old proverb, "As soon as we are born, we are old enough to die." Death is thus an "end" of human *Dasein* in the sense that it may cut short my existence at any moment. In other words, my life is not a long, smooth, well-laid-out road, at the end of which the event of death occurs, but death permeates as it were my existence from the moment I am "thrown" into the world.

Among Christian thinkers no one has perhaps more profoundly experienced and expressed the "being-toward-death" of human *Dasein* than St. Augustine. "From the first moment that we find ourselves in a mortal body," writes the Bishop of Hippo, "something happens within us which steadily leads us toward death. . . . Each one of us is nearer death a year hence than he was a year ago, nearer tomorrow than he was today, nearer today than yesterday, nearer in a little while than he is now, nearer now than a short while ago. Each span of life shortens the length of life, and that which remains of it becomes smaller and smaller with every passing day; and thus our entire lifetime is nothing but a racing toward death, in the course of which no one is permitted to stop for a little while or to slow down his walk: all are forced to keep in step, all are driven on to the same speed."[18]

Since death not only completes *Dasein* but also terminates it, I can never have an adequate experience or understanding of the actual transition from life to death. I may have a more or less detached

---

[18] St. Augustine, *De civitate Dei,* XIII, 10.

and somewhat abstract experience of the death of others, but such an experience — no matter how much I may be stricken by the death of a beloved person — is of no relevance for the understanding of my own death. I can only learn to understand that I have to die my own death and that no one can relieve me of this my personal and private destiny. Kierkegaard's reflections on death, especially those attributed to Johannes Climacus in the *Unscientific Postscript* (cf. p. 47), have undoubtedly lent their persuasiveness to Heidegger's argument.

To envisage death as a genuine potentiality of the Being of *Dasein,* it is necessary to consider the way death appears in the context of everyday existence. In the no man's land of the anonymous *Man* the stark reality of death is obscured or neutralized. One reads about deaths in the obituary columns of the daily newspapers, one attends public funerals, one observes certain rules and conventions laid down by *das Man,* and one tries at the same time every possible trick to reduce the actuality of one's own death to some such abstract and detached proposition as "all men are mortal." The result is the self-estrangement of *Dasein* from its genuine potentiality of Being. The authentic understanding of my own "being-toward-death," on the other hand, restores to me my true selfhood; it personalizes me, and it also imparts to me true insight into the Being of my fellowmen. In virtue of the "resoluteness" (*Entschlossenheit*) with which I face my own death I am freed from the bondage of those inconsequential concerns and activities which engulf the everyday existence of *das Man.* By overcoming in my "freedom-toward-death" the self-delusions of *das Man,* I can at last arrive at an understanding of my *Dasein* as a "whole."

Heidegger's second question, referring to the problem of the "authenticity" of *Dasein,* calls for an ontological analysis of the three phenomena of "conscience," "guilt," and "resolve." The "call" of conscience appeals to the selfhood of man; it calls him back from the anonymity of *das Man.* This call itself issues from the innermost self of man and is generated by "care." "Conscience reveals itself as the call of Care," says Heidegger. "Guilt" points to an intrinsic and original deficiency or privation of *Dasein.* Only by entering into the prospect of guilt can man open himself to his authentic potentiality of existence. And he projects himself into this potentiality by his "resolve," thus imparting to his *Dasein* an authentic lucidity. "Resolve" makes possible genuine "choice"; it begets action in concrete situations and the strength to master them.

Resolute, authentic *Dasein* lives in the fulfilled moment and has become capable of relating itself to future, past, and present, the three dimensions of "temporality." They unveil temporality as a "being-outside-itself" (an *ex-statikon*) and are therefore called by Heidegger the three "ex-stases."

The authentic understanding of "Being" is grounded, according to Heidegger, in "historicity" and is transmitted in the history of civilization. "Historicity" designates the specific kind of motion or movement that occurs in human history, in contradistinction to any kind of physical and mechanical motion. History, the recorded annals of the "happenings" (*das Geschehen*) of human *Dasein,* places man within the monumental frame of the social and national community. The true historian is capable of disclosing the history of the past in its potentialities with such forcefulness that its implications for the present and the future become evident. He is, in the words of the German romanticist Friedrich Schlegel, "a retrospective prophet." In his discussion of these problems of historiography Heidegger specifically refers to Nietzsche's essay *On the Use and Abuse of History* (cf. p. 76 ff) and states that the authentic historian should be able to present a synthetic unity of "monumental," "antiquarian," and "critical" historiography.

IV

The analyses of Part One of *Being and Time* were to unfold "the transcendental horizon" of the problem of Being. Part Two was to present a critical inquiry into the central doctrines of Aristotle, Descartes, and Kant, and to point the way for contemporary philosophy to overcome the subjectivism of modern thinking. The several essays which Heidegger published since the appearance of the first part of his major work in 1927, are all organically related to these fundamental themes of *Being and Time*. There is, however, an unmistakable shift of emphasis from existence to "Being," and Heidegger, furthermore, shows increasing interest in the interrelation of philosophy and poetry. In the essay *On the Essence of Truth* he describes the philosopher as "a wanderer into the neighborhood of Being."

The interrelation of philosophy and literature, Heidegger declares, was closest in ancient Greece, especially in the age of the Pre-Socratics.

Man was then the "guardian" of Being and dwelled in its intimate proximity. And this closeness to "Being" is the distinguishing mark of the true philosopher and the true poet in every age. Their creative thinking has its source in the "ground of the Truth of Being."

The problem of Truth as such, Heidegger states, is inseparably linked with the problem of Being. But the original meaning of Truth has become obscured in the course of the history of philosophy. The Greek term ἀ–λήθεια describes truth as an "un-covering" or "un-veiling" (*Entbergung*) as opposed to the "concealment" (*Verbergung*) of untruth. Truth as such, according to Heidegger, is essentially one and indivisible. He subsequently criticizes and tries to refute as incomplete and inconclusive the scholastic saying, *veritas est adaequatio rei et intellectus* (truth expresses an adequate assimilation of the intellect and the thing), a criticism which seems to indicate that Heidegger misunderstands the implications of this time-honored definition. For, as Etienne Gilson points out, to understand this scholastic sentence correctly, it is necessary to call attention to the meaning it has "in the existential ontology of St. Thomas Aquinas. . . . The assimilation of the intellect to reality which defines truth, is legitimately affirmed in a doctrine in which the intellect, in the process of reflecting on itself, finds itself capable of becoming reality. . . ."[19]

When Heidegger speaks of the "overtness" (*das Offene*) in which the vast realm of beings is "opened up," he evidently (yet unwittingly) repeats in modern phraseology Aristotle's and St. Thomas's *"anima est quodammodo omnia"* (the human soul is in a way all things).[20] The knowing intellect receives into itself the "form" of the thing known and in some way "becomes" that thing by a process resulting in a mysterious synthesis of the knower and the object known. All knowledge, in other words, leads to an expansion or enlargement of the being of the knowing subject.

According to Thomistic doctrine, all things are knowable only, however, because they are ontological manifestations of the supreme knowledge of God: *Scientia Dei est causa rerum* (God's knowledge is the cause of all things). In short, without the Eternal Ideas of

---

[19] "*L'adéquation de l'intellect au réel, qui définit la vérité s'affirme légitimement dans une doctrine où, réfléchissant sur soi-même, l'intellect se découvre capable de devenir la réalité: secundum hoc cognoscit veritatem intellectus, quod supra se reflecti-sur.*" Etienne Gilson, *Le Thomisme* (Paris: Vrin, 1948), pp. 326 and 331.

[20] St. Thomas Aquinas, *Summa Theologica*, Ia, qu. 14, a. 1.

the Divine Intellect there would not only be no knowable objects, but no objects at all. Both the knowing subject and the known object participate in the plenitude of the Divine Being.[21] And St. Thomas would certainly agree with Heidegger that only in this kind of "overtness" an adequation of a thing and an intellectual proposition has meaning and becomes possible. This "overtness" is the enduring and indispensable condition not only of all propositional truth, but of all human civilization, all human knowledge, and all purposive action.

The problem of Truth in all its magnitude was, according to Heidegger, faced for the first time when some of the early Greek thinkers in profound astonishment asked the question, "What is all that which is?" This question marked not only the beginning of the history of philosophy and metaphysics but also of history and civilization. To ask such a question the thinker had first to withdraw from the everyday view of things, in a way analogous to the withdrawal described by Plato in the famous parable of the "cave."[22] Liberated from the fetters of *das Man,* the philosopher ascends into the light of the "sun" of Truth. When he finally descends again "into the cave," he is able to convey to his fellowmen the insight he has gained.

Truth thus consists in the "uncovering," in the bringing back into "the open" that which is. Man, in the process of this "uncovering" of the being of things, enters into *Dasein*. The early Greek thinkers revealed for the first time what it means to be or to exist "in truth." And while this insight into the Truth of Being liberates man for authentic existence, the previous "concealment" of the Truth of Being had held man imprisoned in untruth and error. True philosophy, Heidegger concludes, is always obedient to and a servant of "Being."

V

Heidegger's Hölderlin essays[23] are reflections and meditations on philosophy and poetry and their interrelation. Hölderlin, who gave

---

21 Cf. the author's *A Realistic Philosophy*, p. 93 f.

22 Cf. Plato, *Politeia* (*The Republic*), VII, 514a, 2 to 517a, 7.

23 Friedrich Hölderlin (1770–1843) was a German poet affiliated with both the classical and romantic periods of German letters. A native of the province of Swabia, he studied Protestant theology at the University of Tübingen and in his youth associated with Schiller, Schelling, and Hegel, although as a poet and thinker he stands all by himself. Like the hero of his novel *Hyperion* he lived as a "hermit" in the midst of a society which could offer no satisfactory answer to his longing for a unified *Weltanschauung*. In tragic isolation he sought in vain to bridge the chasm between

such profound expression to his insight into the metaphysical nature
of poetry, is for this reason for Heidegger "the poet of the poet." In
Heidegger's view, Hölderlin felt himself to be an intermediary between "the gods" and the people, trying to communicate to men what
he had learned of "the gods," and to "name the holy." The age in
which Hölderlin lived and wrote is, with only minor modifications,
also the age and cultural environment of Kierkegaard, Nietzsche, and
Heidegger: an age in which "the old gods" have sunk into oblivion
and "the new God" has not yet appeared. God "withholds His
presence," and "holy names are lacking."

In the modern age "the God remains afar," no matter how hard
man labors to fill the void by the invention of substitute "gods." In
such an age the one necessary thing is, according to Heidegger, to
persevere and to be ready for the time when the word that could
reverently and convincingly "name" the High One will be granted
again. The Hölderlin essays, says Heidegger, "make no claim to be
contributions to research in the history of literature and aesthetics.
They arose from a necessity of thought."

Poetry is for Heidegger what it was for Hölderlin: not an embel-
lishment of human existence and not a mere phenomenon of culture
but rather the deepest "ground of human history," guiding and
inspiring human beings by the verbal expression of its insights and
visions. God is, whether man knows Him or not. What singles the
poet out among mortals is the fact that he is "open" for the reality
of the divine and, while singing its praises, rises into its closest
proximity. The poet's joyfulness is born of his nearness to the holy,
but the loneliness of his worship and his remoteness from his fellow
men, whom he yet deeply loves, makes his poetry replete with overtones of sorrow and sadness.

VI

The most important of Heidegger's essays, aside from the *Letter
on Humanism,* is the lecture on the nature of *Metaphysics* (1929)

---

subjective experience and objective reality; in vain he tried to find refuge and consolation
in nature, in art, and in love, the three symbols and sublimations of his frustrated
quest of the divine. In the idealized forms and figures of ancient Greece he visualized
that serene harmony which was denied to him and his age. An unhappy love affair
left his mind clouded with an incurable melancholy, and from a brief sojourn in
France and Spain he returned as an aimless wanderer, spending the remaining thirty-
seven years of his life in mental derangement. In the dynamically moving force of
his Greek meters and free rhythms he resuscitated the religious individualism of Pindar's
odes and anticipated the hymnic language of Friedrich Nietzsche.

with its *Postscript* (1943). Here the philosopher analyzes the concept of "nothingness," viewed as a metaphysical category and in its relation to the problem of "Being." To pose the problem of "Being," Heidegger contends, one must first have faced the problem of "nothingness." The discussion of "nothingness" is thus intended as a preliminary step leading to the elucidation of metaphysics.

The one specific mood in which "nothingness" is experienced is "dread." "What effect has — nothing?" Kierkegaard had asked. "It evokes dread." For Heidegger "nothingness" is a strange and bewildering metaphysical phenomenon. Though it cannot be actually apprehended, it is much more than a mere vague feeling or emotion. In this frightening experience all things seem to slide away from the grip of man: the "nothing" seems to annihilate them (*"das Nichts nichtet"*). But this sinking away of things may and should be followed by a second and reverse movement: man's rediscovery ·of the true nature of things and his subsequent turning back to them with his newly gained love and understanding. Once he has been threatened and stirred to his depths by the engulfing terror of nothingness, he now is prepared for a new and radically different approach to reality. Things, after having been tested in the contrast to nothingness, are revealed in the total "otherness" of their true being.

Metaphysics is defined by Heidegger as the "questioning beyond" the things that are, in order to regain them in their full reality and totality. The traditional technical term for such a "questioning beyond" is, of course, "transcendence." Without transcendence, that is, without the metaphysical inquiry, knowledge and learning become a mere statistic and positivistic accumulation and classification of data.

Metaphysical inquiry, Heidegger says, began with the question, "What is the Being of all that is?" This query brought man into "the open": his horizon widened immeasurably, and both history and civilization received a solid foundation. And this momentous process has to be repeated by every genuine thinker in every historic epoch.

In the *Postscript* to the lecture on metaphysics Heidegger dwells in particular on the distinction between *science* and *philosophy,* contrasting scientific "calculation" (which he calls "the will to will" or "the will to power") and philosophico-metaphysical thought. In metaphysical speculation the phenomena and problems which the philosopher proposes to analyze and interpret can never be made "objects" in the sense in which one speaks of the objects of scientific research. The reason is that in the approach to metaphysical data the Being of the thinker is always involved and implied. He can neither step outside his own Being nor outside "Being" itself and thus achieve a scientific "objectivity." "All the historical and philosophical disciplines (*Geisteswissenschaften*)," writes Heidegger, "and even those which deal with organic life, must, in order to be strict, of necessity be inexact."[24]

Heidegger concludes his inquiry into the nature of metaphysics by describing the true philosopher as the one who obediently and faithfully responds to the "call of Being," the one who dedicates his life to the maintenance of the Truth of Being. Only this attitude on the part of the philosopher can succeed in kindling an identical single-minded devotion in others. The true philosopher and the true poet strive to find the word which enunciates the Truth of Being. And "dread," opening up for man the abyss of "nothingness," may then cause him to listen to this Word in speechless silence. For "nothingness is the veil of Being."

VII

The *Letter on Humanism* was written by Heidegger in answer to certain pertinent questions which M. Jean Beaufret, of Paris, had asked in a communication of November 10, 1946. It clarifies some of the terms and concepts which Heidegger uses in his various writings and attempts to refute some of the objections and accusations of the philosopher's critics.

At the outset Heidegger once more insists on the essential difference between the scientific and philosophical approach to reality. Modern philosophy, he argues, is haunted by the fear of losing its dignity and validity unless it can make itself into a "science." But such a transformation would entail the surrender of the very essence of thinking. Is it fair, Heidegger asks, to call "irrationalism" the endeavor to bring thought back into its own element?

In reply to M. Beaufret's question, *"How can we restore the true meaning of 'Humanism'?"* Heidegger points out that true humanism (and he obviously regards his own philosophy as an endeavor aiming at the restoration of true humanism) is concerned with the essence or nature of man, so that the *homo* may again become *humanus*. Humanistic thinking should thus be engaged in the task of leading

---

[24] Heidegger, *Die Zeit des Weltbildes.* In *Holzwege* (Frankfurt am Main: V. Klostermann, 1950), p. 73.

man back from the inhuman and antihuman to the human and there-
with to the original sphere of his own being.

The *humanitas* of man rests then on his very nature. But how is
human nature properly defined? Karl Marx believed he had discovered
human nature in the "social man." For him the totality of man's
natural needs and wants (food, clothing, procreation, economic subsistence) is secured and safeguarded in and by Society. The Christian,
on the other hand, defines man's *humanitas* by setting if off from
Deitas (the Godhead). In the Christian economy of salvation man is
"the child of God," listening to the call of the Father in the incarnate
God-Man, and following this call. Man, in the Christian view, is "not
of this world," inasmuch as "this world" is merely a transitory passage
to the plenitude of supernatural life.

If "humanism" is defined as the endeavor to enable man to recover
in freedom his *humanitas* or his human dignity, then there are as
many different kinds of "humanism" as there are different concepts of
the "freedom" and the "nature" of man. Their common denominator
is the conviction that the *humanitas* of the *homo humanus* is determined by a definite interpretation of human nature, of history, of the
world, of reality as a whole. Every such "humanism" is grounded in
metaphysics, that is, it presupposes a knowledge of the most general
nature or essence of man. But, Heidegger asserts, the question as to
the Truth of Being and the question as to the way in which man is
related to the Truth of Being are inaccessible to metaphysics.

Perhaps even more important, however, is the question whether or
not the nature of man is situated in the same dimension as the animal
nature. In other words, does our questioning proceed in the right
direction when it tries to understand and define human nature by
referring it back to the nature of plants and animals, simply adding
something specifically "human"? Is the definition of man as "rational
animal" a really satisfactory and exhaustive description? To be sure,
such a definition will always make it possible to arrive at correct
predications concerning man, but it would seem that within such a
frame of reference man remains cast in the molds of the natures of
plants and brutes, notwithstanding the fact that he is said to be marked
off from them by a specific difference. Heidegger is convinced that
this traditional definition implies an underestimation of human nature.
Traditional metaphysics, he claims, always thinks of man in terms of
homo animalis rather than specifically in terms of man's *humanitas*.

According to Heidegger, the aberrations of naturalism and biologism are not overcome by merely grafting on the physical and physiological nature of man an immortal soul, and on the soul a spiritual, personal existence. The fact that physiology and chemistry can investigate man scientifically as a natural organism does not prove that human nature is constituted or even conditioned by this scientifically analyzed body.

None of the "humanistic" definitions of man, Heidegger asserts, does justice to his true dignity. And he admits that to the extent that the analyses contained in *Being and Time* call attention to these shortcomings of "humanism," the philosophic position advanced there may well be called "antihumanistic." This, however, does not mean that it is antihuman. On the contrary, Heidegger's position is antihumanistic precisely because "humanism" in the accepted usage of the term does not esteem highly enough the *humanitas* of man.

As had been stated in *Being and Time,* man is "thrown" into the Truth of Being, so that in the ex-sistence of his *Dasein* he should be the guardian of Being and that in the Light of Being the things that are might appear in their true nature. Whether and how God, history, and nature enter into the Light of Being — this matter is not for man to decide: he is simply called to be in all humility the "shepherd of Being."

But what is "Being" (*das Sein*)? It is neither God nor the ground or cause of the world (*Weltgrund*), Heidegger answers. It is vaster and broader than everything that is (*das Seiende*), but it is nevertheless closer to man than any existent, be it rock, animal, a work of art, an angel, or even God Himself. "Being" is nearest to man, but this nearest has become his farthest because he has lost his relationship to Being in its plenitude and is clinging to things and beings rather than to "Being." And this loss of his relationship to Being in its plenitude is the real reason why modern man — rootless and homeless — moves in the *void of nothingness*. When man forgets the Truth of Being in the midst of the noisy crowd of existents, his *Dasein* disintegrates.

Parmenides' ancient saying, ἔστιν γὰρ ἔιναι ("Being certainly is"), implies that existents never really and fully "are." Philosophy has never advanced beyond this insight, says Heidegger. The latest thinker who deeply experienced the homelessness of modern man — his separation from "Being" — was Friedrich Nietzsche. But his way out of this modern dilemma was the abortive attempt to put metaphysics upside down. And yet, in the nearness of Being alone the question can and must be asked and decided whether night and darkness shall remain or whether the day of holiness will dawn again and the divine epiphany will once again become possible. "Or how shall modern man be able even to ask in earnest whether God is near or withholds Himself if he refuses to think in that dimension in which alone such a question can be asked? . . . This dimension, however, is the dimension of the holy. . . . Perhaps what makes this present age different from other epochs is the fact that the dimension of the holy is closed to it. And perhaps this is the very thing which makes this age not only unholy, but un-whole and un-hale (*heillos*)."[25]

It seems to Heidegger that any true "humanism" understands the *humanitas* of man from his nearness to Being, from his "ex-static" dwelling in the neighborhood of Being, and from his "care" for and about Being. The real meaning of "humanism" can thus only be restored by a redefinition of the term, and such a redefinition requires first of all a more genuine understanding of man's nature and *Dasein*. But then the question may be asked whether a humanism which sets itself up against all the historical forms of "humanism" can still legitimately be called by the same name?

This question provides Heidegger with an opportunity to answer those critics who have accused him not only of teaching an antihumanistic but an antihuman philosophy and who for good measure have added to their indictments the charges of irrationalism, atheism, and nihilism.

"Because," says Heidegger, "we have spoken out against 'humanism,' they fear that we defend the in-human and glorify barbaric brutality. For what is more 'logical' than the assumption that for him who opposes 'humanism' there remains only the affirmation of inhumanity?

"Because we have spoken out against 'logic,' they conclude that we demand that the rigor of thinking be abandoned and that in its place the irrational arbitrariness of blind urges and emotions be enthroned. For what is more 'logical' than to assume that he who speaks out against 'logic' defends the a-logical and anti-logical?

"Because we have spoken out against 'values,' they profess their horror in view of a philosophy which presumably exposes to contempt the highest goods of humanity. For what is more 'logical' than to assume that a thinking which denies 'values' must of necessity proclaim the worthlessness of everything?

---

25 Heidegger, *ibid.*, p. 103,

"Because we have stated that the Being of man is a 'being-in-the-world,' they believe they have discovered that we have degraded man to a mere this-worldly creature and have thereby plunged headlong into the philosophy of Positivism. For what is more 'logical' than to conclude that whoever asserts the 'worldliness' of man leaves room only for the 'this-worldly' and denies the 'other-worldly' and with it any kind of transcendence?

"Because we have called attention to Nietzsche's saying that 'God is dead,' they declare that we teach atheism. For what is more 'logical' than to assume that he who has experienced the 'death of God' (in the present age) is a thoroughly god-less individual?

"Because in all these matters we have spoken out against that which mankind regards as sacrosanct, we are accused of teaching an irresponsible and destructive 'nihilism.' For what is more 'logical' than to assume that he who denies the truth of existing things and beings, places himself on the side of non-being and preaches 'nothingness' as the sole meaning of reality?

"What is going on here? . . . With the aid of the much heralded logic and *ratio* they argue that what is not positive must of necessity be negative. . . . And they are so filled to the brim with 'logic' that everything that runs counter to the customary drowsiness of thinking must be branded as a damnable negation. . . . But does the *'contra'* which is advanced against certain conventional opinions necessarily mean pure negation? . . .

"To advance arguments against traditional logic . . . simply means to pay attention to that 'Logos' which manifested itself early in the history of human thought. . . . What good are all the 'systems' of logic as long as they remain . . . neglectful of the task of inquiring into the nature of the 'Logos'?

"Our argumentation against 'values' does not want to assert that all those things which are commonly designated as 'values,' such as culture, art, science, human dignity, the world, God, and so on, are worthless. It should rather be seen and understood at long last that we deprive things and beings of their dignity by designating them as 'values.' By estimating something as a 'value,' this valued thing or being is reduced to a mere object of human evaluation. That which amounts to something in its own Being is . . . more than a mere 'object of value' for a subject. Every valuation, whether positive or negative, is a subjectivation. . . . Calling God the 'supreme value' means to degrade the nature of God. Thinking of God in terms of 'value' is the greatest blasphemy imaginable. . . . To argue against 'values' . . . means therefore to protest against subjectivism and to confront thought with the light of the Truth of Being. . . .

"The statement: the essence of man rests on his 'being-in-the-world,' implies no decision as to whether man is a this-worldly or other-worldly being in any theologico-metaphysical sense. In this definition of the nature and condition of man nothing is said as yet concerning the existence or non-existence of God. . . . But with the clarification of the meaning of 'transcendence'[26] a sufficiently clear concept of *Dasein* is gained to make it possible to ask how human *Dasein* is ontologically related to the existence of God. . . ."[27]

To think the Truth of Being, Heidegger concludes his inquiry into the meaning of "humanism," is to think the *humanitas* of the *homo humanus*. If, however, man's *humanitas* is thus centrally located in philosophy, will it not become necessary to supplement the knowledge of Being (ontology) with general and specific directions for doing (ethics)? There is no doubt that in this age of technology man, who has been handed over to the impersonal forces of the featureless col-lective, can be brought back to a personal steadiness of his badly shaken existence only by a moral ordering of his planning and doing.

"Man, in so far as he is man, abides in the neighborhood of God" (ἦθος ἀνθρώπῳ δαίμων). Thus reads Heidegger's translation of an ancient saying of Heraclitus. And to give the meaning of these words added emphasis, he tells an anecdote related by Aristotle: "We are told of some words that Heraclitus is said to have spoken to a group of strangers who had come to see him. Drawing nearer, they observed Heraclitus as he was warming himself at a bake-oven. They stopped in surprise and, as he noticed their hesitation, he encouraged them to come in, saying: 'Here, too, the gods are present.' "[28]

The strange visitors, so Heidegger interprets this anecdote, are somewhat taken aback at the sight of the great thinker. They had expected to meet him in surroundings bearing the marks of the extraordinary. And their curiosity had hoped to make this meeting an occasion for some entertaining chatter. Perhaps they had expected to find the philosopher wrapped up in deep thought. And what do they find? A homely, commonplace locale; an oven in which bread

---

[26] Cf. Heidegger, *Vom Wesen des Grundes*, p. 28, n. 1.

[27] Heidegger, *Über den "Humanismus,"* loc. cit., pp. 95–101.

[28] Cf. Aristotle, *De partibus animalium*, A 5, 645, a 17.

is being baked; and a plain, ordinary individual — a philosopher who warms himself at the stove! As there is nothing sensational about the sight of a shivering thinker, the curious visitors lose all desire to step nearer. Do they have to pay a visit to a great philosopher to be treated to such an uncouth spectacle? Heraclitus, who reads the disappointment in their faces, tries to speak words of encouragement. He asks them to enter, and he adds, "Here, too, the gods are present."

Not unlike those men who paid a visit to Heraclitus, Heidegger means to say, we are used to looking for philosophic thought in the form of the extraordinary, accessible only to the initiated. And we are used to measuring moral action by successful practical accomplishments. What is the real measure of thought? And to what law or norm does the action which it begets conform?

Thinking itself is an action, replies Heidegger; an activity more potent and more pregnant with consequences than any kind of *praxis*. Thinking permeates all doing and making. Thinking aids "in the building of the House of Being," and the nature of Being will some day make it possible for us to meditate on the meaning of "house" and "abiding in the house." Only in so far as man has his abode in the Truth of Being can he receive directives from the heart of Being, directives which he may then accept as his law and rule and compared with which all other "laws" are merely poor artifacts.

It is time, Heidegger states at the end of his "epistle" on humanism, that we cease demanding of philosophy the impossible: "Thought is on its descent into the poverty of its nature as a preliminary tool. It gathers language into the simplicity of speech. Speech is the tongue of Being, as the clouds are the clouds of the heavens. Thinking expressed in speech leaves inconspicuous furrows in language. These furrows are even more inconspicuous than those which the tiller of the soil leaves on his slow progress through the fields."[29]

VIII

Where, it must be asked — if one is to interpret correctly Heidegger's contribution to philosophic thought — does the German philosopher take his stand in the historical dialectic of *essence* versus *existence*? Heidegger himself emphasizes that what he means by "ex-sistence" differs from the traditional Aristotelian and Thomistic concept of *existentia* (i.e., actuality) as distinguished from *essentia* (i.e., inner

---

[29] Heidegger, *loc. cit.,* p. 119.

potentiality). "The nature of *Dasein* lies in its ex-sistence." he states.[30] As has been pointed out, ex-sistence means a "standing out" into the Truth of Being. The nature of man is neither determined by the *esse essentiae* nor by the *esse existentiae,* but by the "ex-stasis of *Dasein.*"

Existence, as the term is traditionally used, predicates *that* something is. Essence (*Wesen*) predicates *what* something is: it refers to a thing or a being's nature or to the "internal possibility" (*interna possibilitas*) which makes it of necessity what it is. A philosophy whose basic concept is the *essence* of things and beings is an essentialist philosophy. And a philosophy which centers in the *existence* of things and beings is an existentialist philosophy.

The exemplary prototype of all *essentialist* philosophies is the essentialism of Plato. In Platonism, that which is eternal and immutable is not things and beings (*ta onta*), but that by which things and beings are measured, that with which they are to be compared in order to determine whether or not they correspond to their particular essences. Thus there is, for example, an immutable essence of the State which provides the measure and standard for all actual states. There is an essence of Art which makes it possible to measure and judge all individual works of art. And there is also an essence of man, an essence which every human being carries within himself and which permits him to determine whether or not his existence corresponds to the essential human nature. It is man's task to realize this human essence, that is, to translate into existence his "internal possibility": to become existentially what he is essentially.

Philosophy, by advancing from existence to essence, moves from the dimension of time to the dimension of eternity: at the moment it arrives at the world of eternal essences it has transcended the world of changeable and contingent things and beings. Thus, in Platonic essentialism, the reality of the essence precedes the borrowed and inferior reality of existence, since this latter is nothing but the imperfect realization of the enduring, immutable essences.

As Max Müller points out,[31] in Plato's essentialism the relationship between eternity and time, essential and existential reality, constancy and change, remains unexplained. In Platonism, there are two distinct

---

[30] Heidegger, *Sein und Zeit,* p. 42.
[31] Cf. Max Müller, *Existenzphilosophie im geistigen Leben der Gegenwart* (Heidelberg: F. H. Kerle, 1949), *passim.*

worlds: an ahistorical, eternal world of essences or "Ideas," and a less real, defective, and changeable world of existences.

St. Thomas Aquinas calls essence that which determines the place which every existent occupies in the totality of Being. The position of everything in the whole of creation is thus preordained. And every human action receives its norm and direction from this universal and hierarchical order of Being.[32] The moral imperative of Thomistic ethics enjoins every human being to act in such a way that he safeguard for every existent its essential place in the ordered universe and that he aid in restoring this universal order whenever and wherever it has been disturbed or perverted. Man is called upon to realize his own essence by his actions, so that he may conquer, occupy, and maintain his essential place in the created universe, a position which is preassigned to him both by his own essence or nature and by the essences of all other existing beings. There is, furthermore, in Thomistic philosophy a hierarchy or gradation of values, strictly corresponding to the hierarchy of Being: God ranks above man; man's spiritual nature above his material nature; man above brutes; the brutes above plants. Preordained also is the range of human freedom: man can decide freely for or against what is "right," that is, what is in accordance with the hierarchical, universal order of things.

It is Heidegger's contention that in this grandiose Thomistic philosophy of order the central theme of all philosophy, namely, "Being," is not made the real object of the philosophic inquiry. "Being," he says in effect, is recognized in Thomism as the light that illumines with its sheen everything that is and thus makes philosophy and philosophic questioning possible, but "Being" itself is not subjected to a thoroughgoing philosophic analysis. The investigation, he asserts, rather abruptly leaps from the discussion of the universal order *in* Being to the Creator of this order *above* Being. Does this not mean, however, to continue the thinking in the essentialist categories of Plato and Aristotle rather than to think in specifically *Christian* categories? Christianity, Heidegger argues with Pascal and Kierkegaard, does not demand that I give at all times preference to the higher value in the universal hierarchy of Being: it simply commands that I love my neighbor. And who is my neighbor? Can any universal order answer this question for me? My neighbor is the one who is nearest to me at this moment. He is the one whom no one helps if I do not help him. He is the one who needs *me*, no one and nothing else.

In short, the Christian category of "the neighbor" is a *historical category*, whereas the schema of essential inner possibilities and of a hierarchy of order and of values is ahistorical. It merely enunciates what is to be done or left undone always or at any time. But the individual Christian may have to sacrifice all his "inner possibilities" for the sake of one specific historical and personal mandate which God imposes upon him in this particular historical situation, at this particular moment. Freedom in the highest sense is therefore the taking upon myself of a task which is uniquely and exclusively *my own*. This is what Heidegger means by an "existential decision" or "choice"; this is for him the authentic mandate of an "existential ethics." And this is also why he designates "historicity" as the fundamental category of existential thinking. Kant's "categorical imperative," which enjoins me to do what every other human being would do if he were placed in my position, is thus the exact opposite of the "existential imperative," which tells me to do what I alone and no one else can do.

It is Heidegger's claim that the modern historical consciousness can no longer remain satisfied with the ahistorical propositions deriving from a static order of essences. He is convinced that the significance of historical change and becoming must find its expression in a new approach to ontology; that philosophy must acknowledge and incorporate in its queries the profound changes that have occurred and are occurring in the essential meaning of religion, morals, politics, economics, art, literature, and in various other provinces of human thinking, doing, and making. By this Heidegger does not mean to suggest that the essences which underlie these phenomena of human history and civilization are without enduring reality but rather that their reality must be approached and interpreted in accordance with the changing historical functions which they fulfill in human life and civilization. The "Truth of Being" calls for different forms of realization and revelation, and such a task, according to Heidegger, can only be accomplished by a new "fundamental ontology."

The German philosopher shows himself equally opposed to Positivism and Idealism: Positivism, he contends, suffered shipwreck because it concentrated its attention exclusively on the finiteness and contingency of matter. Idealism suffered shipwreck because it contemptuously denied the finiteness and contingency of human *Dasein* and was bent on submerging the individual existence pantheistically in the absolute and infinite spirit. Heidegger's philosophy is laboring with the problem of giving verbal expression to a new experience of both the finite and the infinite.

There is no doubt that Heidegger has a high esteem for Christian theology, although he insists that it refrain from engaging in purely philosophical and metaphysical argumentation. If he disavows a primary interest in the problem of the existence of God, he does so as a philosopher who is more concerned with "Being" than with "existence." In this disavowal he deviates of course from Thomism as well as from traditional Catholic doctrine. The alternative of theism or atheism, he states, does not face the philosopher in his inquiry into the nature of "Being." God, in other words, is not directly and immediately encountered on the philosopher's way from existents to the ground of "Being."

Again, it may be asked, what is "Being"? In Heidegger's terminology, it certainly does not signify the "pure act" (*actus purus*) which for Aristotle and St. Thomas describes the nature of the "Being" of God (the *"Ipsum esse subsistens"*). "Being" for Heidegger is that reality which is encountered in everything that is and which makes possible everything that is. "Being" is the historical evolution of this all-pervading reality toward its actual existence. If "Being" were identical with God, says Heidegger, then this Deity would be a "becoming" or "emerging" God, which is "nonsense." Therefore, "Being" is not to be identified with the *Ipsum esse subsistens* of Thomistic philosophy. Neither is it the *ens commune* (which is merely an *ens rationis*). In scholastic terminology, Heidegger's "Being" is the actuality of the essence (*actus essentiae*), from which the individual essences issue as *modi* of its contingency. Although the transcendent God is not encountered in the realm of strict philosophy, "Being" is His image and similitude (*imago et similitudo Dei*).

IX

One question of great importance is in the end left at least partially unanswered by Heidegger: the question as to how "Being" is related to "nothingness." Which of the two is the ultimate "ground" of existents? It seems to be Heidegger's conviction that, since what at first appears as "nothingness" is ultimately revealed as "Being," all existents are ultimately grounded in that immense realm of "Being" which reveals itself behind the veil of nothingness and which restores to man all things and beings, including his own authentic *Dasein*.

"Without Being there can never be any existent," says Heidegger. Being as such, however, is so far above and beyond all the things that are, that "it *is* without any existents" (*es west ohne das Seiende*). Here, it would seem, the horizon opens toward the divine Being.

"God creates everything out of nothing; and that which He wants to use He first reduces to nothing," wrote Kierkegaard in his *Journals*. For Christianity, too, nothingness is thus in a way "the veil of Being," that is, a transitory phase in the process of man's spiritual self-realization with the aid of divine grace. Thus understood, nothingness is not only the "veil" but, strictly speaking, the opposite pole of Being. Christianity teaches not only that everything that is was created out of nothing but also that everything would sink back into nothingness the moment God were to withdraw His all-sustaining creative power. This is why Nietzsche's or Sartre's "man without God" moves in a meaningless void which he vainly and desperately tries to populate with the stillborn creatures of his own whims and fancies. And since in Christianity, as in no other religion, man's existence is absolutely grounded in God, the atrophy of faith in God must of necessity lead to the most horrible experience of the abyss of annihilation and nothingness. But in this hour of total abandonment there rings out as it were a final appeal to man's freedom: he may definitively choose either the powers of this world, as a sordid substitute for the real ground of his being, or he may regain his selfhood by striking roots again in the Being of the Living God.

CHAPTER FIVE

THE APE OF LUCIFER: JEAN-PAUL SARTRE

I

THREE major intellectual forces are today struggling for the soul of France: Christianity, Marxism, and Atheistic Existentialism. The chief representative of the latter movement is Jean Paul Sartre (1905 —), while the theistic-Christian branch of French existentialism has found its most convincing spokesman in Gabriel Marcel (cf. Chapter Seven).

Sartre began his career as a free-lance writer and philosopher in 1924; for a number of years he taught in the French secondary schools, was active in the French *résistance* movement of the Maquis during World War II, and achieved international renown after the publication of *L'être et le néant* (*Being and Nothingness*), his major philosophic work, in 1943.[1] In the several novels and stage plays which appeared before and after that date, Sartre exhibits his brilliant gifts as a writer and a master technician, his unfailing instinct for the requirements of the stage, a remarkable lucidity of artistic form and literary style, and a sure grip on the problems of both normal and abnormal human psychology. Sartre's philosophic writings reveal, on the one hand, his talent for rational analysis and logical precision, while, on the other, they often either offend or intrigue — depending on the mentality and taste of the reader — by a certain flippancy and frivolity which the author displays in the discussion of serious philosophic problems.

L'être et le néant is a book of over seven hundred large and closely printed pages. After its publication, the philosophy of existentialism, which up to 1943 had been known and discussed only in the circles of the sophisticated French intelligentsia, became almost overnight a topic of daily conversation and disputation. Sartre and a group of disciples started the publication of *Les Temps Modernes,* a periodical which was to provide a platform for the expression of their philosophic and literary ideas.

---

[1] Cf. Jean-Paul Sartre, *L'être et le néant* (Paris: Gallimard, 1943).

L'être et le néant bears the subtitle *Essai d'ontologie phénoménologique;* it reveals as Sartre's goal a "phenomenological ontology" centered in human existence. Aside from Heidegger and Husserl, the philosopher names Hegel and Freud as his chief precursors.

Several years before Sartre presented his "phenomenological ontology" he had made the phenomena of "being" and "existence" the subject matter of a novel entitled *La Nausée* (Nausea, 1938). This work is no novel in the ordinary sense; it has the form of diary notes which are said to have been found among the literary remains of Antoine Roquentin. A sort of Socratic soliloquy, it aims at the step-by-step *dénouement* of "existence." "Prior to these past few days," writes Antoine Roquentin, "I had really never felt what it means 'to exist.' . . . Ordinarily, existence hides itself. It is here, round about us, within us: we are it, and we cannot speak two words without speaking of it, but in the end we never grasp it. . . . Existence is not something which can be thought from a distance: it overwhelms you brusquely . . . it weighs heavily on your heart like a fat, loathsome beast."[2]

Existence is for Sartre pure contingency: it means simply "to be there; existents appear, they are encountered, but they can never be inferentially deduced. I believe there are people who have understood this, but they have been trying to overcome this contingency by inventing a Necessary Being who causes himself (a *causa sui*). No Necessary Being, however, can explain existence. . . . There is not the least reason for our 'being-there.' . . ." Every existent is *"de trop"*: superfluous, absurd. "And I, too, am *'de trop.'* And yet people are trying to hide themselves behind the idea of law and necessity. In vain: every existent is born without reason, prolongs its existence owing to the weakness of inertia, and dies fortuitously."[3]

The existence of Antoine Roquentin gravitates toward the *Café Mably* with its glittering atmosphere of bohemian libertinage. In 1945, in a conversation with the French philosopher Roger Troisfontaines, Sartre frankly admitted that he was passing most of his days, "from morning till night," in the *café*. Accused by Troisfontaines of mistaking the atmosphere of the *café* for that of normal human living, Sartre replied: "Your interpretation is all wrong; in the *café* I am more absorbed (*engagé*) than at home. In my room I feel the desire to stretch out on my bed. In the *café*, I work. It is there that I have

---

[2] Sartre, *La Nausée* (Paris: Gallimard, 1938), p. 162 f.
[3] Cf. Sartre, *ibid.*, pp. 163–170.

composed all my books." Asked what in particular attracted him to
the *café,* the author added, "It is this atmosphere of indifference: the
others are there without bothering about me, and I do not care about
them. . . . The burden of a family would be intolerable for me."
Sartre's universe, Troisfontaines concludes his comments on this
conversation, "is a world seen from the point of view of the *café.*"[4]

What is the philosophic meaning of Antoine Roquentin's encounter
with the phenomena of "Being" and "existence"? Sartre and the hero
of his novel are concerned with the things of everyday life because
of their conviction that the meaning of "being" and its relationship
to human existence can be discovered in them. In philosophic idealism
human consciousness is the epistemological center of the world of
being and of the being of the world. Everything that is, is nothing
but an artifact of the human mind. Sartre, in *La Nausée,* makes this
formidable mental bastion of philosophic idealism the object of his
attack. Like most modern existentialist thinkers he starts out from
an anti-Cartesian position but, unlike the others, he relapses in his
later works into the idealism of Descartes.

In *La Nausée* the center of the world is not man or human consciousness, but the massive extramental universe as it is symbolized in the
seemingly most insignificant objects of everyday life. To ridicule
philosophic idealism, Sartre introduces the figure of the "autodidact,"
the omnivorous reader, the peddler of dead ideas: "The reading matter
of the 'autodidact' gets more and more on my nerves," writes Antoine
Roquentin; "suddenly I remember the names of the authors he has
recently perused: Lambert, Langlois, Larbalétrier, Lastex, Lavergue.
This is like an illumination. Now I understand his method: he is
reading in the alphabetical order."[5] The encyclopedic brain of the
"autodidact" is filled with shadows and spectres, not with realities,
and the home and origin of these shadows is the void of nothingness
or, what amounts to the same thing, the Platonic "realm of ideas."

What strikes and overwhelms Antoine Roquentin is the brutal
reality of existing things, in contrast to the phantomlike reality of
ideas. The experience which makes him aware of the naked "being-
there" of existents is *la nausée,* the "great disgust" (Nietzsche). And
what makes this experience so terrifying is the fact that dead objects
actually have the power of limiting the freedom of a human being to

---

4 Roger Troisfontaines, *Le Choix de Jean-Paul Sartre* (Paris: Aubier, 1945), p. 52 f, *n.*
5 Sartre, *La Nausée,* p. 48.

deal with them at will. "The objects," remarks Antoine Roquentin, "should not concern us at all, for they are not alive. One makes use of them, one puts them back into their place, one lives among them . . . and yet, they affect me. This is intolerable. I am afraid of entering into a relationship with them, just as if they were animal organisms."[6] As this world of "dead" objects confronts man with silent and stubborn hostility, there arises in the human consciousness a horrible, oppressive fear of the obscene nakedness of the "being-there" of things.

Antoine Roquentin has made the shocking discovery that all being spends and wastes itself on a prodigious scale, but that it does so gratuitously, without any meaning or purpose. Man faces the fearful sight of this colossal, inert mass of being, and he simultaneously experiences himself as the only existent that is aware in his consciousness of the extent, the weight, and the ultimate meaninglessness of this gigantic realm of being.

In a preliminary way *La Nausée* introduces the main themes of *L'être et le néant*.[7] In his philosophic analysis of "existence" Sartre logically confines himself to a phenomenological investigation of the only empirically known being that can consciously experience what it means "to exist," namely, man. It is human consciousness which makes possible this experience.

Sartre states with Brentano and Husserl that consciousness always posits an object: it is of necessity consciousness of *something;* of something which is different from and beyond consciousness. This "transphenomenal being" Sartre calls the "in-itself" (*l'en-soi*), and he opposes to it the "for-itself" (*le pour-soi*) of human consciousness. Nothing can be said of the *en-soi* except that *it is*. Sartre's work is therefore not primarily concerned with this "being-in-itself" but rather with the phenomenological analysis of the structure, the projects, and the limitations of human consciousness.

---

[6] *Ibid.*, p. 25.

[7] The reader may gather from the following brief analysis that Sartre is familiar with the principal teachings of Aristotelian and Thomistic thought and that he follows several of its premises and procedures up to a certain point. He then abruptly and arbitrarily plunges into unwarranted and illogical conclusions and develops what has been justly called an "upside-down metaphysics" and an "inverted theology." The thing which strikes the critical reader as peculiar is the nonchalance with which Sartre presents as dazzling discoveries of his own many ideas which are almost commonplace with both Aristotle and St. Thomas Aquinas. He gives no credit whatever to that philosophic tradition which constitutes a substantial part of his own reasoning.

One characteristic element of human consciousness, according to Sartre, is negation, its capacity of saying "no." This possibility of negation enters into man's questioning of himself and of the world. The "nothingness" of negation, that is, the possibility of not-being, is lodged like a worm in the very core of being: "Nothingness haunts being."[8]

Human consciousness, says Sartre, is discordant, divided in itself. It knows of itself, but it does so in such a way that this knowledge and the knower are neither entirely different nor entirely identical. When, for example, I perceive a tree, I am conscious of the tree and, in addition, I am conscious of the fact that I perceive a tree. I and the tree are two different things. But my perception of the tree, and my being conscious of this perception are neither two entirely different things nor are they entirely identical. What then lies in between these two phenomena: my perception, and the consciousness of my perception? Nothing (*rien*), replies Sartre. And this "nothing" separates the two phenomena to such an extent that they can neither converge nor become entirely separate and independent. They are both linked and held apart by an "abyss of nothingness" which is unbridgeable. Owing to this split in his consciousness, man, Sartre concludes, is divided in himself, never fully himself. The *"en-soi,"* that is, the objective world of things, on the other hand, is undivided, impregnable, massive, unshakable. In the *en-soi* the fullness and security of being manifests itself.

Confronted with the massivity and ontological integrity of the *en-soi,* man experiences himself not only as discordant and fragmentary but also as *free.* Freedom, in Sartre's view, thus results from the fact that man is not self-sufficient, not fully real and therefore actually inferior to the fullness of being of the *en-soi.* Man's freedom, in other words, is a consequence of his ontological inferiority, of a diminution of his being (*une décompression d'être*). But, understanding himself as thus divided and incomplete, man strives to fill this lacuna in his being: he aspires to the plenitude of the *en-soi,* but in doing so he wants to retain the consciousness of his own self, his prerogative as a *"pour-soi."* For what good would it do him to attain to the fullness of being without being conscious of it and thus without being able to enjoy it?

The goal of all human striving is thus an ideal "self," combining the

---

[8] Cf. Sartre, *L'être et le néant*, p. 40 ff.

fullness of being with the fullness of consciousness. Man, says Sartre, is nothing but this striving to become *"l'en-soi-pour-soi"* or, in other words, the striving to overcome the debility of his being by *divinizing* himself. But such a goal is impossible of attainment: the *"en-soi-pour-soi"* is by definition a self-contradictory concept: it attempts to unite two types of being which by their very nature exclude each other. Man is therefore, Sartre concludes, "a futile passion" (*une passion inutile*).[9]

Man, in his futile pursuit of his flighty and fugitive self, "is not what he is, and he is what he is not," Sartre asserts with paradoxical pungency. "We are existents who can never catch up with themselves."[10] No matter how passionately man forges ahead in this endless chase, the fullness of being forever escapes him. But if he knows that this is so, why does he continue such a hopeless race? Because, answers Sartre, man cannot do otherwise: "to exist" means for man to realize himself in action, to storm ahead toward an impossible goal. Although he knows that all his projects are destined to suffer shipwreck, although he knows that he spends himself in vain, he is condemned to continue in activities which constantly annihilate his past, his present, and the projects of his anticipated future. Man, in short, is "condemned" to a freedom which weighs upon him like an inescapable fate.[11]

Man *is* his freedom, says Sartre, and therefore this freedom is *absolute*. It extends to anything and everything; it leaves no room for any kind of determinism. No one can relieve me of this burden: neither I myself, who am this freedom, nor any of my fellowmen, nor a god, because there is no God. All the modes of my being equally make manifest my freedom; all of them are projects in the pursuit of my ideal "self." Absurd, irrational projects, to be sure, but I am precisely this kind of absurdity.[12] Human freedom, therefore, is not a blessing, but a curse and a horrible yoke.

Sartre next proceeds to trace the "nihilating" function of human existence in all directions and dimensions. In every one of them man is separated from himself by the insurmountable barrier of nothingness. Trying to overcome this obstacle to his self-realization, he projects the various possibilities of his existence into the warp and woof of the world, of time and history, of past, present, and future. Man is his own past, and he is not his own past. He can neither catch up with his past nor with his future because he remains

---

9 *Ibid.*, p. 708.   11 *Ibid.*, p. 565.
10 *Ibid.*, p. 253.   12 Cf. *ibid.*, p. 558 ff.

separated from both by that "nothingness" which always intervenes between him and time. Man is thus relinquished, abandoned by his past: it avails him nothing. But the absolute dictate of his present freedom commands him and compels him to assert himself, to *make himself,* that is, to invent and set up motivations and values to sustain his life.

Constantly checkmated in his projects, constantly thrown back on his fragile momentary existence, man, in his dereliction (*délaissement*), experiences dread and anguish. He knows that he is completely alone, absolutely on his own, under the fearful pressure of his own responsibility. The freedom to which he is "condemned" frightens and worries him. He would like nothing better than to rid himself of this burden, by shifting responsibility for his actions either to the determining forces of environment and heredity or to the decree of a superhuman power: by becoming either a nonconscious and nonresponsible being or a being subject to a superior law and necessity. But such attempts at escape — materialistic determinism as much as religious predestination — are essentially dishonest (*de mauvaise foi*) and foredoomed to failure. Man is what he makes himself, and he alone is responsible for what he makes himself.

Sartre enters a new dimension of human existence when he discusses the "being-for-others" (*l'être pour-autrui*). Every philosophic idealism, he affirms, suffers shipwreck in view of the actual existence of "the other." The world of idealism is a world without human beings. The existence of "the other" confronts me with a new and different set of experiences and shatters the solipsism of any idealistic dreamworld. At once I make the astounding discovery that certain things are no longer centered in me but in "the other." As a consequence of the existence of "the others" even those things which constituted my own personal world are slipping away. The unity of my world undergoes a process of dissolution. Lifeless things, such as a road, a lamppost, a letterbox, are no longer oriented toward me but toward another or toward those others who make me one of their number.

Two principal attitudes are possible in regard to the phenomenon of "the other," says Sartre. The first is illustrated by the phenomenon of *love.* Here I recognize and acknowledge the beloved as a free subject, but "the other" in this case regards me as an *en-soi,* that is, as an object or thing. To please, to attract, to fascinate the beloved, I try every possible means to present myself as a perfectly fulfilled and integrated being. But the beloved, if he loves me, demands in turn that I acknowledge in him the attribute of absolute ontological plenitude, and neither of us is willing to enter into a reciprocal relationship on such fictitious and self-contradictory premises.

The second principal attitude in regard to "the other" is illustrated by the phenomenon of *sexual desire*. Here "my regard" transforms the other into an object or thing of which I try to gain possession, whose freedom I try to appropriate. But blinded by carnal passion, I completely lose sight of my original aim: instead of enjoying the anticipated rapture of possession, I either forget "the other" in the auto-intoxication of lust or I sadistically subdue and enslave him. In neither case is the desired union with the other a possibility.

Out of these futile efforts is born a deadly hatred. Not only in love and sexual lust but in all human relationships my own projects may at any time be crossed and paralyzed by the projects of "the other." Therefore, Sartre claims, the original and natural attitude among human beings is not love, harmony, and peace, but hate, conflict, and strife. Rather than tolerate the freedom of "the other," I resolve to annihilate it and him in mortal combat. And yet, what will all this profit me, even assuming that I were to kill all men? It would not alter the fact that at one time they existed and made me an object of their own projects. Thus even this mortal hatred is futile and absurd: it is nothing but a final, abortive effort at self-assertion, born of utter despair.

The total strangeness of "the other" finally confronts me in the phenomenon of *death*. Death is not part of the ontological structure of human consciousness: it can never become part of my projects; I can neither experience nor anticipate death; it is, in short, not encountered among the possibilities of my existence. What, then, is death? It is simply the nonsensical destruction of all human possibilities, the absurd annihilation of the human self. Far from imparting any meaning to human life, death rather reveals most clearly that life in its totality is absurd: "It is meaningless that we were born; it is meaningless that we die."[13]

Every human being, Sartre avers, is animated by the radical desire to become God.[14] As a means for their self-deification and to demonstrate to themselves their creative powers, men make use of the various devices of the arts and sciences. But, as has been pointed out, all such hopes and endeavors are chimerical because the idea of

---

[13] *Ibid.*, p. 631.   [14] *Ibid.*, p. 653.

God, the *en-soi-pour-soi,* is self-contradictory. If there were a God, says Sartre, he would either have to be an *en-soi* and thus possess the fullness of being, but his massive objectivity would then be deprived of consciousness: he would be incapable of any rational, purposive activity. Or, if God were a conscious and personal being, he would be a *pour-soi* like man: he, too, would be divided in himself and invaded by nothingness, the inevitable companion of consciousness. This God also would then be condemned to a mad and futile pursuit of an illusory and impossible goal. Therefore, concludes Sartre, there is no God, there can be no God. And man's passionate desire to become a god himself remains *"une passion inutile."*[15]

It would seem that man's sorry and sordid lot of being condemned to a life of futility and absurdity might plunge him into abysmal despair. But the conclusions at which Sartre arrives are quite different. Beyond despair, he tells his readers, entirely new perspectives are opening up, perspectives which even impart an ethical substance to human action. To reach this point of a new departure, man must first of all renounce what Sartre calls *l'esprit de sérieux.*[16] This "spirit of seriousness" prevails, says Sartre, if one seeks *in the world* a point of departure and of support or if one measures one's own reality and value in the terms of one's belonging-to-the-world. It is no accident, he claims, that both capitalists and revolutionaries are possessed by *l'esprit de sérieux:* they think only and know themselves only as particles of a world which either fulfills their desires or blots out their very existence. Thus, every materialism is, according to Sartre, *sérieux* by definition. Materialism simply denotes the abdication of man in favor of the world. Within this frame of reference there is no possibility of escaping the world's crude force: assimilated to the world, man becomes hard like a rock, dense and opaque like all those things which constitute "the world." Man's subjectivity adapts itself to the lifeless objectivity of the *en-soi.* Karl Marx, whom Sartre calls *"le prince des gens sérieux,"* was well aware that man becomes definitively *sérieux* as soon as he regards himself as merely one object among others.

The values which *l'esprit de sérieux* pursues are, in Sartre's view, purely illusory. He claims that his "phenomenological ontology" has demonstrated once and for all that the attempt of the *pour-soi* to become an *en-soi,* without ceasing to be a *pour-soi,* is "the vanity of

---

[15] *Ibid.,* p. 708.   [16] Cf. *ibid.,* p. 669.

all vanities." Such an ambition, he maintains, is both chimerical and self-contradictory. The only true and absolute value is embodied in a *freedom* which affirms itself in its profound contingency and turns this contingency into a personal adventure. It seizes itself in the very vacuity of its being ("*néant d'être*"), a being "which is not what it is and which is what it is not," and which therefore remains forever estranged from itself. And thus, by a "radical conversion" (amounting to an absolute renunciation of *l'esprit de sérieux*), freedom affirms itself and posits its own foundation. Henceforth, man truly appears as that being to whom all values owe their existence, and freedom appears as the creative "nought" to which the world owes its existence. Man thus has assumed his "absolute freedom" and endows it with the quality of the master value. By doing so he will in rare moments become sufficient unto himself: he will be like a god, an *en-soi-pour-soi*. In the perspective of this "radical conversion" the modes of human action matter little, provided only that man acts, that he "engages himself," and that he entertains no illusions whatsoever as to the goals or ends which he sets for himself. Only in the measure in which he still clings to *l'esprit de sérieux* does man condemn himself to despair, for then he discovers immediately "that all human activities are equivalent . . . that all of them are equally doomed to ultimate failure." On the basis of an ethics of "engagement," on the other hand, any kind of action can be justified, if only the agent is courageous or reckless enough to be consistent: "Thus it makes little difference whether a man is a drunkard or a leader of nations."[17]

II

A *critique* of the main tenets of Sartre's philosophy, as set forth in *L'être et le néant,* will necessarily have to begin with pointing out the complete arbitrariness of many of the French thinker's assumptions and assertions. Among such postulatory and unproven *points de départ* are the concepts of the *en-soi* and *pour-soi;* the reduction of human existence to the sphere of consciousness; the contention of an aboriginal state of hate and strife between man and man; the way the concept of "nothingness" is used (or abused); the apodictic denial of the existence of God; and the proclamation of the absoluteness of human freedom.

The entire structure of *L'être et le néant* rests on the arbitrary

---

[17] *Ibid.,* p. 722.

postulate of an absolute and massive "being-in-itself" (*en-soi*). With a grand sweep Sartre replaces the several philosophic dualisms of the past by a simple phenomenological monism: the "being" and the "appearance" of things are identical or, in other words, things *are* exactly what they *appear* to be; there is no "within" and "without," no hidden "nature" or "essence" of things. And since the thing-phenomenon thus presents itself wholly and absolutely, it can be studied and described both as an ontological and phenomenological datum. This description Sartre calls a *"phenomenological ontology."*

The traditional dualisms of act and potency and of substance and accident share the fate of all the others: they disappear in Sartre's ontology. Since the phenomenon is the entire reality of a being, "everything is in act," and the appearance of a thing is its total essence. The essence merely ties together the successive "apparitions" of existents and is thus itself nothing but a phenomenal appearance.[18] Now if it could be shown that "being" is not only encountered in the massive objectivity of an *en-soi* but also in the conscious ego of the "subject" as well as in the interrelation between object and subject, Sartre's entire argumentation would be immediately invalidated. If finite beings subsist owing to their relation to the infinite Being of God, a divine creative act becomes a reasonable and plausible ontological or metaphysical proposition.

All the arguments which Sartre adduces against the creation of the world and of man by an omnipotent God amount to an apodictic postulatory denial of such a *"creatio ex nihilo."* A rational justification for this denial is not even attempted. Sartre simply asserts that the created world would by its very subsistence detach itself from its "creator." It would immediately claim for itself an absolute autonomy (*"aseitas"*). He argues that, if this were not the case, the act of creation would of necessity have to be coextensive with the spatiotemporal reality of the world, so that the world would then become undistinguishable from its author or would be completely absorbed by him and in him. The question which Sartre fails to ask is whether a world which is both subsisting *and* created being (that is, a world of relative and limited autonomy) is not conceivable. If the answer is in the affirmative, then a *"creatio ex nihilo"* is possible and plausible.

The *en-soi* of the world is for Sartre radical and absolute contingency; it is uncreated, without any *raison d'être,* without cause, and

---

[18] Cf. *ibid.,* p. 12.

entirely *"de trop"* in view of any conceivable "eternity." Contingency thus signifies in Sartre's opinion the absence of a *raison dêtre,* that is, a complete absurdity. This is, to say the least, an unusual concept of contingency. Ordinarily, a being is said to be contingent if it does not have its *raison d'être* in itself but in something else. If it has no *raison d'être* whatsoever — either in itself or in another — a being cannot even be called contingent: it does not and cannot exist at all. God is said to be the Absolute Necessary Being because He has His *raison d'être* in Himself, in virtue of the perfect plenitude of an essence which is its existence. Sartre's *en-soi,* on the other hand, cannot be termed necessary in this sense: since it is wholly without *raison d'être,* it is, strictly speaking, "absurd."

All of Sartre's observations concerning *human existence* are confined to the one sphere of *consciousness.* His anthropological views are thus as limited as those of Descartes, his remote intellectual ancestor. Like Descartes, he strips the human ego of its ontological and psychological richness and vitality by reducing it to a mere *res cogitans.*

In his phenomenological analysis of the "being-for-others" (*l'être pour-autrui; l'être-avec*) Sartre mingles half-truths with fully grown falsehoods. Man's physical and physiological nature — this much is true — acts for its own good in its striving for self-preservation and for the perpetuation of the species. But there is in man, aside from this purely biological vitality, a moral and spiritual life principle which relates the individual self socially to "the other" in service and in love. In Sartre's thinking "the other" never appears as a "thou" but always as the enemy or the stranger who wants to subdue and dominate me. Is it not truly amazing that in a philosophy which calls itself not only "existential" but "humanistic," no mention is ever made of the phenomena of friendship, conjugal and filial love, moral obligation, mutual understanding? There is only the alternative of either the annihilation of "the other" by me, or my own annihilation by "the other." There is never a question of both mine and "the other's" participation in a "we" that is ontologically superior to either of us individually.

Sartre's world is, in short, an absurd and impossible universe, populated by contingent and isolated beings, all self-enclosed and merely physically juxtaposed in a metaphysical and moral vacuum. The neighbor is "the other," and he is the enemy, and since God (if he existed) would be "the absolute other," he would logically be the most formidable and the most hated enemy. "Hell," Sartre writes in *Huis-clos* (*No Exit*), "that is the others." And Orestes, in *Les Mouches* (*The Flies*), asserts that "being can only affirm itself against its Creator." Sartre's freedom, like that of Lucifer, aims at self-deification, without and against "the others," without and against God. It is a freedom which annihilates every value in order to be able to choose itself in absolute autonomy as the one and only value.

"Behind Sartre," writes Roger Troisfontaines, "there opens up a satanic abyss. . . . It is, however, the great merit of Sartre to have described that 'nothing' which is man without divine grace. . . . *Either* man — contrary to truth — claims for himself the self-sufficiency of the deity: he chooses himself in isolation, in contempt of the others and of the Creator; he wants to become a god without God: this is presumptuous egotism; theologically speaking, it is hell. *Or* — in conformity with the laws of being — man . . . accepts the divine life in Christ, in communion with all his brethren; he desires to become godlike with God: this is humble love; theologically speaking, it is heaven. Everything depends on our choice between these two modes of divinization." The choice between *"Non serviam"* and *"Ecce ancilla Domini"* is the choice between hell and heaven.[19]

Sartre repeatedly defends himself against the charge of being a materialist. While there is no doubt as to the justification of the charge, it is equally obvious that Sartre's materialism differs from both the primitive atomistic materialism of past ages and the dialectic-historical materialism of Karl Marx. His is a subtle and refined cryptomaterialism which likes to hide behind deceptive disguises. Sartre, for example, opposes an "absolute freedom" to the massive, material *"en-soi."* But one soon finds out that the "values" which this "freedom" creates are all fictitious and illusory, reflections merely of human "projects" and thus without objective reality. These pseudo values closely resemble the ideological "superstructures" of Marxian materialism, and it is therefore hardly surprising that several of the spokesmen of French communism have shown themselves eager to welcome Sartre into their ranks. The philosopher, however, flatly declared his opposition to the party dogma of historic determinism.

To communist attacks which took sharp issue with some of the most flagrant inconsistencies in Sartre's thinking, the philosopher

---

[19] Cf. Roger Troisfontaines, *op. cit.*, pp. 68–90, *passim*.

replied in an essay entitled *Matérialisme et révolution*.[20] Revolution, he says there, is always an individual or collective act of freedom. If everything follows a predetermined course, then the call for freedom and the revolt of the proletariat become meaningless. While this sounds like a valid argument against historic materialism, it might well be asked why anyone should rise and fight for a freedom which, according to Sartre's own original thesis, is as void of ultimate meaning as existence itself.

The way Sartre manipulates the concept of "nothingness" reveals that he faithfully follows his own precept: to renounce *L'esprit de sérieux*. It is true in a sense that man, in virtue of his freedom of saying "no" injects an element of "nothingness" (or rather "negation") into the realm of being. It is equally true that man has the faculty of comparing that which has been and that which is with that which he ideally projects into the future. But to say that the use of negation in the statement that the present is *not* the past or that the past is *not* the future or that the future is *not* the present, annihilates one or several of these dimensions of reality, amounts to a mere *jeu d'esprit*, a juggling of words. The use of negation in such instances, far from entailing a diminution of being, may actually bring about an extension of the human and historico-cultural horizon and may thus lead to an enrichment of being. In short, all dimensions of reality, though not alike in appearance and content, are equally essential for human existence. And to lay stress on one of them does not mean to "annihilate" the others. A genuine phenomenological analysis in Husserl's sense would attempt to illuminate progressively the various aspects and dimensions of reality as reflected in human consciousness.

Finally, Sartre's assertion that the idea of God is self-contradictory is an unfounded and unproved assumption. He claims that the existence of God is impossible because it involves the idea of a being who is infinite self-consciousness and at the same time self-identical or a perfectly integrated, undivided self. Consciousness, however, is always divided in itself; even in self-consciousness there is a division between the self as knowing and the self as known. And since the plenitude of being (the *en-soi*) is undivided, consciousness is *eo ipso* excluded from it.

What validity is there in this kind of reasoning? The idea of God,

---

[20] Cf. Sartre, *Situations* (Paris: Gallimard, 1948), Vol. II.

says Sartre, is self-contradictory. This is, of course, precisely what he has to say once he has endowed the *en-soi* with the massive density and inertness of matter. From an *en-soi* thus conceived the qualities of a *pour-soi* are excluded by definition. If, however, the *en-soi* were conceived not as matter but as *spirit,* the attribution of thought and reflection would present no difficulty and could be logically and ontologically defended. The "self-contradiction" would disappear. In other words, a spiritual *en-soi* would of necessity be an *"en-soi-pour-soi"*: it would be transparent to itself and identical with itself.

Sartre moreover applies to the idea of God univocally the characteristics of an intramundane contingency, so that such a "god" would find himself subjected to all the conditions of the *"réalité-humaine."* But God's "hold" on the totality of the world cannot be and hardly ever has been understood in this manner. God neither looks at the world from without (whether under the aspect of "object" or "subject"), but by His creative act He confers upon the world its reality: He calls into existence that relation to Himself which is the world. The divine creative act, understood as issuing from the divine essence posits and "holds" the world in its totality. No subject and no object can ever limit either the being or the knowledge of God, simply because it is the divine creative essence itself which constitutes the world in its every aspect of objectivity and subjectivity.

The simple truth is that the finite human mind can never have an adequate idea of God's infinite mind. But it is reasonable to assume that the latter has none of the limitations and imperfections of human consciousness. Sartre's "argument" proves thus only one thing, namely, that the divine mind cannot have the same ontological structure as human consciousness. It does not, however, in any way support the postulate of Sartre that the existence of God is a logical and ontological impossibility.

III

Before Sartre espoused his "moral" philosophy in the series of novels entitled *Les chemins de la Liberté* (*The Ways of Freedom*), he had published *Les Mouches,* a play which forcefully underscores the central theme of his infernal gospel of hatred and revolt. The plot is a modern variant of the ancient Greek tale of Orestes[21] who,

---

[21] Cf. the dramatic versions of Aeschylus, Sophocles, Euripides in ancient times; and the modern psychological treatment of the same theme in Goethe's *Iphigenia.*

as a small child, was taken from his homeland, after Aegisthus, the tyrant of Argos, had slain Agamemnon, Orestes' father, and married Clytemnestra, his mother. Grown to manhood, Orestes returns to Argos and, aided by Electra, his sister, kills both Aegisthus and Clytemnestra and is thereupon pursued by the Furies, the goddesses of retribution.

Sartre uses this piece of Greek mythology to illustrate what he means by absolute human freedom. Argos, the petty, provincial Greek town (which in Sartre's play takes the place of the austere setting of ancient Mycenae) is inhabited by puritanical bigots who bask in the musty and moldy atmosphere of bourgeois hypocrisy. These are the people *"de mauvaise foi";* their guilty consciences are symbolized by "the flies" which swarm all over the city and befoul the homes of the citizens.

When Orestes returns home, he finds Argos in deep mourning. For the past fifteen years the inhabitants have been torturing themselves in doing penance for their coresponsibility in the assassination of Agamemnon, their king. Aegisthus, the killer and adulterer, does not himself believe in this cult of repentance and remorse. He has instituted and perpetuated it in Argos because he is convinced that the fear and terror generated by such a morbid religious cult are the most effective means to keep his subjects in abject obedience. And this conviction is shared by Jupiter, the "god," who rules over the people of Greece. Jupiter, too, can maintain his power only as long as human beings are weighed down by a guilt complex, as long as the fact remains concealed from them that in reality there is nothing at all that could justify their sorrow and remorse.

While away from home, Orestes has been instructed and "enlightened" by an eminent "pedagogue" who, a Greek Voltaire, has "liberated" his pupil from the bonds of faith, love, and religion. This "liberation" makes it possible for Orestes to challenge the tyrannical hold which both Aegisthus and Jupiter have on the people's consciences. From an initial state of lethargy Orestes is aroused by Electra who, in defiance of the king's orders and in mockery of the sinister cult of remorse, performs a dance of rejoicing on the occasion of the annual popular observance of the Day of Atonement. Orestes begins to realize that up to this day he has not really lived his own life. When he realizes that he has to choose between obedience to the law of Jupiter and rebellion against this law, he chooses the latter.

Jupiter, the "god," and Aegisthus, the adulterous tyrant, are cut out of the same cloth. Both know of only one supreme value: order! "For the sake of order," says Aegisthus, "I have killed my king; I wanted order to prevail, and I wanted it to prevail through me. I have lived without desire, without love, without hope, but I have created order." And Jupiter, after the assassination of Aegisthus and Clytemnestra, offers the kingship to Orestes with only one stipulation: he is to perpetuate the regime of "order." Orestes refuses. In place of "resignation and vile humility" he chooses the passionate hatred of the rebel. He dedicates himself to the task of "liberation." After the double murder he is unrepentant. But he is not quite at ease in his newly gained freedom. He knows that "everything has changed. There was some warmth about me, something which is now dead. How empty everything has become. . . . And this anguish: do you believe that I will ever get rid of this gnawing anguish?"

Electra is in the beginning as revolutionary in her advocacy of absolute emancipation as Orestes; without her aid and inspiration the might of Jupiter could not have been broken. But in the end she weakens: the horror of her deed haunts her, and she seeks refuge in repentance and in renewed submission to the abandoned law. Orestes has freed himself from the avenging Furies, but he knows that his freedom, which absolves him from any obligation to God, man, and nature, is the precarious freedom of an exile. He is willing, however, to accept its burdens together with its privileges: "I am condemned henceforth to accept no other law but my own. . . . My crime belongs to me; I claim it as my own in the face of the light of the sun: it is my pride and the mainstay of my existence."

In his preface to *Les Mouches* Sartre claims that he has "attempted to demonstrate that self-abnegation and self-accusation is not the attitude the French were permitted to take after their military defeat. . . . And for the Germans, too, such an attitude is sterile. By this I do not wish to imply that the memory of the faults of the past should disappear from their minds. No. But I am convinced that self-accusation cannot gain for them the forgiveness of the world. That forgiveness can only be brought about by a total and absolute resolution to create a future in freedom and in deed, by a firm will to build this future in common with the greatest possible number of men of good will." This sounds eminently reasonable. But is it more than an afterthought, a belated rationalization of the blasphemous thesis of this play? This thesis proclaims without any ambiguity that man, because of his absolute freedom, has nothing to repent, nothing to feel sorry for. "The man," says Sartre, "who has been smitten by his freedom as by a flash of lightning, is beyond good and evil and beyond the reach of anyone who would dare to give him orders."

The thesis of *Les Mouches* is neither political nor philosophical: it expresses an ethico-religious conviction. The real object of the rebellion of Orestes-Sartre is God and the moral law and order sanctioned by Him. His Jupiter is described as the Creator of the world, the Lord of nature, the supreme Lawgiver. "I have created you," Jupiter tells the rebellious Orestes, "and I have created all things. Behold these planets pursuing their paths in an orderly manner, without ever colliding with each other: I have regulated their course. Listen to the harmony of the spheres, this tremendous song of praise, mightily resounding from the four corners of the universe."

The "god" whose "death" Nietzsche announced had actually never been alive. The same is true of the "god" against whom Sartre's Orestes rises in revolt. This deity inspires no love, but only abject fear and the sadness and hopelessness of despair. Nothing but the magic wand of his freedom can save man from the nightmare of this pseudo divinity. But Sartre no doubt consciously and intentionally constructed this caricature of the Christian God and of Christian morality. To what end? To justify in the rebellion of his hero his own rebellion against Christianity.

"Two centuries of crisis in religion and science were needed," Sartre writes in an essay on Descartes, "so that man could regain his creative freedom . . . , so that at last the truth upon which all humanism is based might appear: man is the sufficient reason for the existence of the world." Sartre's Orestes has discovered the secret that freedom, the gift of God to man, can be turned by man against the divine giver: "I am your king, you shameless worm," says Jupiter; "who, after all, has created you?" "You," Orestes admits with sovereign contempt, "but you should not have created me *free*." "I have given you your freedom, so that you might freely serve me," replies Jupiter. "That's possible," sneers Orestes, "but it has turned against you. . . . I am a man, Jupiter, and every man has to find his own way. . . . What is there between you and me? We shall pass by each other like two ships. . . . You are a god, and I am free: we are equally alone in our anguish."

Sartre's Orestes is a kinsman of all those self-styled "supermen" in past and present who have been preaching the gospel of *self-redemption*. They include historical figures, such as Simon Magus, the gnostic mystagogue, Faustus, the Manichaean, the German Georg Sabellicus (who called himself Dr. Faustus and "Magus Secundus"), Schopenhauer, and Nietzsche, as well as characters of religion, mythology, and literature, such as Lucifer, Prometheus, Faust, and Zarathustra. Sartre merely carries this ancient gnostic theme to a point where self-redemption turns into a blasphemous and sacrilegious "counter-redemption": Orestes is the "Superman" who achieves his freedom by matricide and who in his rebellious pride makes bold to become the liberator also of his fellowmen by taking upon himself their guilt and their remorse. The perversion of the Christian idea of redemption cannot be carried any farther.

Human existence and human freedom, according to Sartre, grow out of and are nourished by despair. Sartre does not wish to affirm that man can in freedom choose between good and evil but rather that man's absolute freedom rises "beyond good and evil." And, like Nietzsche's Zarathustra, he is not insensitive to the horrors which this kind of freedom entails. Orestes, trusting exclusively in his own powers, defiantly invites the curse of Jupiter. His freedom is the freedom of Lucifer, born of stubborn pride and the refusal to serve.

IV

Sartre's philosophy as much as that of Nietzsche expresses the terrifying experience of man's forlornness in a world without God. In his lecture on *Humanism*[22] Sartre tries to assuage this terror by reassuring his readers, telling them that there is no reason for getting very excited about the lamentable state of the world and of man in the world. Nothing is really lost as long as man is courageous enough to rid himself of all nostalgia for things which are gone and cannot be brought back. Everything can still be arranged satisfactorily if only man realizes the strength of his freedom; this strength will then enable him to start a new existence and a new world, both centered in himself rather than in God: "Before you come alive, life is nothing; it's up to you to give it a meaning, and value is nothing else but the meaning you choose."[23]

In all his rapturous praise of human freedom it never occurs to Sartre to inquire into the nature of freedom itself. He takes it for

---

[22] Sartre, *L'Existentialisme est un humanisme* (1946) — English edition: *Existentialism,* translated by Bernard Frechtman (New York: Philosophical Library, 1947).

[23] *Ibid.,* p. 58.

granted that man can freely posit something which did not exist previously; that he can freely forge new chains of causality. Even if that were true (and it is only partially true), the question of how freedom comes into the world and into man or the question of how it becomes possible for man to be or to posit a new beginning, remains unanswered. Sartre ceases his questioning before he has even faced the real problem of freedom.

What is freedom? This is the fundamental question, and it cannot be answered without asking with Heidegger the equally fundamental question, *What is truth?* Since it is truth that shall make us free, the nature of freedom cannot be understood unless it is seen in its relation to the nature of truth. But the problem of truth has no place in Sartre's thinking, for the barbarically primitive statement that truth is what I posit as true cannot in earnest be regarded as a philosophical answer.

Sartre makes much of his dogmatic assertion that "existence precedes essence." He even claims that all existentialism teaches the absolute prevalence of existence over and prior to essence. Man, he says, is "a being who exists before he can be defined by any concept. . . . At first he is nothing. Only afterward will he be something, and he himself will have made what he will be. Thus, there is no human nature, since there is no God to conceive it."[24]

In evident contrast to Heidegger, Sartre uses the terms *"existentia"* and *"essentia"* in their scholastic-Thomistic meaning. But with the aid of modern psychological and psychoanalytical analysis, he totally misrepresents Thomistic metaphysics and then attempts the demolition of this absurd construct of his own mind.

Sartre's relationship to Heidegger is rather complex, but Heidegger himself has guardedly attempted to ward off responsibility for this self-styled disciple. Max Müller goes farther: he points out that Sartre has completely perverted the meaning of Heidegger's thought in every important point. While in Heidegger's view man is the witness, the servant, "the shepherd" of Being, for Sartre man is the autonomous creator and master of Being. Man's absolute freedom knows of no obedience, no service, no humility, no response to Being. Resting on no essence or human nature, man finds himself alone and forlorn in the nothingness of his empty existence, trying to fill the void with his illusory projects, and actually existing only in this process of projecting and acting.

---

[24] *Ibid.*, p. 18.

For Heidegger the essence of truth is freedom. Sartre's "postulatory atheism" demands that "God be dead," so that human freedom may be born. In Heidegger's philosophy freedom is grounded in the Truth of Being. In Sartre's philosophy both Being and freedom are grounded in nothingness. Heidegger is seeking a new approach to the truth of traditional Western metaphysics. Sartre offers his antimoralism and antitheology as substitutes for Christian morality and religion.

CHAPTER SIX

SHIPWRECK OR HOMECOMING?

THE EXISTENTIALISM OF KARL JASPERS

I

AMONG all those thinkers, past and present, who may roughly be classified as "existentialists," the German philosopher Karl Jaspers (1883 —) comes closest to a systematic and integrated presentation of his philosophic creed. This is so despite the fact that, in contrast to Heidegger, Jaspers does not acknowledge the need for an ontology, that is, a fundamental discipline embracing the totality of being. The "philosophy of existence" — a title to which the philosophy of Jaspers definitely lays claim — must be satisfied with the illumination of the possibilities of individual, concrete existence in its freedom, uniqueness, and ineffability.

Karl Jaspers[1] is not only a prolific writer but a thinker whose many works reveal the wide range of his interests and the prodigious scope of the intellectual tradition which is his heritage. His early studies in medicine, psychology and psychiatry, and his practical clinical experiences yielded two important works, one dealing with psychopathology and the other with the psychology of different philosophies of life.[2] Among the major publications of Jaspers, the philosopher,

---

[1] Karl Jaspers was born in the east-Frisian city of Oldenburg as the son of a banker. He studied law at the Universities of Heidelberg and Munich, and medicine at the Universities of Berlin, Göttingen, and Heidelberg. He wrote his doctoral dissertation at Heidelberg on *Heimweh und Verbrechen (Nostalgia and Crime,* 1909). After having held an assistantship at the local Psychiatric Clinic, he was appointed professor of psychology at Heidelberg University in 1916 and professor of philosophy in 1921. For political reasons he was relieved of his academic duties in 1937, was reinstated after the collapse of National Socialism, in 1945, and was named an "Honorary Senator" of the University of Heidelberg in 1946. In 1948, he accepted a call to the University of Basel in Switzerland.

[2] Cf. *Allgemeine Psychopathologie* (Berlin: Springer, 1913; 4 ed., 1946); *Psychologie der Weltanschauungen* (Berlin: Springer, 1919; 3 ed., 1925).

are three series of lectures,[3] comprehensive studies on Descartes and Nietzsche,[4] and two monumental presentations (the second still unfinished) of the sum total of his own philosophic position.[5]

Those intellectual ancestors whose influence can be traced in the thinking of Jaspers include — aside from Kant, Kierkegaard, and Nietzsche, who are specifically named — such ancient and modern thinkers as Plotinus, Giordano Bruno, Spinoza, and Schelling. Kant in particular is for Jaspers the philosopher *par excellence* (*"der Philosoph schlechthin"*). The infrequent references to the Aristotelian and scholastic tradition are largely negative and betray the lack of an intimate, first-hand acquaintance with this important branch of Western thought.

Philosophy begins for Jaspers not with an inquiry into the problem of being but with an inquiry into the specific *situation* in which the philosopher finds himself in the world. The reason for this point of departure lies, Jaspers states, in the fact that the problem of being cannot be resolved by way of a rational analysis. It is impossible to conceive of a doctrine of being which, in virtue of its rational convincing force, could command universal assent. Everything that I experience as essentially real owes its reality to the fact that I myself exist as an individual. The primary philosophic task, therefore, is the "illumination" (*Existenzerhellung*) of the personality of the one who asks the philosophic questions.

When, for example, I ask such questions as "What is being?" or "Why is there something rather than nothing?" or "Who am I?" these queries arise from my personally and historically determined situation. My questions and my answers will fit only this situation in its relativity and particularity and thus cannot be of general and absolute validity. This situation contains some known and knowable as well as some unknown and unknowable elements: it is rooted in an unfathomable past and tends toward an impenetrable future. It has neither a readily definable origin nor a definitely recognizable end. I find myself in the midst of things, immersed in a movement that is apparently undetermined and undeterminable.

---

[3] Cf. *Vernunft und Existenz* (Groningen, Batavia: Wolters, 1935); *Existenzphilosophie* (Berlin: W. de Gruyter, 1938); *Der philosophische Glaube* (München: R. Piper, 1948).

[4] Cf. *Nietzsche* (Berlin: W. de Gruyter, 1936); *Descartes und die Philosophie* (Berlin: W. de Gruyter, 1937).

[5] Cf. *Philosophie* (Berlin: Springer, 1932), 3 vols.; *Philosophische Logik I: Von der Wahrheit* (München: R. Piper, 1947).

Although at first glance everything seems very matter of fact and almost self-evident, I soon begin to wonder as to myself and the world which surrounds me and of which I am a part. What does it really mean, I ask myself, when I state that *I am* or that *the world is?* I know from experience that everything is transitory; I know that I myself was not at the beginning of things and that I shall not be at the end. And I am anxious to find in this incessant flux a statically fixed point which would permit me to arrive at some objective certainty concerning myself and the world. I am looking for an answer that will give me a firm hold on myself and on life, because the incertitude of my present situation fills me with doubt and anxiety. I have come out of one darkness in which I was not yet, and I am on my way into another darkness in which I shall be no more. In the narrow span of light in which I find myself, I am concerned about myself and about things, but the reasons for such concern are as yet a mystery to me. And so I search for some kind of "being" whose existence does not exhaust itself in transitoriness and which may thus impart stability and permanence also to my own self.

Can science and scientific knowledge possibly be of help in showing me a way out of my existential incertitude? Philosophy evidently differs from science in that it lacks a factual, objective basis on which to build the structure of its insight. Is philosophy then for this reason inferior to science? Experimental science claims to base its findings on tested "facts." This claim, however, is only partially justified: all the "exact" sciences start from certain presuppositions which they take for granted without attempting to demonstrate their truth. All scientific "theories" are intellectual constructs which are open to change and correction on the basis of newly discovered "facts." Even if these theories approach a maximum of probability, they never yield absolute certitude; they never penetrate to the full depth of being; they never explore "the whole" of being. Direct scientific "intuitions," such as are occasionally encountered in higher mathematics and in formal logic, are so limited in scope, so fragmentary and so incommunicable that no doctrine of universal and absolute validity can be founded upon them. Science, in short, remains confined to a kind of surface knowledge of the objective world: it cannot grasp and comprehend being as such, and it cannot provide an answer to questions concerning the ultimate values and ends of human life. Philosophy and science are thus equally incapable of sustaining any absolute, dogmatic, or final certitude of knowledge.

Thus, in my search for a secure anchor of being, I am thrown back again on my own concrete self. Here at least I seem to be able to get hold of an authentic reality of which I have an immediate experience. While the being of things is unconscious of itself, I, the thinking subject, am conscious of the being that I am. The very fact that I am able to say, "I am," differentiates my being from the being of everything else. The being of things is inaccessible to me because my very knowledge of them deprives them of their independence; my knowledge relativizes them by transforming them into a reality *for me*. No being can thus be known objectively or "as it is in itself." This is true even of my own being: to the extent that I have a rational knowledge of myself, I am not, strictly speaking, myself. The proper starting point of philosophy is therefore my personal existence, such as it is given to me in the immediate experience of my concrete situation: "The situation is the beginning . . . of philosophy. . . . It is for me the one and only form of reality. . . . My thinking starts from it and returns to it."[6] I must accept my concrete situation in its entirety and in its necessity, and I must try to "illuminate" it as completely and profoundly as possible. Here, if anywhere, do I have a chance of finding my search for "being" answered and rewarded.

What, then, is this personal, concrete "existence" in a given situation? It is, says Jaspers, the hidden ground of my self, that which never becomes an object and which therefore can neither be rationally known nor conceptually defined. It is the origin (*"Ursprung"*) out of which I think and act and of which in rare moments of insight I am indubitably certain.

The meaning of "existence" is further "illuminated" when it is contrasted with *"Dasein,"*[7] the simple "being-there" of empirical reality. And what is the meaning of *Dasein* in the terminology of Jaspers? It signifies the pure givenness of the temporal life and the conditions of the world as experienced by all, philosophers and nonphilosophers alike. It is that which is generally designated as the "reality" whose laws and structures are studied by science: "The whole of *Dasein* is the world. . . . The world is *Dasein* which confronts me as the always determined being of objects; I myself am *Dasein* as far as I am an empirical being."[8]

---

[6] Jaspers, *Philosophie*, I, p. 3.

[7] The term *Dasein*, as will be seen, is used by Jaspers in a sense totally different from that connected with it by Heidegger.

[8] Jaspers, *Philosophie*, I, p. 28.

Human *Dasein,* according to Jaspers, is of the same order as the universal *Dasein* of the world: it can be regarded as an "object" among other objects and can thus be analyzed, studied, described, and explained. Such a scientific exploration of human *Dasein* forms the basis of psychology and the several anthropological disciplines which take their place side by side with the natural sciences. The empirical reality of the world and the empirical reality of human *Dasein* are inextricably intertwined. They cannot even be conceived independent of each other: "Neither is the world . . . without me who knows it, nor can I be without the world in which alone I am what I am. There is no world without me, nor am I without the world."[9]

Human *Dasein* is not "existence," says Jaspers, but man in his *Dasein* is "possible existence" *(mögliche Existenz).* Man is "that being who is not but who can be and ought to be and who therefore decides in his temporality whether or not he is to be eternal. . . ."[10] As "possible existence," man is capable of taking steps, of positing acts which either bring him nearer the fulfillment of his being or, conversely, carry him away from his being, toward nothingness. While the being of human *Dasein* is transitory, the vitality of human "existence" is immortal. While *Dasein* is absolutely temporal, existence is both temporal and timelessly eternal. "*Dasein* realizes itself in the being of the world; possible existence is in the world as in a territory in which it can manifest itself."[11]

How does "possible existence" realize itself? How does it attain to full self-possession? By the decision of an existential choice, answers Jaspers. Existential consciousness is the consciousness of personal freedom of choice. "Existence is real only as freedom. . . . Freedom is . . . the being of existence."[12] When I cease to observe myself psychologically, when I begin to act with positive enthusiasm and in virtue of a certitude which grows out of my very being — at that moment I decide what I am going to be. "In the act of choice . . . , in the original spontaneity of my freedom . . . I recognize myself for the first time as my own true self."[13] Thus "freedom is the beginning and the end in the process of the illumination of existence."[14] Only in those moments when I exercise my freedom am I fully myself; only in my free acts do I have the certitude of absolute being. And no abstract intellectual operations nor any emotional, sentimental, or instinctive impulses can ever impart to me a comparable experience.

[9] *Ibid.,* I, p. 62.   [11] *Ibid.,* II, p. 1 f.   [13] *Ibid.,* II, p. 180.
[10] *Ibid.,* II, p. 2.   [12] *Ibid.,* II, p. 177.   [14] *Ibid.,* II, p. 177.

In the act of freedom there is no "docility" regarding any object; everything lies ahead of me in a fluid state of possibility, and it is I who by a creative *"fiat"* impart actuality to one possibility or the other. I break out of the limitations of my *Dasein* and decide what I choose to be. The act of freedom is thus an absolute beginning, a spontaneous source and origin of true personal authenticity. Existence creates itself in this act, fertilizing the desert of being with the life-blood of personality. And freedom carries with it and within it its own certitude: not in the *cogito* (I think) but in the *eligo* (I choose) lies the guarantee of existence, so that the *Cogito, ergo sum* (I think, therefore I am) of Descartes becomes an *Eligo, ergo sum* (I choose, therefore I am) in the formulation of Jaspers. "In choosing I am, and if I am not, it is because of my failure to choose."[15]

Existential freedom is undefinable. The attempt to resolve the problem of freedom by objective rational analysis can never succeed because it fails to recognize and respect the nature of freedom. "Freedom proves itself by my action rather than by my insight," says Jaspers.[16] Since my free decision is unconditioned, existential choice cannot result from any objective conflict of motives. Nevertheless, the free act is not a blind act: man is conscious of his action, he knows what he is doing, and without such knowledge there would be no freedom. But the faculty of choosing among several known possibilities is not yet freedom in the full and true sense because it is a pure faculty or power without a subject matter or a substantial content.[17]

My freedom, furthermore, presupposes my being conscious of a law or a hierarchy of values. Freedom of choice, that is, a human act of freedom in the strict sense, is impossible without a law. But this law — the indispensable condition of my freedom — must be an internal, personal law rather than an external, universal norm: "Existential choice is not obedience to an objectively formulated imperative," but my obedience to an internal imperative. Since the world is inexhaustible in its contents and since science is by its very nature incomplete and fragmentary, I must act without first acquiring a complete and exact knowledge of all the factors involved in my decision. Otherwise I will never get beyond the stage of deliberation. I must either act now, at this present moment, in this particular situation, or I must absolutely refrain from action, and that means (for Jaspers)

---

[15] *Ibid.*, II, p. 182.
[16] *Ibid.*, II, p. 175.
[17] Cf. *ibid.*, p. 178.

I must refrain from living. Existential freedom chooses to act, that is, it chooses to live.

It is obvious, of course, that in his doctrine of freedom Jaspers defends a strictly anti-intellectualistic position. For any rational philosophy freedom of action is inconceivable without a prior intellectual knowledge which can deliberate and weigh motives. For Jaspers, on the contrary, it is precisely the absence of any rational, objective knowledge that makes freedom of action possible. Objective knowledge for him means constraint: "The science of not-knowing (*das Wissen des Nichtwissens*) is the condition of freedom. . . . If we knew of an intelligible answer to the question, 'Whence guilt, strife, and evil?' the possibility of existence would be deprived of its genuine, original experience. . . . The breakdown of every theodicy becomes an appeal to the spontaneous activity of our freedom."[18] No action that is conditioned by an external motive or end can be a free action; to be free, it must be "unconditioned."

The question then arises: how is any intelligible discussion of existential freedom as well as of other existential realities possible if none of them can be expressed and articulated objectively or conceptually? Jaspers answers that any such discussion can only be in the nature of a "sign language": it does not make the existential reality directly visible, but it points the way toward its seizure; it is an appeal rather than a revelation or expression of its being. The discussion of existential realities, in other words, serves to awaken the individual; it acts as a potent stimulus in the individual's efforts at self-realization.[19]

To be free means to be one's self; freedom is loyalty to one's self. This self has a history, and the act of freedom is the epitome or the fulfillment of the self's "historicity," bringing to fruition its past and in anticipation preparing its future. The "historicity" of my self narrows down somewhat the margin of individual freedom: whereas for Sartre human freedom is absolute, for Jaspers it is limited by the individual's historically molded personality. In other words, my past actions carry a substantial weight in regard to both the possibilities of my future and the actual decisions of my present. Thus freedom and necessity meet and fuse not only in my present and future choices but in the very individuality of my existence. Each and every decision establishes a new foundation for the formation of my real historical

---

18 *Ibid.,* III, p. 78.
19 Cf. *ibid.,* II, p. 430 f.

self: I am bound by the decisive character of my choices; in virtue of these choices I have become what I wanted myself to be.

The historical weight of my "original choice" is so great that all my subsequent choices are restricted by the fact of this historical continuity. This explains, says Jaspers, why the life of each individual is burdened by some necessary, inevitable "guilt." My present faults are deeply rooted in the historical structure of my being. The original, absolute choice, by which I have become what I am, was the one and only fully autonomous act in the self-determination of my existence; it predestines or predetermines to some extent what I am now and what I shall be in the future. My aboriginal freedom which in its very nature is boundless in its desire for complete self-realization — regardless of the claims and rights of others — weighs upon me like an "original sin." This radical tendency of my original freedom to become absolute, imparts to it the character of an original guilt. And this original guilt becomes thus the source of all the particular faults of my present and future.

In freedom I seize my existence. Freedom "is" existence, says Jaspers. But no matter how free, how independent and personal my existence may be, it never can subsist apart from that *Dasein* which is its natural environment and which provides the medium and the sustaining subject matter for its action. In view of this linkage with *Dasein,* existence finds itself exposed to two mortal dangers: it may mistake *Dasein* for the actual ground and depth of being and may thus lose itself or be dissolved in it; it may, for example, attach itself with complete abandon to the objects of sense as if they constituted the fullness of reality — or existence may behave as if *Dasein* were altogether unreal, of no value and significance whatsoever. The proper attitude maintains a precarious "tension" (*Spannung*) between these two extreme possibilities.

Dasein as such, isolated from existence, is essentially incomplete, fleeting, relative, evanescent: a contingent and transitory "nullity" (*Nichtigkeit*). Man therefore succumbs to a monstrous delusion if he regards it as an absolute reality, if he endows it with the attributes of stability, necessity, permanence, and absolute universal validity. Without the substantial content of the "historicity" of the concrete and personal human existence, *Dasein* is an empty shell. If, on the other hand, it is filled with this personal content, it immediately acquires "an absolute weight and value" and becomes "infinitely important." *Dasein,* in short, is indispensable "as an expression or manifestation of existence." By freely appropriating it, existence, as it were, incorporates *Dasein;* it becomes part of existence or even one with existence. "In this 'seizure' existence fulfills its destiny by realizing its being."[20] The unity of "existence" and *Dasein,* in which the individual self becomes manifest, constitutes for Jaspers man's "historicity," and "historical consciousness" is the conscious experience of this unity.[21]

The unity of existence and *Dasein* in the concrete, historical self — a unity in which the depth of being has become incarnate in an irreplaceable manner — signifies for Jaspers the fusion of the "eternal" and the "temporal." "Eternity," in other words, is not the plenitude of an existence outside or above time, nor the infinite extension of temporal existence, nor an infinite duration of human existence after death in a life beyond: "eternity" becomes incarnate in "time"; it manifests itself in the fulfilled moment. As soon as the weight of eternity is received into the temporality of *Dasein,* the eternal envelops and permeates the temporal. As far as my personal existence is concerned, I then exist *in* time, *above* time, and *beyond* time. Such an eternal existence in the fulfilled moment is realized in the unconditioned, necessary, and singularly authentic *act of freedom,* an act in which the individual overcomes the constraints of his temporality by deciding himself "in time, for eternity."[22] Prompted by my vital urges and my desire for lasting happiness, I seek permanence in time, and in the unconditional act of freedom I can satisfy this desire: I can introduce eternity into time.

II

In the act of freedom my existence not only takes possession of itself but it also enters into *communication* with other existences. I cannot really become myself in isolation, says Jaspers, but only in communication and collaboration with others. Not only do I become myself in this "loving strife" of communication with others, but the same is equally true of the others: they also attain to self-realization and self-possession in communication. Self-realization in communication is, according to Jaspers, like a *"creatio ex nihilo"*: a new richness of being is acquired and revealed. And, conversely, the absence or the refusal of communication leads to a corresponding absence or loss of being.[23]

---

[20] Cf. *ibid.,* II, p. 122 ff.
[21] Cf. *ibid.,* II, p. 424.
[22] Cf. *ibid.,* p. 207 f.
[23] *Ibid.,* II, p. 58.

The reasons with which Jaspers explains the need for communication in the process of self-realization follow the line of argument of the Hegelian dialectic: I am an ego, says Jaspers, only by setting myself off from a nonego, by asserting myself in the face of "the other," by opposing myself to "the other." This kind of self-assertion, however, leads me to the edge of "the abyss of absolute estrangement" in regard to "the other." And my desire for the unity of being urges me to bridge this abyss in the union of "being-with-the-other." Thus communication originates and is consummated.

Existential communication differs from all objectively verifiable relationships among human beings. It surpasses ordinary friendship, affection, and love as well as reciprocal esteem, mutual psychological understanding, and a mere unanimity of thoughts, convictions, and aspirations. All these have their proper place in *Dasein,* not in "existence": they are all insufficient to link existences in the profundity of their unconditional freedom. This does not mean, however, that existences can enter into a relationship of full and unrestricted immediacy. Such an immediacy of communication is prevented by the temporal condition of existences, that is, by their embodiment in the contingency of *Dasein.* But it is in these conditions and circumstances of ordinary, everyday life that "communicative situations" arise — in the various forms of mandate and service, in discourse, in social relations, and in social and political action. These contacts and relationships within the structure of *Dasein* are, as it were, "the body" or the material substrate of existential communication, the visible and tangible manifestation of its "invisible soul."[24]

What in particular, asks Jaspers, entices and attracts my "will to communication?" He answers that it is not so much what "the other" *has* as what he *is:* I want to reach "the other" in the original and irreducible ground and substance of his freedom. My own freedom, in other words, is in search of the freedom of "the other"; my own self requires other selves with whom to enter into a dual relationship of opposition and unification. "I cannot become myself," writes Jaspers, "if the other does not wish to become his self; I cannot be free if the other is not free."[25] In genuine communication those who enter into the existential relationship "open themselves" and "reveal themselves" to each other without reservation in the original depth of their being,

---

24 Cf. Jaspers, *Vernunft und Existenz,* p. 63.
25 Jaspers, *Philosophie,* II, p. 57.

ready to see and to be seen, to penetrate and be penetrated, to mold and be molded in a reciprocal give-and-take. In order to gain "existence" I am willing to forsake all my attachments to empirical goods and values, so that I may become free to experience sympathetically the profound existential truth of "the other."

Existential communication does not lead, however, to a fusion of existences. Such a fusion would entail the submersion of the individual in the collective, as happens, for example, in the undifferentiated being *en masse* of primitive or totalitarian societies. True communication, on the contrary, respects and preserves the distinctions between individual and individual and between their existential truths. Existential truth, therefore, is as multiform as are the individuals in whom it is incarnate. And these various existential truths are not only equally legitimate but they mutually necessitate and supplement each other. My existential truth, in other words, is inalienably my own, and the choice which I am called upon to make is not between different forms of truth but between existence and nonexistence, between *my* truth and the absence of truth, between *my* faith and the absence of faith. And since I am identical with my truth, I cannot "objectivate" it by placing it outside myself and regarding it as one object among others.[26]

Like existence, communication is thus undefinable and ineffable: it cannot be expressed in abstract concepts; it carries with it a certitude which is objectively inconceivable and unknowable. What can be objectively known, seen, and appreciated is the material effects of existential communication; its "existential" consequences, on the other hand, are beyond the reach of any objective criterion. "The consciousness of possible existence alone is capable of perceiving their truth in the bond of communication."[27]

Jaspers, like Kierkegaard, Nietzsche, and Heidegger, is aware of the dangers which threaten human existence when it surrenders its inalienable personal prerogatives to the impersonal, soulless anonymity of the masses. The existing individual, even in communication, must always preserve the integrity of his "self." His "being-with-others" must be in the nature of a voluntary, personal "engagement." "He who only loves 'mankind,'" writes Jaspers, "loves nothing but an empty abstraction; he only loves truly who loves this particular human being. . . . I destroy communication if I seek it in a communion

---

[26] Cf. *ibid.*, II, p. 419 f.   [27] *Ibid.*, II, p. 423.

with the greatest possible number."[28] Such a communion must of necessity lose in depth what it gains in numerical extension. True communication always brings to light something in human beings which makes them feel that they did not meet each other by chance in the domain of *Dasein* but that they have been related to each other from eternity.[29]

III

The philosophic search for being moves, according to Jaspers, in three main directions: toward "the world," toward "possible existence," and toward "transcendence." The search for the world leads to "world-orientation"; the search for possible existence leads to the step-by-step "illumination of existence"; and the search for transcendence leads into the proximity of the fullness of being. Philosophy must "transcend" the world of objects because no being that is given to man as an object of his research embodies Being in its fullness.

The *Dasein* of everyday life in its satiety and complacency is without transcendence. In the immanence of *Dasein* I am capable of experiencing pleasure in the brutal vitality of things and beings, but I remain empty in my satiety, helpless and forlorn in sudden loss, shiftless in the flux of time. The blind vitality of human life differs, however, from the kind of vitality which we observe in animals. The animal is not helpless, not forlorn, not empty. It lives fully and securely within the limits of its specific nature. Man, by foregoing transcendence, does not and cannot acquire the singular strength and security of the animal nature. If he renounces the prerogatives of his human existence, he immediately becomes less than an animal. Man, in short, cannot "be there" like other existents: he either transcends his "being-there" (*Dasein*), or he descends below the animal level by losing himself and his possibility of transcendence.

All transcendence originates in the disquietude which man experiences in view of the incompleteness, finiteness, and transitoriness of *Dasein*. "The idea," says Jaspers, "which actually seizes transcendence in consequence of the fragmentary nature of every communication and of the shipwreck of every form of truth in the world, has almost the force of a proof of the existence of God: presupposing that truth *must* be, this idea encounters transcendence on the basis of the experienced insufficiency of any concept of truth."

[28] *Ibid.*, I, p. 16; II, p. 438.
[29] Cf. Jaspers, *Vernunft und Existenz*, p. 62.

Transcendence is realized in the three dimensions of world-orientation, the illumination of existence, and the metaphysical penetration of the realm of being. To these three dimensions correspond the three existential impulses of (1) exploration of the world in order to learn what being is; (2) exploration of the interrelationship of the world and myself as an agent in the world; and (3) the search for God. If any one of these impulses is silenced, philosophy ceases to function. For it is precisely in my capacity as a philosopher that I study the disciplines which make possible world-orientation; that I am engaged in the illumination of my existence in the world; that I have an open mind for the metaphysical lucidity and transparency of things.

Jaspers at times uses the terms "Transcendence" and "God" synonymously. The deity to which the philosophy of Jaspers has reference is, however, neither the transcendent God of theism nor the immanent God (e.g. Spinoza's *"Deus sive natura"*) of pantheism. Both of these ideas of God are, according to Jaspers, equally at fault in that they are "ontological": both imply that metaphysical truth is firmly and objectively established, valid always and for all. "After Kant," says Jaspers, "all ontology stands condemned."[30] "We can neither conceive Transcendence as an individual God, separated from the world, nor can we say that 'all' is transcendent or that God is the being which contains 'all.' "[31] Such an alternative is valid only for the human reason, not for human existence.

Existential philosophy finds it equally impossible to endorse faith in the God of a "revealed religion" founded upon the claim that God has manifested Himself once and for all in human history, and supporting this claim by the promulgation of fixed dogmas. Existential freedom is strictly personal, and its truth is always incomplete; it therefore excludes and rejects any truth established once and for all and of supposedly timeless and universal validity.

As to atheism, it is likewise unacceptable for the existential philosopher: it sustains a negative ontology of its own and is as dogmatic and intolerant as any sectarian religion. Since the existential philosopher can thus neither endorse the religious nor the atheistic position, he has to live by the *tertium quid* of a "philosophic faith."

Although religion is inaccessible to strict philosophy, it is nevertheless of eminent value and significance for human existence. Jaspers points out that in the religious sphere two fundamental attitudes are

---

30 Cf. Jaspers, *Existenzphilosophie,* p. 17 f.
31 Jaspers, *Philosophie,* I, p. 52.

encountered: defiant self-assertion and trusting self-surrender (*Trotz und Hingabe*). Prometheus is a symbol of *Trotz;* Job is a symbol of *Hingabe.*

The Christian faith in the contents of revealed religion absolutizes, according to Jaspers, a world-historic occurrence of vastest implications for the life of all. This "absolutizing" of a segment of history leads to the establishment of the institution of the One True Church, commanding an absolute authority and sustained by divinely authorized and revealed scriptural documents. From the point of view of philosophy, Jaspers asserts, this process entails the loss of "existential historicity" because "philosophic faith" can neither be absolutized nor institutionalized. It is and remains alive only in the vast realm of individual minds and in their continued discourse through the ages. While religious faith is dogmatic, "philosophic faith" is undogmatic.

To demand universal acceptance of the contents of religious faith as an embodiment of universal truth leads, according to Jaspers, to intolerance and makes true existential communication impossible. On the other hand, Jaspers finds in the biblical religion many sublime truths which can be utilized for the synthetic structure of "philosophic faith." Among these he mentions specifically the idea of the one God, the unconditional choice between good and evil, the emphasis on "love" as the basic reality, the confirmation of the presence of the eternal in finite man, the idea of an ordered but contingent universe, and the idea of God as man's ultimate refuge and anchorage.[32] In this connection Jaspers attributes special significance to the fact that none of the great thinkers of the West, including even Nietzsche, could have elaborated his philosophy without an intimate acquaintance with the Scriptures. No other book, Jaspers affirms, can ever serve as a substitute for the Bible.

Although "philosophic faith," then, differs in many respects from religious faith, both are grounded in "transcendence," and a philosophy without faith in transcendence ceases to be philosophy in the true sense. And as to the individual philosopher, "a faithless philosopher is an existence-less philosopher."[33]

The individual who is "open" (*aufgeschlossen*) to the sign language of tradition and of his surrounding world is able to discern in these realities the handwriting of God. "The voice of God becomes audible

---

[32] Cf. Jaspers, *Der philosophische Glaube* (München: R. Piper, 1948), p. 82 and *passim.*

[33] Cf. Jaspers, *Existenzphilosophie*, p. 81 and *passim.*

in the freedom of personal conviction; it has no other organ to make itself heard by men. Whenever man decides himself out of the depth of his being, he believes he obeys God, without knowing in an objectively guaranteed way what it is that God wills."[34]

Divine Transcendence is correlated to human existence, and only when man faces Divine Transcendence can he take hold of his own existence. Transcendence itself testifies to the fact that "the world is not founded upon itself but points beyond itself. If the world were all that there is, there would be no Transcendence. But if there is Transcendence, then there is in the being of the world something that points toward it."[35]

As might be expected, Jaspers makes at least partially his own Kant's critique of the traditional proofs of the existence of God.[36] He denies that they are intrinsically conclusive, but he admits their usefulness as tools in preparing the way for an intellectual approach to the problem of Transcendence. These traditional proofs, Jaspers argues, proceed from various empirical realities of a cosmic, psychological, and moral nature; they stress the contingency of the world, the imperfection of human planning, of human projects and accomplishments; and they thus lead the human intellect in the end to the edge of an abyss where either nothingness or God is experienced. But, Jaspers adds, all search for God presupposes already the idea of God: "A certitude of the existence of God, may it be ever so intangible, is a presupposition, not a result of the philosophic argument."[37]

Much of what Jaspers says concerning God, transcendence, and reality follows at least in part the traditional doctrines of Christian philosophy and theology. The statement, for example, that "actual reality excludes all potentiality" seems in line with Aristotelian and Thomistic thinking. And Jaspers evidently stays within the same doctrinal frame when he calls transcendence "the true aboriginal unity . . . behind the unity visible in the mirror of the world." That reality, he continues, "out of which and in which is everything that we are and everything that exists for us, is itself infinite and perfect," whereas "all immanence is broken and torn by fissures. . . . Transcendence is, above all, that power in virtue of which I myself exist;

---

[34] Jaspers, *Der philosophische Glaube*, p. 57.

[35] *Ibid.*, p. 17.

[36] Cf. the author's *A Realistic Philosophy* (Milwaukee: The Bruce Publishing Company, 1944), pp. 77–90.

[37] Jaspers, *Der philosophische Glaube*, p. 30 f.

precisely in my freedom I exist only in virtue of this power."[38] In his own somewhat heavy and involved language Jaspers speaks here of the finiteness and contingency of both *Dasein* and human existence, of their dependence on the transcendent, divine Reality.

Jaspers is also familiar with what Christian theologians call the "apophatic" or "negative" way (*via eminentiae; via negationis*) of arriving at some predications concerning the "hidden" nature and attributes of God. But while Christian theology teaches an *"analogia entis"* (analogy of being), an analogy between Creator and creature, in virtue of which God can be known analogically by natural human reason, Jaspers denies with the Neo-Platonists this principle of analogy. While he pays tribute to the attempts of "negative theology" to acquire a knowledge of God by determining what He is *not* rather than what He *is,* Jaspers insists that a valid knowledge of God is neither positively nor negatively obtainable. God is simply the "totally Other" and therefore totally different from anything that is known or knowable.

In my attempt to discover in Divine Transcendence the ground of everything that is, it seems to me at times "that God reveals Himself to my vision, but . . . He almost immediately disappears again; when I try to seize Him, I seize nothing; when I try to penetrate to the source of being, I fall into the void. Never can I make His Being a content of my consciousness."[39] God is thus "that which cannot be thought" (*das Undenkbare*), "an empty abyss," as far as human reason is concerned. "Transcendence," Jaspers concludes, "can neither be determined by any predicate, nor represented as an object, nor arrived at by any conclusion. All the categories can, however, be utilized to signify that Transcendence is neither quantity nor quality, neither relation nor causation, neither one nor multiple, neither being nor nothing."[40] But, although Transcendence remains without any determination, although it can neither be known nor thought, it is nevertheless present in thought according to the fact *that* it is, not according to *what* it is. "It is that which it is," is all that can be said of its being.[41]

How is "Transcendence" related to the individual human existence? Existence, says Jaspers, always falls short of its goal in its attempt

---

[38] Jaspers, *Existenzphilosophie*, p. 66.
[39] Jaspers, *Philosophie*, III, p. 3.
[40] *Ibid.*, III, p. 38 f.
[41] Cf. *ibid.*, III, p. 67.

at self-realization, and its unsated freedom urges it incessantly on to go beyond that which it is. In Transcendence, on the other hand, there is neither privation nor freedom because there is a fullness of being which leaves nothing to be decided and nothing to be newly acquired.[42] In turning toward "Transcendence" I seek being as such, that is, being in its unicity, being as it is not encountered in any particularized existent. "Transcendence," asserts Jaspers, "is beyond all form."[43]

To elucidate further what he means by "Transcendence," Jaspers makes use of a term which recurs again and again in his discussion of metaphysical problems: he speaks of *"das Umgreifende"* (literally, that which "envelops"). Everything we know, Jaspers contends, appears to us within the frame of a "horizon," and that which "envelops" all horizons is the unknowable *"Umgreifende."* The latter comprises, first of all, the *"Umgreifende"* that is the world; second, the *"Umgreifende"* of my own self; last, the total *"Umgreifende,"* that is, Transcendence in the strict and final sense. There is, however, transcendence in the sense of a "going beyond" in every one of these three phenomena: in the illumination of existence, in world-orientation, and in metaphysics.

There is transcendence in the illumination of my existence: this means that there is in my ego an unknown zone which "envelops" my knowledge of my own being. I am linked with an enveloping *Dasein* which is without limits and of which I therefore can have only a limited and incomplete knowledge. My "consciousness in general" (*Bewusstsein überhaupt*), Jaspers affirms with Kant, unifies and organizes those objects which my mind encounters. And by the activity of my mind (*"Geist"*) I am capable of creating ideal syntheses by means of which I try to get hold of everything that is real and intellectually conceivable. But even these ideal syntheses are only fragmentary and preliminary, never definitive, always subject to revision, correction, and addition, owing to new experiences.

There is transcendence in world-orientation: this means that outside myself the unknown "envelops" me on all sides. This unknown is "being-in-itself" (Kant's *"Ding an sich"*). While the forms of the perceived object derive, according to Jaspers, from the subject, that which fills these forms with content derives from extramental reality, and to this matter which is furnished to my mind from the outside

---

[42] *Ibid.*, III, p. 5.   [43] *Ibid.*, III, p. 39.

I cannot add even the smallest grain of dust. While "being-in-itself" is unknowable, it manifests itself indirectly: it is experienced as the outer limit of human consciousness, a limit which is sensed, felt, and thought but which cannot be intellectually penetrated.

Both existential illumination and world-orientation are not self-sufficient. Their limited horizons therefore call for the all-enveloping horizon of total and absolute Transcendence. "My own being," says Jaspers, "relates itself . . . to that Transcendence by which it is given to itself and on which it founds its existence." This ultimate *"Umgreifende,"* however, is even more radically unknowable than the "being-in-itself" of the world. The latter manifests itself at least indirectly in the experience of "the limit." Absolute Transcendence, on the other hand, is inaccessible to any experience and any research. It *"is"* without ever being seen or known.[44]

Human existence, in the act of freedom, touches authentic, unconditioned being, but in doing so it remains profoundly aware of its limited autonomy, of its dependence on a higher and fuller reality without which it could not sustain its own being. I know that I can realize myself only in relation to and in virtue of Transcendence and that at the moment I should claim absolute autonomy I would sink into a bottomless abyss. Transcendence alone offers existence the possibility of a boundless expansion of the self: "In Transcendence, freedom seeks its fulfillment . . . , its perfection, its expiation, its redemption."[45]

How can human existence attain to Transcendence? What acts are possible on the part of the individual in regard to this end? Transcendence, answers Jaspers, can be felt in certain "limit situations" (*Grenzsituationen*), that is, in fundamental human situations which "are felt, experienced, and thought on the boundaries of our *Dasein* and whose common denominator lies in the fact that . . . there is nothing firm, no indubitable absolute, no support which could withstand the test of thought and experience." In the "limit situations" everything "is fluid, in the restless movement of its constantly being-called-in-question; everything is relative, finite, split into opposites; never the whole, never the absolute, never the essential."[46] The dreadfulness of this experience cannot be overcome by any human planning and calculating. As the "limit situations" call upon what is most

---

[44] Cf. Jaspers, *Vernunft und Existenz,* p. 30 ff.; *Existenzphilosophie,* p. 15 f.

[45] Jaspers, *Philosophie,* III, p. 5.

[46] Cf. Jaspers, *Psychologie der Weltanschauungen,* p. 229 f.

fundamental in man, the proper human response is an entirely different sort of activity, namely, "the realization of the possible existence within us." In such "limit situations" as extreme suffering, decisive struggle, the consciousness of guilt, and the imminence of death, I may become truly what I am in the depth of my being: "In my solitude, I feel the nearness of God, and yet, He is never actually there. He is near, but only as an outer limit of my existence."[47] "We become ourselves by entering into these limit situations with open eyes. . . . To experience limit situations and to exist is one and the same thing."[48] In this experience man becomes not only conscious of the enveloping frame and "limit" of his existence but simultaneously of the enveloping presence of the transcendent Absolute.

The being of Transcendence "becomes audible for the individual in the form of 'ciphers' or *symbols,"* and human existence can experience Transcendence in the reading of these "ciphers." Philosophy in its search for being seizes the "ciphers" as possible *"vestigia Dei,"* as signs and signals pointing toward the ultimate depth and plenitude of Being. But such a "seizure," such an "enlightening certitude" of the Divine Reality has, according to Jaspers, nothing in common with empirical perception and with objective, rational knowledge. In this experience "the search becomes the finding." God is "already present wherever and whenever I seek Him. . . . Presence and search are one."[49] And such seeking and finding is, in Jaspers' view, not helped but hindered by any positive religious rites and cultic observances. The search must of necessity proceed by way of doubt, disquietude, and distress rather than by way of "a daily assurance that God is there." Official worship, cult, and religious propaganda lead away from rather than into the neighborhood of the "hidden God." We can approach God only individually, in the most personal of all human acts. The unique God may then reveal Himself, but only to me: He will reveal Himself as *my* God rather than as the God of all the world. And thus *my* existence will be elevated toward *my* Transcendence.[50]

It is, says Jaspers, the function of philosophic *metaphysics* to prepare the way for the experience of Transcendence. Since, according to Jaspers' conviction, "a creative metaphysics is no longer possible," there remains only the task of appropriating and reinterpreting the historic-

---

[47] Jaspers, *Philosophie*, III, p. 126.   [49] *Ibid.,* p. 3.
[48] *Ibid.,* II, p. 204.   [50] Cf. *ibid.,* III, p. 121.

ally conditioned metaphysics of the past. The most important function, however, of any metaphysics is the reading of the "ciphers." The language of the "ciphers" is the sign language of the transcendent Reality: "The 'cipher' is for philosophy the form of transcendent Reality in a world in which everything can be 'cipher,' but in which nothing has the power of compelling reason to accept any particular thing as 'cipher.' "[51] The world, nature, and man, the starry firmament, human history, and human consciousness — they are not only given narrowly circumscribed in their empirical value: they are all capable of acquiring the significance of "ciphers." And it is metaphysics which deciphers Transcendence as it manifests itself symbolically in these finite realities.

In becoming "cipher," the realities of the world, hitherto opaque, become transparent: they "break open," as it were, and in an infinite perspective they allow a glimpse of the Absolute Being of Transcendence. Religious myths and dogmas as well as the rational arguments of natural theology (theodicy) are valid as "ciphers," says Jaspers, provided they do not claim to be more than that. The danger is precisely that man, in accepting them, "objectivates" them: that he places Transcendence in an objective space above and behind the world and thus tries to separate that which is inseparable.[52]

While empirical reality imposes itself upon me with the force of necessity, the same is not true of Transcendence: I may decide to listen to its voice, or I may refuse to listen and choose to remain enclosed in the crude and mute reality of *Dasein*. In other words, the "cipher" imposes upon me no definite, compelling conclusion regarding Transcendence; its language is equivocal and ambiguous, lending itself to different interpretations. It is for this very reason, asserts Jaspers, that the reading of the "ciphers" is an essentially personal act: "If I am existentially deaf, I am unable to hear the language of Transcendence."

IV

Man, as long as he lives, is faced with the alternative of the conquest or loss of his self. In view of the possibility of self-annihilation he is overcome by dizziness, fright, and dread. But the threat of annihilation may point the way to "existence." "There is no freedom without the threat of possible despair."

---

[51] Jaspers, *Existenzphilosophie*, p. 76.   [52] Cf. Jaspers, *Philosophie*, III, p. 152.

There are in human existence contradictions ("antinomies") which cannot be resolved, opposites which cannot be reconciled or neutralized. There is freedom linked with dependence, communication bound to solitude. There is no good without an admixture of evil, no truth without falsehood, no happiness without grief, no life without death. While history presents us with many evidences of progress, it simultaneously offers the spectacle of progressive destruction. "If there were a chance that technical progress could bring about the total destruction of all human existence, there is hardly any doubt that even this end might be attained." Finally, death comes to every living being, annulling all individual and social accomplishments, exhausting all possibilities and modes of life. It is, however, the privilege of man that he can freely and lovingly accept and embrace such a precarious world and existence with all their possibilities, risks, and prospects — fearful, tragic, and sublime.

Jaspers illustrates the tragic antinomies of existence by what he calls "the law of the day and the passion of the night": the law of the day "imparts order to human life; it demands clarity, coherence, fidelity, reasonableness. It insists that something worthwhile be realized in the world, constructed in time; that temporal *Dasein* be given a definite content in virtue of the eternal and the infinite. But the passion of the night breaks down every order and plunges man into the abyss of nothingness. . . . The law of the day knows the night only as a limit. . . . In action, it thinks of life only, not of death. But the passion of the night is lovingly and fearfully related to death, its friend and its enemy."[53] Day is bound to night, and what has been made to stand out in clear profile in the one is converted into the dark abyss of the other.

What, then, is the ultimate term of this polarity and perpetual "tension" of human existence? "The ultimate," says Jaspers, "is shipwreck" (*Das Scheitern ist das Letzte*).[54] Human existence in the world is destined to suffer shipwreck. The unity and unification of the world is rationally conceivable but, in practice, it is an abortive enterprise. Even in its desire for Transcendence, existence meets with the antagonistic "passion of the night" which cannot be reconciled with the good "law of the day." But man is capable of giving a meaning to shipwreck and existential despair: existence uses both to gain access to Being and Transcendence. Ultimate shipwreck thus becomes

---

[53] *Ibid.*, III, p. 105.   [54] *Ibid.*, III, p. 220 f.

the supreme "cipher" which imparts value to all the others: in shipwreck Transcendence becomes translucent. Therefore, says Jaspers, in the face of the menacing forces which bear down upon my existence, it is my duty not only to continue the struggle but to intensify its vigor. In shipwreck, consciously experienced, affirmed, and surmounted by my forward thrust toward Being, my existential freedom reaches its vital sphere. The bonds which tied it to *Dasein* are cut, and with its newly released energy it takes hold of Transcendence. "The non-being of all being that is accessible to us," concludes Jaspers, "that non-being which reveals itself in shipwreck, is the Being of Transcendence."[55]

"It is sufficient," says Jaspers, "that the One be. My own being which perishes completely as *Dasein,* is indifferent to me, provided I remain in constant ascent as long as I live." The existential philosophy of Jaspers thus ends on a strong Neo-Platonic note.

V

Karl Jaspers' existentialism is a philosophy of "becoming" rather than a philosophy of "being." As such it is anti-intellectualistic and voluntaristic. Like many other Germanic thinkers (Jacob Böhme, Lessing, Fichte, Hegel, Schopenhauer, Kierkegaard, Nietzsche, etc.), Jaspers values more highly the *élan* of an endless seeking and striving than the tranquillity of possession — regardless of whether it be a question of truth or being or God. The "becoming" is said to be better, more perfect, richer in content than the "become." Such a view is, of course, neither sustained by common sense nor by philosophic reasoning. Movement and becoming are as such incomplete, deficient realities; they are partial or particularized being, aspiring toward the fullness of being. The same is true of the movement we call human action. Man moves physically, morally, and intellectually in view of an end, in order to attain to a greater richness of his own being and existence as well as in order to enrich and enhance the being he finds in the surrounding world. It is self-contradictory and nonsensical to assume that the fulfillment of such a striving leaves man poorer than he was in the state of striving.

Any truth that is objectively and unquestionably established and for which universal validity is claimed is for Jaspers a stifling yoke. Life — the life of the spirit in particular — is in his view a perpetual

---

[55] *Ibid.,* III, p. 234.

becoming. Once it is arrested, death ensues. As far as the sphere of moral action is concerned, the German philosopher asserts that it is spiritual suicide to submit to any objective, universal rule of thought and conduct. The authentic act of freedom is unmotivated. Both religious and "philosophic" faith must dispense with or pass beyond all "motives of credibility," such as historical testimony and miracles. The act of faith is for Jaspers unrelated to any *"praeambula"* that would make it appear to the intellect as reasonable, just, and obligatory. Faith, according to Jaspers (who in this respect agrees with Martin Luther), rejects all rational motivation and justification. Thus, in the philosophy of Jaspers as in the "dialectical theology" of Karl Barth there exists a radical antagonism between faith and reason. The act of faith is generated by an impulse of freedom, rationally unjustifiable.

It is interesting, however, to note the amount of reasoning Jaspers has to make use of in order to demonstrate the supposed weakness of human reason. "Jaspers deprecates every 'philosophic system,'" writes Joseph de Tonquédec, "every universally valid 'doctrine,' every teaching that can be objectively transmitted. And after having made these statements, he writes three volumes of philosophy. Whether he admits it or not, he certainly attempts to teach his contemporaries the one and only way of truth, the only correct attitude regarding reality, the only way to attain to being and to relate oneself to Transcendence."[56]

Jaspers, furthermore, rejects any attempt to define rationally the nature of man. "What man is, cannot be determined ontologically," he writes.[57] But is such an ontological determination not implied in the discussion of man's *Dasein*, of his unique position in the universe, of "consciousness in general," of human *"Geist"* and *"Vernunft,"* or in the assertions concerning freedom, conscience, and "possible existence"? All such statements are evidently meant to be of universal validity, that is, they are meant to be predicable of each and every human being.

To see, as Jaspers does, reality exclusively in its aspect of "becoming," means to disregard the highest forms of reality. Even Bergson, the philosopher of the *"durée"* and the *"élan vital,"* acknowledged that the highest forms of spiritual life are characterized by quietude and utter simplicity. He pointed to the testimony of Christian saints

---

[56] Joseph de Tonquédec, *L'Existence d'après Karl Jaspers* (Paris: Beauchesne, 1945), p. 100.

[57] Jaspers, *Philosophie*, III, p. 187.

and mystics whose lives are centered and anchored in the profound depth and tranquillity of the Divine Reality. Thus it would seem that individual beings become more perfect the more they approach and approximate the immutability of the Divine Being.

The "existential freedom" which Jaspers espouses appears equally indefensible from the psychological and metaphysical point of view. Freedom loses its meaning and vanishes when one tries to detach it from both rational knowledge and motivation. Jaspers asserts that the authentic act of freedom is an *"Ursprung,"* that is, a first beginning. If that were true in an absolute sense it would metaphysically imply a kind of being that posits itself, an *ens a se* and *per se,* that is, a divine being. Jaspers does not claim with Sartre that human freedom is "absolute," but it is difficult to see why, on the basis of his premises, he should not arrive at an identical conclusion. As against Jaspers' contention that there are encountered in man acts which are totally unconditioned, it must be stated that freedom as much as knowledge is bound to the specific modes by which the intellect and will of a particular subject are constituted. As Joseph de Tonquédec points out, the scholastic axiom, *Quidquid recipitur, ad modum recipientis recipitur* (whatever is received [into the mind] is received according to the mode of the recipient), is equally valid for knowledge and for action: *quidquid agitur, ad modum agentis agitur* (whatever is done [by an agent], is done according to the mode of the agent).[58] "Man stands in need of certitude," adds the same French critic, "and this is not the first time that a skepticism regarding knowledge issues in a mysticism of action. . . . Knowledge is not a screen placed in front of being . . . , it is, on the contrary, the only means for the apperception of being in its reality."[59]

The existentialism of Jaspers — and this is a great merit and definitely a step forward — is equally opposed to determinism, positivism, and scientific materialism, on the one hand, and to the Cartesian and Hegelian types of idealism, on the other. Jaspers centers his philosophy in the concrete situation of the concretely existing and unique individual (St. Thomas' *individuum ineffabile*), emphasizing the elements of personal courage, risk, and venture, and the anguish which the individual experiences in view of imminent shipwreck and death. What counts in the drama of human existence is not the generalities

---

[58] Cf. Joseph de Tonquédec, *op. cit.,* p. 118.
[59] *Ibid.,* p. 119.

of scientific laws but the unique and irreplaceable value of human personality. While all this is, of course, not as new as it might appear at first glance, the fervor and convincing force with which it is restated are indicative of a healthy and encouraging trend in contemporary philosophy.

In the existentialism of Jaspers, however, as much as in that of Kierkegaard, the reaction against the many aberrations of modern philosophy overshoots the mark. While it is perfectly true that thought is not being, that thinking the good is a far cry from being good or doing the good, the conclusion that thought is void of being is entirely unwarranted. The fact that knowledge does not comprise or exhaust the totality of being, hardly justifies the assumption that knowledge is impotent and reality unintelligible. The *tertium quid* in the dialectic of idealism (i.e., the contention that thought and reality are identical, or that thought creates reality) versus agnosticism (i.e., the assertion that thought is totally incapable of having any certain knowledge of reality) is the acknowledgment of the capacity of thought to take hold of the being of reality, but imperfectly or only to a certain degree. The epistemological presumptuousness of the idealist and the epistemological despair of the "existentialist" are both unrealistic because they both misjudge the nature and the capacities of the human intellect.

"He who wants to be true must take the risk of erring and of placing himself in the wrong," writes Jaspers; "he must push matters to an extreme; he must place them on the knife's edge, so that there may be a true and real decision."[60] To carry out this precept with logical consistency would evidently lead to the suspension of all the laws and rules of thought and action. Whatever course of action I may have decided to choose, I can then justify both my deeds and my misdeeds by stating that in my present historical situation I was forced by an internal necessity to act as I have acted; to have enacted *my* truth, in obedience to the commandment of my personal existence. My action was not due, I am bound to say, to an arbitrary movement of my will, but it proceeded from the full authentic depth of my being. And might it not happen that, as in the case of Sartre, this "depth of my being" may have become a prey of the "passion of the night" and may thus have turned against all laws, human and divine?

---

[60] Jaspers, *Philosophie*, II, p. 69.

Human existence itself appears gravely endangered by the assertion that every existing individual has *his* truth, *his* way of reading the "ciphers," *his* Transcendence, and *his* God. This danger can only be warded off by the affirmation of a moral law which, anchored in the supremely "existential" law of Divine Transcendence, guides individuals and groups and makes possible true communication within the frame of a genuine human civilization.

CHAPTER SEVEN

"From Refusal to Invocation":

Gabriel Marcel

I

"There is only one suffering: to be alone," says Rose, the main character in *Le Coeur des autres,* one of Gabriel Marcel's plays. This sentence expresses one of the basic experiences of the most prominent representative of the *Christian philosophy of existence* in France. Though influenced to some extent by such thinkers as St. Augustine, Pascal, Schelling, Bergson, and F. H. Bradley, Marcel stood for a long time alone also as a philosopher, and he developed an "existential philosophy" at a time when he was as yet unfamiliar with the writings of Kierkegaard, Heidegger, and Jaspers.

Born in Paris, in 1889, Marcel lost his mother when he was only four years of age, and in the lonely years of his early youth he learned to communicate with the creatures of his imagination. He wrote his first two plays at the age of eight, and from then on the theater, because of its "significant bearing on other existences," never lost its fascination for him. "In the drama and by means of the drama metaphysical thought seizes itself and determines itself in the concrete," Marcel wrote many years later.[1] Drama and philosophic reflection are for him "two summits of equal height." While his plays — numbering almost an even score — present variations of the themes of human loneliness, misunderstanding, and disappointed love, his longing for communication, friendship, fidelity, and happiness finds expression in his musical compositions and in his philosophic and critical writings.[2]

Marcel's father was a state councilor in the French government,

---

[1] Gabriel Marcel, *Positions et Approches concrètes du Mystère ontologique* (in *Le Monde cassé*), p. 277.

[2] Cf. the bibliographies in *Existentialisme Chrétien: Gabriel Marcel* (Paris: Plon, 1947), p. 208; and Paul Ricoeur, *Gabriel Marcel et Karl Jaspers* (Paris: Editions du Temps Présent, 1947), p. 439 f.

for some time French ambassador at Stockholm, and later on director of the National Library and the National Art Galleries in Paris. "My father," writes Gabriel Marcel in retrospect, "had been brought up in the Catholic religion, but he had detached himself from it at an early age. His intellectual attitude was that of so many agnostics of the end of the nineteenth century whose minds had been imbued with the ideas of Taine, Spencer, and Renan. Catholic thought appeared to him antiquated and infested with absurd superstitions." Yet, "few men, I think, have led a more rigidly disciplined life and have had a higher sense of their professional duties than my father."[3] "Not only my entire childhood but my entire life," Marcel confesses, "were dominated by the event of the sudden death of my mother. . . . In a mysterious way she has always remained present to me."[4]

The aunt under whose guidance Gabriel, after his mother's death, grew from childhood into adolescence, was, he says, "an admirable woman." She was a Jewess, "but her family had renounced any religious beliefs. She herself had embraced Protestantism. . . . She imposed upon me an extremely strict moral discipline. . . . She shared my father's agnosticism, with the difference that his had a moral and hers an aesthetic tinge; the result was that I grew up in an atmosphere of instability and aridity."[5]

At school Gabriel excelled as a student, although he detested the pedagogical system which, it seemed to him, was founded on a radical misconception of reality. "I do not hesitate," he writes, "to attribute to those school years an actual arrestation of my intellectual development as well as the poor state of my health which has remained with me as a heritage of that period of my life. . . . This kind of education produced in my mind a state of revolt. . . . I am tempted to ask myself today whether my aversion to the *lycée* was not responsible for the increasing horror with which the spirit of abstraction filled me as it was cultivated . . . in that school."[6]

Traveling extensively in the company of his father, the young Gabriel Marcel visited the great art centers of Europe and made the personal acquaintance of many prominent political and literary personalities in several countries. He soon familiarized himself with the great Anglo-Saxon and German writers and thinkers of the past and

---

[3] Gabriel Marcel, *Regard en Arrière* (in *Existentialisme Chrétien*), p. 299.
[4] *Ibid.*, p. 303.
[5] *Ibid.*, p. 300.
[6] *Ibid.*, pp. 302, 304.

present. At the age of eighteen he wrote an academic thesis on *The Metaphysical Ideas of Coleridge and Their Relationship to the Philosophy of Schelling* (1908). Two years later he received his credentials as a teacher in philosophy, and he subsequently taught intermittently in secondary schools and colleges at Vendôme (1912), at Paris (1915–1918), at Sens (1919–1922), and, during World War II, again at Paris (1939–1940), and at Montpellier (1941). The intervening years and all his spare time Marcel devoted to philosophic and literary research and to creative writing. During World War I he served with the Red Cross. His special assignment was the search for the missing, a task which involved him deeply in the drama and tragedy of human existence. In recent years Marcel has filled many lecture engagements in several European countries, and in 1949 and 1950 he was honored with an invitation to deliver the "Gifford Lectures" in Scotland.

The strictly philosophic works of Gabriel Marcel are few in number. The presentation of his ideas is informal and unsystematic. Although outwardly these books seem little more than collections of diary fragments and philosophic essays, there is found in them a coherence and continuity of thought which add up to a consistently integrated philosophy of life.[7]

Having been exposed to the influence of agnosticism at home and in school and thus lacking any personal contact with positive religion, Marcel, even as a young man, felt in himself and in his environment an emptiness which oppressed and perplexed him. His philosophic inquiry soon brought him face to face with the phenomenon of religious faith. The opening pages of the *Journal métaphysique,* written in 1914, give evidence of Marcel's early preoccupation with the idea of God. Though himself an unbeliever, he had begun to take a profound interest in the faith of others and to analyze philosophically the inner structure of the *act of faith.* During the war years, at the time he served with the Red Cross and was deeply shaken by the daily inquiries he received from the grief-stricken parents of soldiers missing in action, Marcel turned to psychic research and parapsychology and engaged in spiritistic experiments.

---

[7] Cf. *Journal métaphysique* (Paris: Gallimard, 1947). *Le Monde cassé, suivi d'une méditation philosophique intitulée: Positions et Approches concrètes du Mystère ontologique* (Paris: Desclée de Brower, 1933). *Etre et Avoir* (Paris: Aubier, 1935). *Du Refus à l'Invocation* (Paris: Gallimard, 1940). *Homo Viator* (Paris: Aubier, 1944). *La Métaphysique de Royce* (Paris: Aubier, 1945; originally written in 1917).

In 1928, as a member of the *Société française de Philosophie,* in the course of a discussion on the problem of atheism, Marcel defended the validity of religious faith against the attacks of Léon Brunschvicg. A few months later, he received a letter from the French Catholic writer François Mauriac which ended with the question, "Why, after all, are you not one of us?" This question struck Marcel with the force of a personal call, and shortly afterward (in 1929) he became a convert to Catholicism.

II

Marcel's philosophic inquiry starts out from the experience of the individual's "being-in-the-world." The philosopher is a human being who seeks to illuminate the human situation. My "being-in-the-world" and in history particularizes and limits me. How can I accept my human situation and make it the starting point of my becoming a *human person?* The answer, says Marcel, cannot be given in the abstract, in a theory; it can only be found in steady contact with concrete reality, in personal engagement, and, ultimately, in a personal act of faith. To philosophize in the concrete means to philosophize *hic et nunc;* it means to be seized by reality and to be and remain ever ready to stand in wonderment in view of the unfathomable richness of reality. "The problem of the reality of the external world," writes Marcel, "was among those philosophic problems which posed themselves for me with a frightening actuality. . . . I believe I have never accorded any interest to that extreme form of idealism which denies this kind of reality."[8]

Philosophy is for Marcel a phenomenological analysis with an ontological goal. Philosophic rationalism, he is convinced, misses this goal because it regards as true only that which can be either rationally or scientifically verified. It defines truth as an accord of minds reached by the submission of individual thought to "thought in general." And it is the supreme ambition of rationalism to reconcile and harmonize the partial views of individuals in the absolute and definitive synthesis of a total explanation of the universe. The *religious absolute,* however, can never be related to a truth conceived in this manner. Why not? Because religious experience is always personal and incommunicable. Is the claimed truth of religious faith then purely subjective? Is it irrational, illusory, or fictitious? Is the verifiable truth of reason and

---

[8] *Regard en Arrière, op. cit.,* p. 308.

science the only valid kind of truth? In other words, how can the believer justify his faith? How can he establish its authenticity without having recourse to "objective" criteria? Perfect faith, replies Marcel, rises above the objectivity of the world and of history and experiences God in the pure actuality of an Absolute Presence.[9]

Beginning with the second part of his *Journal métaphysique,* Marcel attempts to find a way to escape the subjectivism and partial fideism implied in many of the earlier passages. While the first part of this philosophic diary evinces a sincere but largely unsuccessful effort to attain to concrete reality without sacrificing certain remnants of Kantian and post-Kantian idealism, the entries of Part II and the opening sections of *Etre et Avoir,* following the lead of such thinkers as St. Augustine and Pascal, seek to discover in the experience of the individual destiny a link with the consciousness of universal history. In that vital act by which I constitute myself as a person in my own historical situation, I simultaneously take cognizance of the universal history of the race and of that Creator-God who is both the "enveloping" and transcendent Reality of myself, of the world, and of my "being-in-the-world." There is, as Marcel emphasizes, no connotation of pantheism in such a view: "Pantheism has never held any attraction for me, above all because it seemed to me incapable of tolerating personal life in its concrete plenitude."[10]

Marcel's discussion of the individual destiny begins with the questions, Why am I in the world? Why am I immersed in matter and in history? It is rather difficult for me, according to Marcel, to accept my human situation with all the checks and limitations imposed upon me by my physical constitution, my family ties, my inherited characteristics, my education, the age and society in which I live, and, in addition, by all those unforeseen events which invade my day-by-day existence and often cross my projects. How can I persuade myself to accept willingly and loyally such a precarious existence? By clearly and realistically recognizing my limitations, answers Marcel, I shall be able to overcome them. But philosophic rationalism can be of no help in resolving the many problems and dilemmas of human existence; all its attempts to this effect must of necessity fail, because it removes all these problems from the concreteness of reality. Its craving for "objective" verification leads to the artificial dualisms of

---

[9] Cf. *Journal métaphysique,* p. 48 f.
[10] *Regard en Arrière, op. cit.,* p. 308.

subject and object, "appearances" and "things-in-themselves," the empirical and the thinking ego, individual thought and "thought in general." What is "thought in general" (Kant's *Bewusstsein überhaupt*) but thought without a thinker, thought emptied of personality? It is thus impotent in regard to the concrete, individual human destiny.

What is impossible for speculative reason becomes, however, an actuality in *the act of faith,* which arouses and rescues the individual from the perplexity, anxiety, and even despair engendered by the uncertainty and instability of the human situation. In the act of religious faith the individual constitutes himself as a person by affirming the infinite personality of *God*. Faith is thus a union of two freedoms: the free appeal of God and the free response and homage of man. In the act of faith man is restored to that unity of which he was deprived by rationalism and idealism. "I now understand my situation in the world by relating it to the creative will of God. I realize my engagement in history by becoming aware of my divine vocation."[11]

The act of faith thus marks the birth of both human personality and human freedom. But what is commonly called the "freedom of choice" is for Marcel only a prelude to the true and authentic "freedom of engagement." In relating myself as a subject to the world and to history, I accept and fulfill the destiny prescribed for me by my particular human situation. In the act of faith I respond to the divine call to become a free person. The Fatherhood of God, in other words, makes it possible for me to become truly myself.

The mutual relationship between human and divine personality is, in the opinion of Marcel, of fundamental significance for philosophy. If such a relationship exists, then the thinking subject is no longer the pure intellect of the Cartesian *"Cogito"* — an intellect detached from all material contingencies — but a concrete human being: suffering, struggling, hoping, and loving. In my personal situation I will then be able to understand and affirm myself as a creature here and now, and everything relating to this situation will then acquire a new weight and significance. That I was born in that particular year in this particular town and country and in this specific social environment: all such previously more or less irrelevant facts will then be understood "existentially," that is, in terms of my irreplaceable existence here and now.

---

[11] *Journal métaphysique,* p. 41.

Whereas for Sartre the human situation — threatened, hemmed in, and potentially frustrated and annihilated by the pressures and projects of "the others" — begets *la nausée,* for Marcel the free acceptance of this same human situation becomes the source of religious humility. And, like Jaspers, Marcel finds in the "tension" which exists between human freedom and the limitations imposed by the human situation the way to "transcendence." This is why Marcel had chosen as a motto for his academic thesis the saying of Hugh of St. Victor, the mediaeval mystic, "To raise oneself to God is to enter into oneself, and not only that, but in the depth of the self to transcend oneself." There exists the closest possible interrelation between the understanding of my human situation, my affirmation of the Fatherhood of God, and the birth of my personality.

But how am I related to those things which exist in the world outside myself? Marcel conceives of this relationship in analogy to the way in which I am related to my body. To explain this relationship, Marcel makes use of the term *"incarnation":* as I am incarnate in my body, so the world is incarnate in me, and God is incarnate in the world, manifesting Himself by means of sensible signs, symbols, and vestiges (Jaspers' "ciphers"). In other words, to conceive of God "objectively," that is, as a separate, objective entity, apart from myself and apart from the world, is an impossibility. Such a concept of God, Marcel claims, would amount to a denial of His very essence, for the "living God" (*le Dieu vivant*) is an "incarnate" God, who is present *per essentiam* in myself and in all things.

In this connection Marcel devotes special attention to what has somewhat inappropriately been termed the "soul-body problem." I am tempted, he says, to regard my body as a mere tool, but a simple reflection convinces me that this is a misconception: my body can hardly be a mere tool, since it is itself a necessary condition for the manufacture of tools. It would be more correct to say that — adopting the terminology of Heidegger — my body is the mode of my "being-in-the-world." And this means that, since I am compelled to rely on my body for the study of the world of objects, my body cannot itself become for me "an object." I can study my body scientifically (i.e., as an object) only by a fictitious detachment or a "disincarnation," by positing with Descartes an artificial dualism between myself as a thinking substance, and myself as a chunk of matter. In reality, says Marcel, the bond which unites me to my body is concrete and existential. My body becomes intelligible only as an incarnate ego if my body and myself in unison have been willed by the supratemporal, suprahistorical, and supramundane creative act of an Absolute Mind. If, on the other hand, this transcendent support is lacking, both rationalism and existentialism turn into atheism; human existence in the world becomes utterly absurd, and man is handed over to forlornness and despair.

The foundation on which the Christian existence rests is supratemporal and absolute. The mystery of my "incarnation" is illumined in the act of faith which "fills the void which exists between my empirical and my thinking self, in the affirmation of their transcendent union."[12] And "from the idea of that God who has willed *me* I can then pass on to the idea of that God who has willed *the world*."[13] I am ready to accept my "being-in-the-world" with its limitations in understanding myself as a creature of God. This newly gained insight into myself is thus not the result of any rational or objective knowledge, but the work of faith, that is, the work of a personal *consecration* of my life. The believer, says Marcel, is like a lover who offers his own self and the whole world to his beloved. In the same way the man who has faith offers to God everything that he is and everything that he has, saying, "All this belongs to Thee." But this act of *consecration* is simultaneously an act of *restitution:* what I offer to God is His already; in offering my gift I discover that the thing offered is His own handiwork, for He is the creator of the gift as He is the creator of myself. The world of sense is no longer estranged from the life of the spirit: it has become a manifestation of the Divine Existence, the Word of God addressed to man.

III

The individual human existence is linked with *time* and with *history*. The world in which I exist is in perpetual flux, moving toward its dissolution. Not only my body, but the entire psychophysical structure of my being is involved in this universal mobility. At times I abandon myself to this flux and allow myself to be carried to new and unknown shores. In my temporary refusal to will and to choose, I hold myself open to exhilarating experiences which may enrich and transform my being. But as long as I let myself thus drift, I renounce judgment and evaluation of my life, and I am in constant danger of losing my real self and substance in the excitement and agility of the moment:

---

[12] *Ibid.,* p. 45.   [13] *Ibid.,* p. 6.

"Nothing is closer to despair, that is, closer to the refusal to exist and closer to suicide than a certain way of celebrating life as it is embodied in the pure instant."[14]

I transcend the fleeting moment by exercising my freedom in a threefold *"engagement"*: in confronting my present, in accepting my past, and in projecting my future. By thus affirming myself in the continuity of my *personality* I oppose myself to the featureless collective (Heidegger's *"das Man"*). In the perspective of the impersonal *"Man"* I cannot confront my present, I rob myself of my past, and I cannot build my future.

Only in voluntary engagement can I impart meaning to that series of events which constitute *my past.* I assume full responsibility for all my past acts, in saying to myself: it is *I* who have acted in this way; *I am what I have done.* In disavowing my past, on the other hand, I disavow myself by introducing into my being one of those unreal dualisms which divide and destroy human existence.

But while I thus depend on my past, my past no less depends on me. It receives its meaning from *my present* as soon as it is incorporated into the whole of my destiny. By affirming my past and confronting my present I am laying the foundations for the possibilities of *my future.* Thus my fidelity toward both my past and my present becomes *creative* in view of my future. To face and accept my future trustingly and with the pledge of *fidelity* means to affirm it with all the uncertainties it entails and with a high sense of responsibility for whatever it may hold in store. In this way *hope* and *fidelity* triumph over time without denying it; they establish and maintain "the ontological permanence of my life."[15]

In virtue of these three distinct phases or temporal dimensions which constitute the act of voluntary engagement, I impress upon my life an enduring orientation which in its continuity supersedes mere temporal succession. The acknowledgment of my individual destiny is then no longer a blind submission to the dialectic of history, but a free appropriation on the basis of valuation, judgment, and choice. And in my choices I am guided by a Light which, while it surpasses and transcends me, is nevertheless more intimately present to me than I am to myself. It is this Light which, while it surpasses time and history, maintains in my own temporal and historical exist-

---

[14] Gabriel Marcel, *Etre et Avoir*, p. 290.
[15] Cf. *ibid.*, p. 138.

ence a continuous and yet flexible orientation. To its sheen I owe the partial illumination of those shadows which accompany me on every one of my steps. And thus I accept humbly, yet freely, my particular limited situation, embodying in my concrete, personal "incarnation" as loyally as possible the creative intention of that God who has willed me.

Once I have freely accepted my human situation and my life has become unified by my fidelity to my vocation as a human person, every one of my acts is organically integrated in the totality of my existence. And it is only in this totality that I acquire my authentic freedom and my full human stature. The refusal, on the other hand, to thus engage and dedicate myself leads to a cumulative loss of both freedom and personality. Authentic freedom manifests itself in choice; it fulfills itself in engagement; and the highest form of engagement is the *act of faith*.

The world is, in the words of Keats, "the vale of soul-making." That means that in the sequence of my choices my freedom may — depending on the nature of my choices — become authentic, or it may die; my personality may realize itself, or it may disintegrate.

Whereas for Sartre man is "thrown" into a hostile world and abandoned to his own devices and projects, for Marcel man, as an "incarnate" being in an "incarnate" world, is not left to realize his destiny in absolute solitude. His voyage through time and history is illumined by certain "values," which are not of his own making but are themselves "incarnate" in "being." "Value denotes the seizure of being by the human intellect," says Marcel. "Value can only be safeguarded where being is safeguarded as a mystery of which I partake from the moment I begin to exist."[16] Whereas in Sartre's philosophy it is the human "choice" which creates values, it is Marcel's contention that it is the values which command a choice. But he adds that a value can only exercise this function if it is recognized and acknowledged as such and if it becomes "incarnate" in the human subject. Thus understood, value is the basis of choice, although it does not determine the choice: the value can always be negated in favor of the absurd. But such a negation is a self-betrayal of human freedom. In the light of the incarnate value, being is encountered, revealing itself in its enduring quality and appealing, like Jaspers' "ciphers," to a creative interpretation on the part of man.

---

[16] *Aperçus sur la Liberté* (in *La Nef*, No. 19, 1946), p. 73.

The mystery of "incarnation" is most sublimely real in the Incarnation of Christ. In His Incarnation man's two great aspirations — his longing for the authentically human and for the divine — are fulfilled. In His humanity, Christ is like unto man and thus satisfies on the *horizontal* plane the need for an incarnation according to the maximal *human* measure. Inserted into historical space and time, Christ's humanity is related to my own temporal existence. In His divinity, Christ calls upon me to surpass all purely human dimensions in a movement of transcendence, a movement toward the fulfillment of all human aspirations in the *vertical* direction. Having taken our departure from our temporal human existence, we are drawn by Christ's Incarnation toward the supratemporal Divine Existence.

IV

In his search for a new and concrete approach to the mystery of "being," Marcel speaks of two different kinds of "reflection."[17] While the "first reflection" has its place in scientific research, the "second reflection" is strictly philosophical.

The "first reflection" proceeds from human experiences that are confined to the categories of "seeing" and "having" (*voir et avoir*). Within these categories the existing subject disappears: in the process of the "objectivation" of the thinking ego and of the empirical contents of consciousness, both subject and object are totally detached from existence. Thus the "thinking substance" of Descartes and the "transcendental ego" of Kant are no longer "real" subjects.

Links between thought and reality are established by dialectics, that is, by questions and answers based on observation and verification. Although the knowledge thus gained is valid and can be communicated, it is a knowledge confined to the sphere of "seeing" and "having," that is, a purely scientific and technical knowledge. Its frame of reference is not the existing individual, but "thought in general," the impersonal thinking of *"das Man."* It is Marcel's conviction that every epistemology which rests on "thought in general" inevitably leads to a "democratization of knowledge" which ultimately means the self-destruction of knowledge. Such an epistemology tends to glorify the purely "technical man," the "man in the street," the "common man." Philosophical and metaphysical knowledge, on the contrary, is essentially opposed to *"das Man."*[18] "The immortal glory

---

17 Cf. *Position et Approches concrètes du Mystère ontologique, op. cit., passim.*
18 Cf. *Etre et Avoir*, p. 182.

of a Kierkegaard or a Nietzsche," writes Marcel, "consists . . . in having demonstrated, not so much by rational arguments as by their lives, that a philosopher worthy of the name is not, cannot be, and must not be a man of the public, of meetings and conventions; that he debases himself to the extent that he allows himself to be deprived of that solitude which is his proper vocation."[19]

The "second reflection" is based upon the first, but it transcends it as philosophy transcends science and technics. Philosophic reflection is aware of the fact that it is deeply rooted in reality and therefore incapable of looking at reality from the outside as upon an object of scientific investigation. Philosophic reflection is not concerned with "problems" but involved in "mysteries." "A problem," states Marcel, "is something which one hits upon, something which blocks one's way. It is wholly 'in front of me' (*devant moi*). A mystery, on the contrary, is something in which I find myself engaged, whose essence it is consequently not to be wholly 'in front of me.' It seems that in this realm (of the mystery) the distinction between the 'within myself' (*l'en-moi*) and the 'in front of myself' (*le devant moi*) loses all significance."[20]

Philosophic reflection, says Marcel, transcends all objective knowledge and all objectivity. But this transcendence carries a meaning totally different from both the negation of the Hegelian dialectic and the "nihilation" (*néantisation*) of Sartre. In Hegel's "logical" progress from thesis to antithesis to synthesis, the antithesis "negates" the thesis, and the synthesis both "negates" and "sublates" (*hebt auf*) thesis and antithesis. The Hegelian synthesis establishes a new logical term, but not a new reality. And in Sartre's dialectic, the proper act of the "*pour-soi*" is "negation." Condemned to freedom, the "*pour-soi*" first exhausts itself in negation and then remakes itself in the ultimately absurd *élan* of a "futile passion." Marcel's "negation" and "transcension" of objectivity, on the other hand, are essentially the endeavor of human thought to escape its limitations by reaching beyond itself into the realm of "being."

Marcel claims that every problem of knowledge becomes eventually involved in an endless regress: that which is sought in the end is always presupposed at the outset. In trying, for example, to arrive at self-affirmation, my reflection tells me that to attain to that end it

[19] *Regard en Arrière, op. cit.*, p. 315.
[20] *Etre et Avoir*, p. 145.

must start out from self-affirmation. Similarly, the validity of my knowledge could never be ascertained in the end if this validity were not taken for granted from the start. "Thus," says Marcel, "the problem of knowledge destroys itself *qua* problem." To avoid such a *petitio principii,* my questioning must pass on from the problematical to the "meta-problematical": it must penetrate to a sphere in which thought and being are no longer separated but partake both of a higher unity. "To posit the meta-problematical means to think the primacy of being in its relation to knowledge . . . , to recognize that knowledge is enveloped by being."[21]

The union of body and soul, the phenomena of evil, of love, of freedom — they all pose no problems: they are mysteries. They "envelop" me; I am enclosed in them. It is equally improper, according to Marcel, to speak of the "problem of being"; there is only a "mystery of being." But if thus everything that is "meta-problematical" is shrouded in mystery, will it not become necessary to resort to a Kierkegaardian "leap" to capture this mysterious meaning? Marcel answers in the negative. The genuine *"Cogito"* is for him ontological (i.e., fraught with "being") rather than epistemological. All vital thought is centered in a *real* subject capable of acquiring *real* knowledge, that is, knowledge of reality.

There remains, however, in the very core of thought an element of obscurity, owing to the mystery which surrounds the manner in which — through the medium of the knowing ego — thought partakes of being. But this mysterious element, though obscure, is not entirely unintelligible. While it is true that a mystery cannot be known in the way scientific facts are known, this does not mean that nothing can be known about it. Since "being" has been the inseparable companion of thought on all of its dialectical exploits, philosophic reflection discovers that genuine thought and knowledge are always grounded in and enveloped by "being." And in this discovery thought finds itself, as it were, in its own home.

The meta-problematical mystery is indubitably real, although its reality cannot be proven either logically or empirico-scientifically. It transcends both objective thought and empirical consciousness and can therefore, like Jaspers' "enveloping transcendent," be misjudged, misinterpreted, or rejected outright. It appeals strongly (yet not irresistibly) to the spontaneity of human freedom: "This philosophic

21 *Position et Approches concrètes du Mystère ontologique,* p. 264.

reflection functions only in virtue and for the sake of freedom. . . . The very idea of constraint is void of all possible meaning in this sphere. . . . I can freely choose the absurd because I may easily persuade myself that it is not absurd, or because I may even give preference to it precisely because it is absurd."[22]

The recognition of the meta-problematical is thus a free act. My reflection, face to face with a mystery, may always degrade this mystery by reducing it to a mere "problem." In other words, I am always free to apply to it the "first reflection" and to close myself to its mysterious call.

The *real* subject is a *free* subject. "It is undoubtedly necessary," writes Marcel, "to renounce once and for all the naïvely rationalistic idea of a system of affirmations valid for 'thought in general' or for any consciousness whatsoever. . . . The ontological order can only be recognized personally by the totality of a being engaged in a drama which is his own, while at the same time it surpasses him infinitely in every sense — a being to whom has been imparted the unique power of affirming himself or negating himself, depending on whether he affirms being and opens himself to it — or negates being and thereby closes himself to it; in this dilemma resides the very essence of human freedom."[23] In the "logic of freedom," says Marcel, objective knowledge also has its place, but only as an initial phase in an "ascending dialectic." Objective knowledge is neither definitive nor total knowledge. In order to remain loyal to itself it must transcend itself and give way to "the ontological mystery."

What, then, is the new "concrete approach" to the ontological mystery which Marcel proposes? Since an objective knowledge of being is impossible, the knowledge which can partially unveil the ontological mystery must be of a different kind. Adopting the method and terminology of "negative theology," Marcel states that, first, this knowledge must be *negative,* that is, a knowledge arrived at by exclusions rather than by positive affirmations; second, it must be *concrete.* The ontological mystery must be surrounded, as it were, by a series of predications, stating what it is *not* rather than what it *is,* until in the end "being" can be envisaged in its transcendent integrity. "Being," says Marcel, "is a sort of ontological permanence, to which we are linked and owing to whose endurance we ourselves endure;

---

[22] Marcel, *Du Refus à l'Invocation,* p. 35.
[23] *Etre et Avoir,* p. 174 f.

it is a permanence which implies or demands a history; it is definitely not the inert or formal permanence of an abstractly valid law."[24]

The ontological mystery includes both *history* and *eternity*. Being as such can neither be phenomenologically described nor psychologically appropriated: it is neither a source of desire nor a theme for discussion nor an object of demonstration. It would be equally erroneous, however, to profess agnosticism in regard to being. All the several negative predications want to emphasize is the fact that "being" is more than any object and any idea: it is more because it is *a presence* of inexhaustible concreteness. It is thus thoroughly positive, and the strength of its reality is such that it "negates all negations." While "being" can neither be observed nor exhausted, it can be *encountered in beings.* In other words, that kind of "being" with which the "second reflection" is concerned and of which it partakes, is not the "universal being" or "being in general" of metaphysics, nor the being of an abstract idea or essence, but always a real and personal being, always *this* or *that* being. The more personal it is, that is, the more it is *a* being, the more it is *real*. In short, the more we recognize the individual being *qua* individual, the more we approach "being as such."[25]

The existential concreteness of being is further enriched by what Marcel designates as the category of *"the encounter."* He illustrates this category by referring to an entry in his *Journal métaphysique:* "I meet someone unknown to me in the train. We talk about the weather and about the war news. But although I speak to him, he remains for me 'someone,' 'this man there.' Little by little ... I learn some biographical data; it is as if he were filling out a questionnaire. ... But the remarkable thing is that the more this man is external to me, in the same degree I remain external to myself. ... I am like the pen which puts down words on a piece of paper, or like a registration machine. ... Yet it may happen that between 'the other' and myself a bond is established as, for example, when I discover that we have a certain experience in common (we have visited the same place; we have been exposed to the identical danger ... , we have read and loved the same book); thus a unity is created in which the other and I are *'we,'* which means that he ceases to be for me a mere 'he,' and becomes a *'thou';* the words, 'thou also,' assume here a most essential significance. We now actually communicate with each other: a vital union is

[24] *Ibid.*, p. 173 f.
[25] Cf. *Du Refus à l'Invocation*, p. 192 f.

formed between him and myself."[26] And from the moment that real communication is established between ourselves, we pass from one world into another, from the problematical world — where the categories of "sameness" and "otherness" in relation to the perceived object are valid — to the meta-problematical world, where these categories lose their meaning. The "given object" is surpassed, and in its place appears the ontological plenitude of the *encountered being.*

The newly discovered "thou" is an *immediate presence* and as such neither a physical fact which can be seized and verified in sense perception, nor an idea which imposes itself on my mind. This presence may therefore always be misjudged, forgotten, called in question, or obliterated. The response to the call of being, in other words, is an act of freedom. The positive response is an expression of fidelity, hope, and love. The negative response, or the refusal to respond, though no less free, is a betrayal of both being and existence.

Marcel takes great care in analyzing the attitudes of *fidelity, hope,* and *love.* They are for him the looked-for "concrete approaches" to the ontological mystery. He wants us to listen to the "ontological call" incarnate in these attitudes. But, he warns, these concrete approaches are always threatened, because the structure of human existence and of the world is such that infidelity and the ensuing despair remain always possible. The acknowledgment of the ontological mystery is a free, creative act, but an act which involves a crucial test and which requires the fearless *"testimony"* of the individual. And thus "we recognize the hidden identity of the way which leads to *sanctity* and the way which leads the metaphysician to the affirmation of being. The reflection on the nature of sanctity is perhaps the real introduction to ontology."[27]

V

Philosophic idealism, according to Marcel, labors under "a fatal illusion when it fails to see that to be a subject is not a fact or a point of departure but rather a conquest and a goal."[28] The primary and basic aspect of the condition of man is, as has been pointed out, his "being incarnate": he is "a being who finds himself united to a body."[29] When I say, "I exist," I refer not to the Cartesian *"Cogito,"*

---

[26] *Ibid.,* p. 49.
[27] *Etre et Avoir,* p. 123.
[28] *Position et Approches concrètes du Mystère ontologique, op. cit.,* p. 296.
[29] *Du Refus à l'Invocation,* p. 236.

but to my "incarnate being," that is, to "this body of mine, of which I can neither say that it is myself, nor that it is not myself, nor that it is an object for myself."[30] Thus there exists between myself and my body neither separation, nor a complete fusion, nor, strictly speaking, a relation, but a *participation*. And my linkage with the world, with "the others," and with *God* has the same mysterious character as my being incarnate in my body. In neither case can this mysterious bond be made the subject of scientific investigation or the object of scientific knowledge.

"Participation" denotes the actuality of human *rapports* as revealed in the reality of "myself," of the "thou," of "the other," and of the "Absolute Thou" (*le Toi absolu*) of God. This means that God is not "somebody" who entertains objectively determinable *rapports* with myself and with the world. The real God is a supremely *personal* God, who can never become for me a "he" (*lui*). "God can be given to me only as an Absolute Presence in the act of worship, and any idea which I form of Him is merely an abstract expression or an intellectualization of this Presence."[31] And so the "problem" of God disappears together with the "problem" of the union of body and soul and the "problem" of the world, to give way to the "mystery" of the "Absolute Thou."

I can regard my body as something that "I have" (an *avoir*), that is, as an object. But I can also refrain from positing such an artificial "alienation" between myself and my body and acknowledge in my body a constitutive element of my *self*. The "I have" then becomes an "I am," and the moment I transcend the sphere of the *"avoir"* my body turns from a tyrant into a servant. The same applies to my linkage with the world: the more I regard the world as a mere spectacle which I watch from the outside, the more the world becomes metaphysically unintelligible and absurd. A scientifically "objectivated" universe, ruled by technology, set apart from man and regarded as a thing in and by itself, becomes a strange monster — incomprehensible, evil, and destructive.

Again, the same applies to my *rapport* with God. But if God cannot be thought as a *"lui"* or as a *"cela,"* am I not thrown back into pure subjectivity? Marcel denies that this is the case, for, he says in effect, the order of the divine mystery is both transsubjective and transobjective. "If God is essentially a 'Thou,' for whom I exist,

---

[30] *Etre et Avoir*, p. 11 f.
[31] *Ibid.*, p. 248.

for whom I count . . . it is easy to imagine that perhaps for my neighbor He is not real in the same way."[32]

Participation is never so much an accomplished fact, says Marcel, as it is an appeal to the will to participate. In other words, the human situation in its dramatic tenseness is and always remains in this earthly life the situation of an *itinerant,* a wayfarer (*"homo viator"*). In this scintillating universe of possibles the only thing that is fixed and certain is *death:* the death of my sentiments and enthusiasms; the death of the being whom I love; and my own death.

Death poses for me the problem of "being-no-more," a thought from which the man of ordinary everyday life (*das Man*) shrinks in horror and cowardice. No dialectic reasoning and no method of concealment, however, can either obscure or enhance the reality and certainty of death. And thus absolute despair in view of this seemingly irreducible mystery remains always a temptation and a possibility. But to human freedom — and only to it — is given the power to triumph over this abysmal prospect by recognizing in death an appeal to being; an appeal which calls for a response that carries me even beyond death itself: "If we speak of an ontological counterpoise of death, it cannot be life as such . . . nor can it be some objective truth. This ontological counterpoise can only reside in the positive employment of a freedom which turns into devoted dedication (*adhésion*), that is, into *love,* which is 'the essential ontological gift.' When that happens, death is . . . transcended."[33]

Thus the "existential dialectic" and the "ascending dialectic of reflection" are joined together on the plane of *salvation.* The appeal to being, which issues from the "I exist," is answered by an "I believe." Human existence is always trapped and human freedom stifled within the limited perspective of any "to have." To have a body, to have a friend, to have faith: as soon as this body, this friend, this faith become "possessions," they turn into possessive attachments. "By this term 'to have,'" writes Marcel, "I mean not exclusively visible possessions . . . but also those ingrained habits — both good and bad — opinions, prejudices, which make us impervious to the breath of the spirit; in short, everything which paralyzes in us what the Apostle calls the freedom of the children of God."[34]

Marcel distinguishes between two modes of "detachment," that of

[32] *Journal métaphysique,* p. 254 f.

[33] Cf. *Etre et Avoir,* p. 244. *Du Refus à l'Invocation,* p. 186 f.

[34] Marcel, *Homo Viator,* p. 128.

the spectator and that of the saint: "The detachment of the saint has its *habitat,* if I may say so, in the very heart of reality; any curiosity regarding the universe is absent from it. This kind of detachment is a participation, the highest that there is. The detachment of the spectator, on the other hand, is the exact opposite: it is a desertion. . . ."[35]

"In the last analysis," Marcel contends, "everything can be reduced to the distinction between that which one 'has' and that which one 'is.' . . . In the precise measure in which I am attached to things, they exert upon me a power which derives from this attachment and increases proportionately with it. . . . The tyranny which my body exercises over me depends . . . in a considerable degree on the attachment which I have for it. . . . I disappear in this attachment; it is as if my body were devouring me; and the same may be said of all my possessions . . . : inasmuch as I treat them as possessions, they tend to suppress me. . . . And this is, strangely enough, the more true the more inert we are in regard to inert objects; and it is less true if we are actively linked to something . . . in a personally creative way as happens, for example, when the gardener cultivates his garden, when the farmer attends to his farm, when the musician plays his violin, when the scientist works in his laboratory. In all these instances the *'avoir'* no longer, if one may say so, tends toward its own annihilation, but toward its sublimation in an *'être.'* Whenever there is pure creation, the *'avoir'* is transcended . . . : the dualism of the possessor and the possessed disappears in a new living reality."[36]

The perspective of *"le voir, l'avoir et la mort"* (seeing, having, and death) is decisively overcome and transcended in that creative reflection which pays homage to reality in an act of absolute engagement, that is, in the *act of faith.* In this act the total reality of my self addresses itself to the totality of being and is absorbed in the presence of that totality.[37]

VI

Man is called upon by being, and he is to respond to this call by a total dedication. This response, taking either the form of *faith* (as opposed to "refusal") or of *hope* (as opposed to "despair"), is always in the nature of a "testimony" (*un témoignage*) manifesting itself in

[35] *Etre et Avoir,* p. 25.
[36] Cf. *Etre et Avoir,* pp. 225, 239 ff.
[37] Cf. *ibid.,* p. 63.

works. Man is "a witness," and "bearing witness" is of his very essence.[38]

What, then, is a witness? Instead of being a mere spectator, looking at facts and events as a stranger from the outside, the witness tests things by receiving them into himself in virtue of a personal act which engages him in his entire being. Such a receptivity is, above all, an existential "overtness" toward the world, toward "the others," and toward God.

Man, the free subject, is, however, capable of transforming his receptivity further by projecting it into those creative works which are his gifts to that realm of being of which his existence partakes. He gives testimony by his works, and in his creative consciousness appeal and response, receiving and giving, fuse: "To work means to become a prey of reality in such a way that we do no longer know exactly whether it is we who work upon reality or whether it is reality that works in us. . . . Wherever creative consciousness asserts itself . . . giving and receiving converge. . . . We give in receiving or, better yet, giving is already a kind of receiving."[39]

On every plane of human existence there is found a vital unity of *passio* and *actio* (*pâtir et agir*: passive receptivity and creative activity). In sense perception the world is received by the senses, and the latter respond by that "work" which psychology so inadequately calls an "image." This "image" is by no means the mental double of the physical thing, just as the work of art is not a photographic double of some segment of the universe. "There is no difference in kind but only a difference of degree or of power between our aptitude to 'sense' and our aptitude to 'create'; both aptitudes presuppose the existence not only of a self, but the existence of a world in which the self recognizes itself, upon which it works, into which it expands."[40] And the intellect, like the senses and yet more profoundly than the senses, is a witness: it receives being, and its act is a creative attestation of being.

Philosophy, too, is a "creative attestation." The thinking being, that is, the philosopher, is "a witness." While the "first reflection" posits the *ens cogitans* as an epistemological subject, as a mere spectator of reality, the "second reflection" reveals to the subject its participation in being. The subject finds itself engaged in a certain

---

[38] Cf. *ibid.,* p. 140.
[39] *Homo Viator*, p. 203.
[40] *Du Refus à l'Invocation*, p. 16.

adventure involving risks and dangers, but oriented toward being and reality.

If philosophy is essentially a "creative attestation," a personal "bearing witness," then the central question of metaphysics must needs concern the one who bears witness, that is, the philosopher. He therefore must begin his inquiry into being by asking, "What am I?" Extricating himself momentarily from the functional mechanisms of the world which is his temporal abode, the philosopher begins to wonder about his own existence, and he interrogates himself concerning his "being-in-the-world." If everything is not to be reduced to a meaningless play of fleeting appearances — "a tale told by an idiot, . . . signifying nothing" — then there must be an absolute ground of *being*. The fervent aspiration to partake of this "ontological mystery may itself already be a rudimentary form of participation."[41] There is no doubt, on the other hand, that the philosopher can arbitrarily deny himself to the call of being: "The pure and simple abstention, in the presence of being, which characterizes a large number of philosophic doctrines, is in the last analysis an untenable attitude."[42]

The authentic philosopher is "the fully awakened human being," says Marcel. Philosophic reflection — the "second" reflection — is the *ensemble* of all those acts in which thought bears witness to the presence of being. Philosophy, too, is thus a kind of *fidelity:* it is the perpetuation of a testimony which at any moment might be revoked. As long as it is sustained, it is a continuous and creative attestation, and it is the more creative the more eminent the ontological value is of that to which it bears testimony.[43]

Explicating in its ultimate consequences the fundamental situation of human existence, that is, the situation of each and every human being, philosophy is universal; but its universality is concrete rather than logical. "There are," explains Jeanne Delhomme in her excellent commentary on Marcel's philosophy, "a thousand different and mutually irreducible ways of saying that Mr. X is an honest man. These thousand ways are as many concrete approaches to the moral value of Mr. X. But, underneath all these differences, it is the same reality that is envisaged, and that which is expressed is the same truth. Similarly, there are a thousand different ways of exploring the ontological mystery; there are an infinite number of concrete approaches

---

41 Cf. *Position et Approches concrètes du Mystère ontologique*, p. 361.
42 *Etre et Avoir*, p. 168.
43 Cf. *ibid.*, p. 174.

to it, none of which exhausts the inexhaustible concrete reality, but each of which testifies to the same presence. Philosophic universality is thus realized by the unanimity (yet certainly not the identity) of testimonials. While *the condition* of the existing being (*d'existant*) is common to all, every existence is *personal*. Philosophy, or the ascending dialectic of reflection, is the concrete unity of these two elements of the ontological mystery."[44]

VII

Gabriel Marcel began with the refusal to acknowledge the traditional rationalist distinction between subject and object. His entire work is oriented toward the recognition of a reality which is both transsubjective and transobjective. This reality he calls the "metaproblematical" or the "ontological mystery." As against the philosophers and philosophies of nihilism and of the absurd he holds that both reflection and existence are steeped in the Truth of Being.

Marcel adds his own voice to that of Kierkegaard, Nietzsche, Heidegger, and Jaspers, warning of the dangers which modern man faces, as the forces of an almost exclusively technical civilization threaten to engulf his personality and thereby to annihilate the very substance of the "ontological mystery." He insists that today perhaps more than in any other historical epoch it is necessary to rescue human existence from these tyrannical forces of the inhuman and the infrahuman, so that the path to the suprahuman and eternal may be found again.

The French thinker also joins his fellow "existentialists" in condemning the increasing degeneration of human relations and the virtual impossibility of genuine communication in a society which in growing measure is losing the understanding for speech and language —the means of communication—and the respect for the individual —the subject of communication. He deplores with Heidegger that social relations in the contemporary world have as their frame of reference the cold egalitarian irresponsibility of *das Man* rather than the personally creative polarity of the "I" and the "thou." On this basis he criticizes the shortcomings of a "democracy" which no longer rests on the twin pillars of Truth and Freedom and which therefore condones relativistic pragmatism, moral license, and mass stupor.

---

[44] Jeanne Delhomme, *Témoignage et Dialectique;* in *Existentialisme Chrétien* (Paris: Plon, 1947), p. 200.

In his praise of the virtues of the private personal existence, of the "ontological weight" of friendship, fidelity, and love, Marcel sometimes seems to forget that there is an "ontological weight" also embodied in the creative manifestations of communal life, in economic and political organisms, in the institutions of science and learning, in the Church and in the State. It can hardly be denied that without at least some of these communal bodies the private human existence would be left unsheltered. There is a middle term, after all, between individualistic anarchy and authoritarian collectivism.

Marcel finally criticizes the aberrations of philosophic idealism, rationalism, and positivism. This critique could be even more convincing if it were implemented by a more positive acknowledgment of the legitimacy of certain indispensable objective and rational requisites and categories of any strictly philosophic and metaphysical reflection which refuses to be led into the blind alleys of either fideism or agnosticism. Marcel himself seems to feel the need for such an implementation when, in the final pages of *Etre et Avoir,* he states emphatically that "it would be foolish indeed to believe that the speculative work of the intellect is a luxury. I repeat: it is a necessity, and not only from the point of view of the intellect, but from the point of view of love (*charité*). I believe that those who with disarming frankness regard Christianity above all as a social phenomenon, as a sort of doctrine of mutual aid, as a sort of glamorized philanthropy, commit a grave and dangerous error. Here again the word 'life' reveals itself as charged with ambiguity. To say, 'it matters little what you *think,* as long as you *live* like a Christian,' is, I believe, to make oneself guilty of the most serious offence against Him who said, 'I am the Way, the Truth, and the Life.' *The Truth.* It is, above all, on this territory of Truth that the religious battle must be fought; it is on this territory that it will be won or lost. And by this I mean that man will show on this territory of Truth whether or not he has decisively betrayed his destiny and his mission, and whether therefore *fidelity* may have to remain the privilege of a small number of elect, of saints, pledged without doubt to martyrdom, and praying untiringly for those who have chosen darkness."[45]

VIII

Immanuel Kant's saying, "It is man's highest task to know what one must be in order to be a human being," can still serve as a

---

[45] *Etre et Avoir,* p. 295.

guidepost for any philosophy of human existence, even if in Kant's own system the existing individual was eventually absorbed by a "transcendental ego" and a "consciousness in general."

Kant wanted philosophy to answer four main questions: (1) What can we know? (2) What are we to do? (3) What may we hope for? (4) What is man? The fourth of these questions is the one that Kant should have asked first, because on the answer to it depend to a large extent the answers to the others. It is also the question with which the thinkers whose teachings have here been discussed are chiefly concerned. And their answers differ according to their positive or negative attitudes regarding "being" and "Truth." Whether they admit it or not, it is their metaphysical concepts, presuppositions, or even prejudices that determine their anthropological views.

In St. Augustine's and Pascal's thinking — that is, long before the modern crisis of human existence gave rise to "existentialism" — philosophy is born of the vital and tragic conflicts and contradictions in the mind and heart of man. The same, with some qualifications, may be said of John Henry Newman's conception of philosophy. And it is this dramatic tension in human life, aggravated by the many new perplexities and uncertainties introduced by the age of science and technology, that again in the modern age, and especially in recent decades, has centered the philosopher's quest in the situation, the condition, and the being of man.

The modern "existential" philosophers are united in their protests against the claims of philosophic idealism and in their attempts to rescue the individual from the bloodless and lifeless generalities of abstract ideas and essences as well as from his submersion in the anonymous, impersonal collective. They are divided, however, in their interpretation of the nature of that personality and that freedom which are to be saved. The Kierkegaard-Nietzsche and the Marcel-Sartre antitheses illustrate perhaps best this parting of the ways: on the one side the preservation and salvation of human personality and human freedom in the supereminent Reality of Divine Existence and Divine Love; on the other side the self-destroying nihilistic frenzy and the final perdition of the man without God. The "Superman" is no antidote against the "collective man": they are not as far apart as it may seem; they rather mutually condition each other, and they are both symptomatic of the ontological dissolution of the human person. Only the God-Man can save man from the clutches of both the Man-God and *"das Man."*

It is not true that man, as most of the contemporary "existentialists" claim, possesses *unlimited possibilities*. Man is, on the contrary, limited on all sides except one: he is, as Kierkegaard, Jaspers, and Marcel have well seen and lucidly described, open toward "transcendence": he is *"capax Dei."* In every other respect and dimension man encounters limits: in his thought and consciousness, in his willing and doing, in his social and political relations. Even in freely willed self-destruction the human limit is not transcended but, on the contrary, radically confirmed.

Within the limits imposed by his situation in the world, man lives, as Jaspers has pointed out, in tensions, conflicts, and contradictions, moving back and forth between the extreme possibilities of salvation and perdition, sanctity and satanic rebellion, self-realization and self-annihilation. In addition, in his striving to explore the secrets and utilize the forces of nature, man commands vast possibilities of economic and scientific planning, possibilities which he turns into actuality in his attempts to gain the technical mastery of life. But these efforts, too, are beset with temptations and dangers. Here, too, lurks for the human intellect and will the possibility of self-betrayal: possessed by the will to power, man may in demonic passion debase his human stature by becoming the slave of those tools and machines which owe their being to his creative genius.

* * *

Pestalozzi, the serene, high-minded, and warmhearted Swiss educator, was no "superman," no "existentialist," and not much of a thinker. But in his calm and sober ways he knew of the intimate and intrinsic values of human existence as well as of the dangers which constantly threaten it. Addressing himself to "the innocence, the earnestness, and the noble sentiments of my age and my fatherland," he wrote in 1814: "Human kind forms itself essentially not *in massa, but individualiter,* from face to face, and in a human way from heart to heart. The education for humanity, the formation of human beings and all the means used to that end are in their origin and essence eternally a concern of the individual and of such institutions as are close to the individual's heart and spirit. They are never a concern of the crowd. Individual man, as he stands before God, his neighbor, and his own self, seized in his innermost being by Truth, and filled with love for God and the neighbor, is the only pure basis of the true ennoblement of human nature."

THE THEMATIC STRUCTURE OF EXISTENTIALISM

ALL philosophy begins — as the ancient Greeks so well knew — with astonishment and wonder. But this attitude may be caused either by the mere fact *that* things and beings are or exist, or it may be caused by a consideration of *what* these existents are, that is, by their essence or nature. A. A. Maurer, in the introduction to his translation of St. Thomas Aquinas' early treatise *De Ente et Essentia,* points out that St. Thomas inaugurated a real revolution in metaphysics when he turned the philosopher's interest "from form and essence, where it had lingered for so many centuries, to the act of existing." It was a decisive moment in the history of metaphysics, he says, "when philosophers became aware of the specific problems which attach to existence as distinct from essence. . . . The Angelic Doctor was the first to recognize the primacy of the act of existing over essence. . . . Even in his youth St. Thomas was regarding being from an existentialist point of view."[1]

Jacques Maritain, following a similar line of argument, asserts that Thomism is "the philosophy of existence and existential realism."[2] He distinguishes between an "authentic," Thomist, and an unauthentic or "apocryphal" philosophy of existence. In the latter category he places all atheistic forms of existentialism in general and the philosophy of Jean-Paul Sartre in particular. Both "authentic" and "apocryphal" existentialism affirm, according to Maritain, the primacy of existence, but whereas the former preserves essences and thereby the intelligibility of existents, the latter denies essences and thus marks the self-defeat of the intellect and despairs of intelligibility. The French thinker finds the basic error of the atheistic existentialists in their

---

[1] St. Thomas Aquinas, *On Being and Essence* (translated with an introduction and notes by Armand Augustine Maurer, C.S.B.; The Pontifical Institute of Mediaeval Studies, Toronto, 1949), p. 9.

[2] Jacques Maritain, *Existence and the Existent. The Christian Answer* (translated by Lewis Galantiere and Gerald B. Phelan; Pantheon, New York, 1948), p. 2 ff.

false presupposition that "existence *alone* is the nourishing soil of philosophy. They treat of existence without treating of being."[3] For the Thomist existentialist (who is a "theist"), on the other hand, essence and existence in their correlation make up the *one concept of being which,* analogically, permeates all things as their very act of existing. Being is "that which is" or "that which is able to exercise existence," and at the summit of all beings, in the unity of "Him Who Is," the intelligibility of essence fuses with the superintelligibility of existence. Thus the entire metaphysics of St. Thomas "is centered not upon essences but upon existence."[4]

While it is of the essence of God to be or to exist (*esse*), "creatures . . . do not exist by their very nature. If they exist, their act of existing is given to them by God. They *receive* their act of existing: God *is* His act of existing. That is why in every creature essence is really distinct from the act of existing, whereas in God the two are identical."[5]

The essence or nature of a thing can be defined, and St. Thomas devotes the first chapter of his treatise *De Ente et Essentia* to the definition and explication of such terms as *being, essence, form,* and *nature.* He does not attempt, however, to define the *act of existing* (*esse*), for the simple reason that this act (which is expressed in English by the verb "to be") "cannot properly be conceptualized or defined. It is . . . the ultimate and most perfect of all acts" and "is grasped . . . as exercised (*existentia ut exercita*), as possessed potentially or actually by a subject."[6] Kierkegaard unwittingly follows St. Thomas when he states that "There is something which cannot be thought conceptually: the act of existing." And Maritain acknowledges that Kierkegaard's "central intuition of the absolutely singular value and the primacy of the act of existing was in the last analysis the same as that which lies at the heart of Thomism."[7]

The conviction of the *primacy of existence* is shared by all existentialist thinkers, ancient, mediaeval, and modern. Their concern with the individual, personal aspects of being, with the mysterious recesses of their own selves, places them in opposition to those philosophers who, like Plato or Hegel, in an attitude of detached reflection, allow the act of existing to be submerged in ideal forms or essences. *Existential thinking* may thus be defined as a type of speculation that is not

[3] *Ibid.,* p. 24.
[4] *Ibid.,* p. 42.
[5] A. A. Maurer, *op. cit.,* p. 15.
[6] *Ibid.,* p. 12n.
[7] Maritain, *op. cit.,* p. 130.

only related to the concerns of actual life but decisive for human existence and human action. It is a kind of thinking that arouses and "makes" the human self. This is of course not quite as new as it may at first appear: both the "Socratic method" (the philosopher acting as a "midwife") and the Christian way of the *"imitatio"* (the "following of Christ") are types of existential thinking. Both have their center of gravity not in pure thought or pure knowledge as ends in themselves, but both gravitate toward "existence," that is, toward a "way of life."

The *modern* Philosophy of Existence may be said to have taken its start from the attacks launched by the "Young Hegelians" against the idealistic "system" of their master. This "existentialist" revolt was greatly encouraged by the Berlin lectures (1841) of the German philosopher F. W. Schelling, who in the final stage of his thinking turned against the main theses of that same philosophic idealism to which he had himself formerly adhered. Among his listeners were Kierkegaard, Bakunin (the Russian anarchist), Friedrich Engels (the coauthor of the *Communist Manifesto*), and Jacob Burckhardt (the Swiss historian).

Against Hegel's "essentialism" (the identification of essence and existence in the general "idea") Schelling insisted that pure thought cannot explain the transition from the "idea" to "nature" or to concrete reality. He calls Hegel's idealism "absolute" in the sense that it posits being without existents (*das Sein ohne das Seiende*). As soon as "the system" attempts to take the decisive step from pure logic to reality, the thread of the dialectical movement of the "idea" is cut, and there remains nothing but "a broad and ugly ditch" between *what* a thing is and the fact *that* it is. Schelling concludes that pure rationality is incapable of ever reaching concrete reality and that Hegel's "pure being" is actually "nothing," just as "pure whiteness" remains an empty concept unless there is something that is white. Thus Schelling's "positive philosophy" begins with "existence": it does not (like Hegel's dialectic) proceed from thought to being, but from existing beings to thought. His starting point is, to use his own words, an "a priori empiricism."

Kierkegaard had undertaken his first trip to Berlin after the completion of his academic dissertation. He wanted to attend Schelling's lectures because he had high hopes that the latter's "positive philosophy" might offer a corrective to those features in Hegel's interpretation of reality which he had found most objectionable. But his *Journals* reveal that he was greatly disappointed. "I am too old to listen to lectures, and Schelling is too old to lecture," he wrote. He evidently found even Schelling's new "positive philosophy" too much steeped in abstract idealism, too far removed from "existence." From then on Kierkegaard turned polemically against any attempt to comprehend reality by way of rational speculation. While he did not deny the universally human, he remained henceforth convinced that it could only be reached by starting from the individual: "What reality is cannot be expressed in the language of abstraction." By making the act of existing the criterion of reality, Kierkegaard thus shifts the problem of being from the abstract to the concrete, from being in general to human existence.

Following Kierkegaard's lead, modern and contemporary existentialism designates as the center of thought *the existing thinker*. But it remains preoccupied with the problem of the interrelation of thought and existence (*essentia* and *existentia*), of "whatness" and "thisness." In stressing, however, the fact that the thought of the existing thinker is determined by the uniquely concrete tasks of his *Dasein*, existentialism claims to be a philosophy of the "I" rather than a philosophy of the "It." While the "abstract thinker" is a "disinterested" theorist, the existentialist thinker is *inwardly concerned*. With this principle of "existential thinking" as a general frame of reference, it may now be attempted to recapitulate in a summary fashion the major themes of existentialism.

1. *Subjective Truth*. It is the common conviction of all modern existentialists that there is no knowledge independent of a knowing subject. Any abstract universality they regard as an illusion of formal logic, and they put in its place a "concrete universality" which they identify with "ethical reality." This means that even in the sphere of thought and knowledge true universality is only possible in the concreteness of moral action, that is, in personal existence. In this sense, they say, "subjectivity" is truth. In other words, for the existentialist, knowledge is not an end in itself, but it proceeds from and terminates in the question, "What does this thought or this knowledge mean *to me*, the knower, the existing thinker?" All true knowledge includes the dimension of existence.

Kierkegaard, for example, does not deny that there is an "objective" truth, an "objective" knowledge, and even (for God) a "system" of objective truth and knowledge. But for the individual human being, he says, the important thing is not the "what" but the "how": the content of knowledge must become the content of personal life; the abstract conceptual truth must be transformed into the concrete inwardness of a spiritual existence. This is why Kierkegaard defines truth as an "objective certitude, held fast in the appropriation of the most passionate inwardness." Knowledge is for him not mere passive receptivity but simultaneously a creative productivity, in which the "how" of the thinker and knower is of decisive importance.

2. *Estrangement.* In Franz Kafka's novel, *The Trial,* human existence is symbolically described as a paradoxical legal process or trial in which man finds himself entangled without being able to discover the precise nature of the charge brought against him. In the same author's novel, *The Castle,* man is subjected to the arbitrary decrees of a mysterious sovereign power, and despite his desperate efforts he cannot penetrate the mystery, that is, he cannot gain access to "the castle." In both instances man appears as a stranger to the world into which he has been "thrown" and in which he is inescapably involved. The same motif of "estrangement" recurs again and again in the poetic work of Rainer Maria Rilke. In the poem, *The Great Night,* for example, the German author vividly describes the human experience of total strangeness and forlornness in regard to lifeless objects. The big city is said to be "inaccessible," and the landscape "darkens unpersuaded" as if the human ego were nonexistent. "Even the nearest things made no effort to become intelligible. The street drew oppressively near, and I found myself a stranger to it." The poet finds himself hemmed in by "angry towers" and "inscrutable mountains." Everywhere man finds himself locked out and alone with himself. He feels himself handed over to uncertainty and insecurity, "exposed on the mountains of his heart."

The animal is sheltered, Rilke asserts with Jaspers, but man is homeless. He is the most helpless and defenseless of all creatures. He is surrounded by a world of utter strangeness and beset by dangers on all sides. If he wants to prevail in the face of estrangement, he must persevere in the midst of danger rather than hide in an illusory security. But in trying to meet the challenges of his surrounding world, man experiences most profoundly the finiteness of his existence, the outer limit of all human striving and achievement. He recognizes, in Heidegger's terminology, his "being thrown" into a place and situation not of his own choosing. In courageous "resolve" he must take upon himself the risks which such a precarious existence implies and thus eventually "transcend" the crisis of estrangement.

The experience of "estrangement" is equally fundamental in the thinking of Sartre. Here, too, the "crisis" begins with the discovery of a hostile objective world (*l'en-soi*), a world of the nonego advancing aggressively upon the ego (*le pour-soi*) which, aided by science and technology, had prided itself of having conquered and subjected the world of matter. But now man witnesses with horror the nonego rising in revolt against the ego. He faces the "totally other" which calls in question himself, his thinking, his doing, and his "values." "Being-in-itself" begins to oppress him like a nightmare, seizing and enveloping him with an iron grip. The constructs of abstract rational thought are crumbling. The "autodidact," the "humanist," the "abstract thinker": they are shaken out of their complacent detachment, their disinterested "objectivity." Antoine Roquentin, the author of the diary in Sartre's novel, *La Nausée,* pities the tragicomical fate of the "autodidact": he does not condemn his noble sentiments but his perverted notion of human existence, his abstract and unreal "humanism" and humanitarianism. Man, Sartre proclaims with Antoine Roquentin, is not an abstract essence or idea that is to be realized but, conversely, the idea of man must grow out of the concreteness of human existence: "Existence precedes essence."

"Estrangement" is overcome in the novel *La Peste* (*The Plague*) by the French writer Albert Camus. The theme is developed negatively in the same author's earlier biographic narrative, *L'Etranger* (*The Stranger*). The "absurdity of existence" is the initial thesis in both works, but in *La Peste* the main characters serve to illustrate a newly discovered meaning of human life. The novel delineates a Jasperian "limit situation": the plague which strikes the North African town reveals in a step-by-step *dénouement* the illusory nature of the most cherished conventions, customs, traditions, and ideologies. Under the hammer blows of fate they dissolve and decompose simultaneously with the bodies of the sick and the dying. But in the sea of general disintegration the eternally human, the authentically "existential" reappears and remains in great purity and lucidity. The "self-estrangement" of man is conquered by the forces of neighborly love and unselfish friendship. Man rediscovers his true self in distress and suffering and in service to his fellowmen. Rieux, the "atheistic" physician, and Paneloux, the Jesuit priest, are like two grand symbols of this "real" reality. They represent the self-evident, matter-of-fact human existence which no longer depends on ideological superstructures. They are the embodiment of a "new order," a kind of hidden "natural law." But this new order is born of chaos and in the abyss of "nothingness."

Man, in "existential experience," learns that all the experiences of his "everydayness" are in the last analysis nonessential, that even in total loss he can preserve the integrity of his human personality. He may gain a new existential authenticity by either forced or voluntary detachment from everyday experiences and earthly possessions.

3. *Existence and Nothingness.* The mysterious and uncanny background of existential thinking appears in the experience of nothingness or "the nought." This experience tears to shreds all the familiar relations and proportions of everyday life; it forces man into an existential "crisis," in which the marks of his finiteness or contingency — his "temporality" and his "historicity" — are strikingly revealed. Face to face with nothingness man enters into a state of "existential despair," from which he may be rescued by "resolve" (Heidegger) or "faith" (Kierkegaard). This experience is impressively described in Miguel de Unamuno's *Life of Don Quixote and Sancho Panza.* Don Quixote is for the Spanish-Basque writer the heroic man who is willing to take upon himself the dangers and risks of total incertitude and who therefore is in the view of "everydayness" a mere fool and phantast. He is blamed by those who live "unauthentically" for having dragged Sancho Panza out of his comfortable life and peaceful pursuits, for having persuaded that simple peasant to leave his wife and children to become involved in mad adventures. "There are small minds," writes Unamuno, "who assert that it is better to be a contented pig than an unhappy human being. . . . But he who has once tasted the flavor of humanity, he will — even in profound unhappiness — prefer the unhappiness of man to the contentment of the pig. . . . It is well, therefore, to cause disquietude in human souls and to kindle in them a mighty yearning."

4. *Existential Anguish and Nothingness.* All modern existentialists stress the creative significance of anguish. The problem is first discussed in Kierkegaard's, *The Concept of Dread* (1844), and the theme is philosophically elaborated by Heidegger who, like Kierkegaard, insists on the distinction between "anguish" and "fear." It is the peculiarity of anguish that it cannot be rationally understood or explained. In existential anguish man is not threatened by something definite (as is the case with "fear"), something that could be named or defined. If the object of anguish could be thus determined, man might be able to rise in defense, ward off the danger, and regain his security. But in existential anguish man's relationship to the world is

totally shaken and becomes wholly questionable. Something utterly mysterious intervenes between him and the familiar objects of his world, between him and his fellowmen, between him and all his "values." Everything which he had called his own pales and sinks away, so that there is nothing left to which he might cling. What threatens is "nothing" (no thing), and he finds himself alone and lost in the void. But when this dark and terrible night of anguish has passed, man breathes a sigh of relief and tells himself: it was "nothing," after all. He has experienced "nothingness."

"If we now ask specifically," writes Kierkegaard, "what constitutes the object of anguish, we must answer: it is nothingness. Anguish and nothingness are correlative." Thus anguish is the necessary effect of the experience of nothingness: the two are inseparable. And it is anguish, according to Heidegger, that arouses man from the false tranquillity of his everyday life and makes him free for the fulfillment of his existential tasks. Anguish, thus understood, is the positive privilege of man; it is "an expression of the perfectibility of human nature" (Kierkegaard). It destroys all artificial security and hands man over to that total abandonment in which "authentic existence" originates. "He who has truly experienced anguish," says Kierkegaard, "has learned to walk as in a dance . . . , while the apprentices of finiteness lose all reason and courage." In the passage through anguish man gains a new kind of security, "a hold in the infinite" (Jaspers).

Boredom (*ennui*), melancholy, and despair are degrees, modes, and variations of anguish. These "moods" too can be authentic and unauthentic. In *authentic ennui* man is seized by a nameless emptiness: everything seems to become equally unimportant and indifferent. And, as in the case of anguish, escape can be sought in distraction, in sensual or aesthetic pleasure. But authentic *ennui* forces man into decision and choice and thus aids him in gaining his authentic existence.

The same is true of *melancholy*: "Whoever sorrows and grieves," writes Kierkegaard, "knows exactly what causes his sorrow and grief. But if you ask the melancholy person as to the cause of his melancholy . . . he will answer: I do not know; I cannot tell." Anguish and melancholy reach their greatest intensity in *existential despair*. But once despair has seized man in the depth of his personality, the possibility of a decisive change can be envisaged: man has readied himself for the "leap" into authentic existence: "To despair truly, he must truly will to despair. But if he truly wills to despair, he is truly already beyond despair" (Kierkegaard). In his freely willed despair man has freely chosen himself in his eternal existential significance. Thus, despair is the "crisis" through which man passes on his way to authentic existence.

The greatest significance, however, of existential despair lies in the fact that in this "mood" the *Dasein* which man is becomes most luminously manifest. The understanding of anguish points the way to the understanding of "being." What is actually dreaded in anguish is man's "being-in-the-world" as such. But because what is dreaded is "nothing," no human being and "no thing" can help man in this dreadful experience. In the night of the nothingness of anguish, however, originates the "overtness" toward existence as such. Nothingness, according to Heidegger, reveals to man "the favor of Being": under the veil of nothingness he becomes a partaker of Being.

5. *Existence and "the Others."* The existentialist thesis asserts that authentic existence can only be realized in and by the solitary individual. The social collective can be of no help in the attainment of this kind of authenticity; it can only retard or frustrate it. This is why "the individual" is the basic category in the thinking of Kierkegaard. The "self" and "the masses" are at opposite poles. And what is true of "the masses" applies equally to "the world." For the existential thinker the world is at best a kind of testing ground of existential authenticity, the matter to be used in the process of self-realization.

Nevertheless, authentic existence cannot do without the world and "the others." It demands, however, a new "existential community" which in turn is to make possible "existential communication." The individual existence of the human person remains therefore always "overt" toward the existence of "the other." According to Jaspers, existence even fulfills itself and becomes authentic in genuine communication: "I cannot become myself without entering into communication, and I cannot enter into communication without being a human self." In existential communication every association which rests merely on habit, custom, or tradition must be either freely affirmed or freely rejected. If affirmed, it must be inwardly appropriated. Because existential communion must be reconquered again and again, it can never become stale and inert.

6. *Situation and "Limit Situation."* Human existence is essentially "being in a situation." Man has not chosen the particular situation in which he finds himself "in the world," and he feels himself oppressed

and hemmed in by a strange and hostile environment. These limitations of his human situation are not only of a physical but also of a psychological nature. In certain moods man feels himself not only as a prisoner in his surrounding world but also, as it were, imprisoned and enslaved by his changing emotional reactions, by his instincts and urges. In his attempts to gain mastery of his "situation" he meets with new and stubborn limitations which he recognizes as conditioned by the finiteness and contingency of his existence. While he may succeed in improving or mastering certain individual circumstances, he inevitably must confess his inability to cope with the most fundamental limits of his human condition, such as he encounters in suffering, guilt, and death. These are, according to Jaspers, integral elements of human existence as such. They are the walls which resist every attack, and they are the causes of human shipwreck. They inject into human life the elements of contradiction, insecurity, risk, and constant danger. The realization that they are an integral part of the lot of finite man shakes human existence to its depths.

"Limit situations" are thus situations in which man faces the insurmountable walls surrounding his existence and becomes profoundly conscious of the many clefts and abysses which cannot be closed or bridged over by any exertion of human thinking. These "paradoxes" of life impress upon man the actuality of his imperfection, his fragility, his homelessness. But by opening his eyes to his precarious human situation, they intensify his efforts toward self-realization.

7. *Temporality and Historicity*. These are, in the view of modern existentialism, the most conspicuous marks of human finiteness and contingency. Attention is called to the difference between "subjective time" and "objective time": the pulse of "subjective time" is faster or slower than that of "objective time" because this pulse depends in the case of the former on the personal experiential content with which time is filled. While the hours filled with gaiety and laughter fly rapidly, those filled with boredom stretch out interminably.

Man plans, hopes, fears, and anticipates, and thus in everything he embarks upon in the present there is implicit an element of *the future*. But man also remembers and at every stage of life's road finds himself confronted with set factual circumstances and with historically conditioned structures and events, and thus in every present there is implicit an element of *the past*. To the deeper view the present moment reveals a rich temporal structure of several dimensions.

The future, the existentialist contends, is not something wholly indefinite that will occur at some later date and therefore does not concern me at this present moment. The future is already alive in human hopes and fears, in human planning and designing: it is a formative force and an integral part of the present. Similarly, *the past* is not something that merely "has occurred" at some earlier date and therefore no longer concerns me at this present moment. In its aspects of both good and evil it reaches into the present and determines it to a considerable extent. *The present,* finally, is not an unextended point in the transition from past to future but the firm bond which ties together the dimensions of time. *Future, past,* and *present* are thus for the "inward temporality" of the human mind three dimensions or directions into which the human sense of time extends and which in their togetherness constitute the present moment. Heidegger calls them the three "ex-stases" of time. And Kierkegaard describes the present moment as the point in which time and eternity meet and intertwine. "Such an (existential) moment," he writes, "though short and temporal . . . is yet decisive because it is filled with eternity. . . . It is, as it were, eternity's first attempt to make time stand still." In the moment, thus understood, there is an absolute "halt" and "hold" in which temporality is transcended and overcome.

While "history" is the recording of the "objective" course of events which have run their course in time, "historicity" is the "subjective" structural form in which man experiences historical events. In his given situation man finds himself always to some extent determined and limited in his action by the past; not only by his own past decisions and choices but by those massive historical structures (states, societies, social and family groups) of which he partakes. He is, says Heidegger, an "heir" who lives in his "heritage." His projects for the future can therefore never ignore or circumvent the historical past. Positively and negatively, in his affirmations as much as in his negations, he must take account of his heritage and is therefore never absolutely free in his existential choices. His existential task in view of his "heritage" consists in penetrating and appropriating the external subject matter of history, so that it becomes part of his authentic inward life. In other words, the impersonal "it" of "objective" history must become a personal "mine" in the appropriation of its contents.

In the category of "the existential" the idea of "progress" becomes meaningless: each generation and every individual in each generation has to face the essentially identical human and moral problems and has to make his own choices. "The truly human," writes Kierkegaard, "no generation can learn from the one that preceded it. In this respect every generation is 'primitive' — its tasks differ in no way from those of every preceding generation, nor does it progress beyond any of them. Thus, for example, no generation has learned from the preceding one *how to love* — none can start at any point except from the beginning." And the same holds true of *faith:* "No generation can begin at a point differing from that of the preceding one; none can start otherwise than from the beginning; and none progresses beyond the preceding one." The task of the individual consists thus not in enlarging or transforming the enduring essence of love or of faith but in intensifying the passionateness of personal appropriation. This, according to Kierkegaard, is not "progress," but a "repetition," consummated in the inwardness of personal existence. In its own inwardness the authentic human being gains an ultimate and absolute value which transcends the fluctuating relativity of history.

This existential interpretation of history is closely related to what Nietzsche called "monumental" historiography. The authentically existing individuals in every age are "contemporaries": they greet each other as they tower like mountain peaks above the dividing valleys. They represent the "continuity of greatness" in the history of mankind.

8. *Existence and Death*. The existential thinker is not interested in death as an "external" event objectively considered but in the way in which the individual is related to *his own death*. He asks himself: what does *my death* signify for this day and this hour of my existence? How does the knowledge of the inevitability of my death (which may occur at any moment) affect my life here and now? The existentialist thus regards death as a constitutive part of *life* and he demands that it be incorporated into the texture and pattern of his existence. He sees in death (if we disregard the lone dissenting voice of Sartre) the decisive motivating power which spurs man on to the highest existential resolve. Any stoic indifference to death, he argues, is not courage but cowardice, a kind of escapism which shies away from the real abyss of life.

To the everyday view life appears as a temporal continuum sufficient unto itself and comprehensible without the prospect or horizon of death. In this perspective death, if envisaged at all, is merely a remote external event that casts no shadow on life. But this view of life, existentialism argues, does not take into consideration the nature and internal structure of human "temporality." As has been pointed out, in his hopes and fears, in his plans, projects, and expectations, man always outruns and outweighs the present moment. The actual present life of the individual receives its meaning and direction from its links with his past and future. If this is the case, then death as the final existential link with the dimension of futurity conclusively implements the individual's past and present. Man, in short, must adapt the pattern of his existence to the prospect of his certain death, his ultimate and inexorable "limit situation."

While the death of the individual is certain, the day and hour of his death are uncertain. The non-authentically existing individual veils and beclouds his knowledge of the inevitability of death by living thoughtlessly and distractedly from day to day and never facing realistically the possibilities and the boundaries of his *Dasein*. And yet, death may occur at any moment and at a time when it is least expected. The authentically existing individual therefore, according to the "categorical imperative" of existentialism, must live in such a way that he is prepared to die at any moment and that such a sudden end does not render his life meaningless. "It is true," writes Heidegger, "that in death existence reaches the end of its course, but does this necessarily mean that it has also exhausted its specific possibilities? An unfulfilled existence also ends while, on the other hand, existence may have reached and surpassed the stage of ripeness even before death puts an end to it."

In the vertigo of the "fear of death" man is overcome by the dreadful thought of "being-no-more," and it is this experience which reveals to him the final and total threat to which his existence is exposed. But this fear of total annihilation may also have a very salutary effect: in existential perseverance in the face of the certainty of death man may reach an absolute "hold" beyond time and death. By forcing man to ask himself as to what is absolutely essential in his existence and by making him free and resolute in his action, death becomes the final challenge and supreme test of existence.

9. *Existence and God*. For Kierkegaard and for theistic and Christian existentialism in general, human existence is grounded in the realization of the eternal in the temporality and finiteness of *Dasein*. The Danish thinker believed that such a realization was possible only in the religious stage of existence and in the religious personality. If God is omitted (as in Heidegger's speculation) or if, God is denied (as in Nietzsche's and Sartre's thinking), then there remains only the yawning abyss of nothingness, a void which cannot

be filled because He who alone could fill it is refused admission.

When man arrogates to himself the title and function of divine creativeness, his efforts are foredoomed to failure: they terminate in "nothing." Since God is the author of "Being" as well as of "beings," no being can exist or be creative without Him Who Is, and wherever He is not, there is the void. These fundamental truths concerning "religious existence" are discussed by Kierkegaard in the *Postscript* preparatory to the elaboration of the third of the "stages on life's road." Here he distinguishes clearly between what he calls "religion A" and "religion B." While "religion A" is described as possibly the highest attainment of "humanity" — a deep emotional awareness of the divine, or an ardent longing for eternal happiness — "religion B" is the highest attainment of a specifically religious inwardness that is informed by faith in the historical revelation and Incarnation of Christ. Whereas "religion A" may exist both in paganism and in a nominal "Christendom," "religion B" is the expression of authentic Christian faith, hope, and love. "The abstraction of religion A," by positing the immanence of human existence as a quasi-religious absolute, cuts itself off from real "transcendence" and leaves the individual enclosed in the circle of finitude. It may be said therefore that "religion A" actually illustrates the futility of all attempts to absolutize the human self. While it is true that "religion A" must be present before the individual can become aware of "religion B," it is equally true that if such an awareness or "awakening" does not ensue, the individual inevitably moves toward his eventual self-annihilation.

Applying Kierkegaard's distinction to contemporary existentialism, it seems evident that both Heidegger and Jaspers have penetrated to the threshold of "religion B." Jaspers emphatically relates human existence to transcendence, but he halts short of "stepping over" the threshold: he confines the human "overtness" toward transcendence to the "limit situations" of suffering, strife, guilt, and death, in which man is "enveloped" by transcendence as by an impassable boundary of his existence. In the context of Jaspers' philosophy, transcendence is thus only experienced under the aspects of "religion A": in crisis, in existential despair, and in "shipwreck." Of the thinkers whose philosophies have been discussed in the preceding pages, Gabriel Marcel is the only one who is familiar with authentic religious existence in the sense of Kierkegaard's "religion B": like Kierkegaard, he sees in Christianity a unique spiritual force which, breaking into the temporal and finite self, consumes it, and raises out of its ashes the eternal and infinite self.

Atheistic existentialism, much against its avowed intention, demonstrates conclusively the utter futility of every endeavor to save man after having abandoned God. It unwittingly testifies to the fact that human existence is inseparable from human nature or essence and that both human existence and human essence must wither away without the supporting force and grace of God, of Him Who Is and Whose essence is His act of existing.

Christianity, by illuminating further the aboriginal relationship between the existence of man and the existence of God, has shown a sure way to save the human person from disintegration and dissolution. The essential Truth, embodied existentially in Christ, the God-Man, secures and consecrates human existence and offers in the call for an *"imitatio Christi"* the direction which points toward its fullest realization. There is no truth in the Christian sense save "existential truth," that is, "living" truth or truth incarnate in the act of existing.

The unity or congruity of theory and practice, of religious doctrine and individual devotion, of essential and existential truth was regarded as a matter of course until the time when philosophy proclaimed its full emancipation from theology and henceforward developed its own autonomous concepts of truth. There was no danger to the integrity of truth as long as Christian thinkers continued to understand philosophic concepts as "preliminary tools," as aids in securing the way to the ultimate, supernatural, and divine Truth. Though granting to philosophy a relative autonomy in its own particular sphere, they still regarded the entire body of rational and natural philosophy as part of a unified theological world view. The danger began when the "emancipated" thinkers set themselves up as final arbiters and judges of supernatural truth. This total emancipation of reason from faith, of philosophy from theology, led eventually to the fatal radical dualisms of thought and extension (Descartes), theoretical and practical reason (Kant), Apollo and Dionysos (Nietzsche), essence and existence (Sartre).

The Christian thinker is always an "existential" thinker in the sense that he is not concerned with abstract and universal ideas and essences that bear no relation to actual life. "He is not so much interested," writes the Swiss Jesuit theologian Urs von Balthasar, "in God as a philosophical *ens a se* as in God, the Father of Christ Jesus;

not so much in the spirit as an abstract principle of general laws and values as in the spirit of the fiery tongues. . . . He is not worried about a synthesis of nature and supernature, knowledge and faith, the secular and ecclesiastic orders, because he knows that he who uncompromisingly abides in Christ is relieved of such worries." And, pointing to St. Anselm of Canterbury, the same author concludes: "In prayer he approaches the mystery . . . and he is fully aware that even God's natural revelation in the created universe and in human reason is a genuine revelation. . . . From the point of view of faith he understands that reason too was created for the sake of faith, and nature for the sake of grace, and that nature and grace in their togetherness are the one interlinked and unified revelation of the One incomprehensible love of the Tri-Une God."

BIBLIOGRAPHY

Barrett, William, *What is Existentialism?* (New York: Partisan Review Series, No. 2, 1947).

Benda, Julien, *Tradition de L'Existentialisme ou les Philosophies de la Vie* (Paris: Bernard Grasset, 1947).

Binswanger, Ludwig, *Ausgewählte Vorträge und Aufsätze zur phänomenologischen Anthropologie* (Bern: A. Francke, 1947), Vol. I.

Bobbio, Norberto, *The Philosophy of Decadentism. A Study in Existentialism.* Transl. by David Moore (Oxford: Basil Blackwell, 1948).

Bollnow, O. F., *Existenzphilosophie* (Stuttgart, 1949).

Brandenstein, Bela von, *Der Mensch und seine Stellung im All* (Einsiedeln: Benziger, 1947).

Bretall, Robert, *A Kierkegaard Anthology* (Princeton: Princeton University Press, 1946).

Castelli, Enrico, *Existentialisme Théologique* (Paris: Etudes Philosophiques I, Hermann & Cie., 1948).

Copleston, F., S.J., *Friedrich Nietzsche. Philosopher of Culture* (London: Burns, Oates, 1942).

D'Arcy, M. C., S.J., *The Mind and Heart of Love* (New York: Henry Holt, 1947).

Delp, Alphons, S.J., *Tragische Existenz* (Freiburg i.B.: Herder, 1946).

Deussen, Paul, *Erinnerungen an Friedrich Nietzsche* (Leipzig: F. A. Brockhaus, 1901).

Diels, Hermann, *Ancilla to the Pre-Socratic Philosophers;* a complete translation of the fragments in Diels, *Fragmente der Vorsokratiker,* by Kathleen Freeman (Oxford: B. Blackwell, 1948).

Farber, Marvin, *The Foundation of Phenomenology: Edmund Husserl and the Quest for a Rigorous Science of Philosophy* (Cambridge: Harvard University Press, 1943).

———— *Philosophic Thought in France and the United States* (Buffalo: University of Buffalo Publications in Philosophy, 1950).

Finance, Joseph de, S.J., *Etre et Agir dans la philosophie de Saint Thomas* (Paris: Beauchesne, 1945).

Flake, Otto, *Nietzsche* (Baden-Baden: P. Keppler, 1947).

Förster-Nietzsche, Elizabeth, *Das Leben Friedrich Nietzsches* (Leipzig: C. G. Naumann, 1895–1904), 2 vols.

———— *The Life of Nietzsche.* Transl. by A. M. Ludovici (New York: Sturgis, 1912–1915).

———— *The Lonely Nietzsche.* Transl. by Paul V. Cohn (London: W. Heinemann, 1915).

Fries, Heinrich, *Die katholische Religionsphilosophie der Gegenwart* (Heidelberg: Kerle, 1949).

Gabriel, Leo, *Existenzphilosophie. Von Kierkegaard bis Sartre* (Wien: Herold, 1951).

Gilson, Etienne, *L'Etre et L'Essence* (Paris: Vrin, 1948).

—— *Being and Some Philosophers* (Toronto: Pontifical Institute of Mediaeval Studies, 1949).

Grene, Marjorie, *Dreadful Freedom: A Critique of Existentialism* (Chicago: University of Chicago Press, 1948).

Haecker, Theodor, *Sören Kierkegaard*. Transl. by Alexander Dru (London, New York: Oxford University Press, 1937).

—— *Der Buckel Kierkegaards* (Zurich: Thomas Verlag, 1947).

Halévy, Daniel, *Nietzsche* (Paris: Bernard Grasset, 1944).

Harper, Ralph, *Existentialism* (Cambridge: Harvard University Press, 1948).

Heidegger, Martin, *Sein und Zeit* (Tübingen: Neomarius Verlag, 1949, 6 ed.).

—— *Was ist Metaphysik?* (Frankfurt a.M.: V. Klostermann, 1949, 5 ed.).

—— *Kant und das Problem der Metaphysik* (Bonn: F. Cohen, 1939).

—— *Platons Lehre von der Wahrheit* (Bern: A. Francke, 1947).

—— *Existence and Being*. With an Introduction by Werner Brock (Chicago: Henry Regnery Co., 1949).

—— *Holzwege* (Frankfurt a.M.: V. Klostermann, 1950).

—— *Erläuterungen zu Hölderlins Dichtung* (Frankfurt a.M.: V. Klostermann, 1951).

Hessen, Johannes, *Existenzphilosophie* (Essen: Dr. Hans von Chamier, 1947).

Hodges, H. A., *Wilhelm Dilthey* (New York: Oxford University Press, 1944).

Hohlenberg, Johannes, *Sören Kierkegaard*. Transl. from the Danish by Maria Bachmann-Isler (Basel: Benno Schwabe & Co., 1949).

Hubben, William, *Four Prophets of Our Destiny* (New York: Macmillan, 1952).

Imaz, Eugenio, *El pensamiento de Dilthey* (México: El Colegio de México, 1946).

Jaeger, Werner, *Paideia: The Ideals of Greek Culture* (New York: Oxford University Press, 1939).

—— *The Theology of the Early Greek Philosophers* (Oxford: Clarendon Press, 1947).

Jaspers, Karl, *Philosophie* (Berlin: Julius Springer, 1932), 3 vols.

—— *Man in the Modern Age*. Transl. by E. Paul (London: Routledge, 1933).

—— *Vernunft und Existenz* (Groningen, Batavia: Wolters, 1935).

—— *Nietzsche* (Berlin and Leipzig: W. de Gruyter, 1936).

—— *Existentialphilosophie* (Berlin and Leipzig: W. de Gruyter, 1938).

—— *Von der Wahrheit. Philosophische Logik I* (München: R. Piper, 1947).

—— *Der philosophische Glaube* (München: R. Piper, 1948).

—— *The Perennial Scope of Philosophy*. Transl. by R. Manheim (New York: Philosophical Library, 1949).

—— *Vom Ursprung und Ziel der Geschichte* (Zurich, 1950).

—— *Vernunft und Widervernunft in unserer Zeit* (München: R. Piper, 1950).

Jolivet, R., *Les Doctrines existentialistes de Kierkegaard à Sartre* (Fontenelle: Abbaye S. Wandrille, 1948).

—— *Introduction à Kierkegaard* (Fontenelle: Abbaye S. Wandrille, 1946). *Introduction to Kierkegaard*. Transl. by W. H. Barber (New York: E. P. Dutton & Co., n.d.).

Jones, W. Tudor, *Contemporary Thought of Germany* (London: William Norgate, 1931), 2 vols.

Jorgenson, Theodore, *Henrik Ibsen* (Northfield, Minn.: St. Olaf College Press, 1945).

Kaufmann, Walter A., *Nietzsche. Philosopher, Psychologist, Antichrist* (Princeton: Princeton University Press, 1950).

Kierkegaard, Sören, *Samlede Vaerker* (Copenhagen: F. Hegel & Son, 1901–1906), 14 vols.

—— *Papirer* (Copenhagen: Nordiskforlag, 1909–1934), 18 vols.

—— *Philosophical Fragments*. Transl. by David F. Swenson (Princeton: Princeton University Press and American-Scandinavian Foundation, 1936).

—— *The Journals of Sören Kierkegaard* (New York: Oxford University Press, 1938).

—— *The Point of View for my Work as an Author*. Transl. by Walter Lowrie (New York: Oxford University Press, 1939).

—— *The Present Age*. Transl. by Alexander Dru and Walter Lowrie (New York: Oxford University Press, 1940).

—— *Stages on Life's Way*. Transl. by Walter Lowrie (Princeton: Princeton University Press, 1940).

—— *Concluding Unscientific Postscript to "Philosophical Fragments."* Transl. by David F. Swenson; completed and edited by Walter Lowrie (Princeton: Princeton University Press and American-Scandinavian Foundation, 1941).

—— *Fear and Trembling*. Transl. by Walter Lowrie (Princeton: Princeton University Press, 1941).

—— *Repetition*. Transl. by Walter Lowrie (Princeton: Princeton University Press, 1941).

—— *The Sickness unto Death*. Transl. by Walter Lowrie (Princeton: Princeton University Press, 1941).

—— *Training in Christianity*. Transl. by Walter Lowrie (Princeton: Princeton University Press, 1944).

—— *Edifying Discourses*. Transl. by David F. Swenson and Lillian

Marvin Swenson (Minneapolis: Augsburg Publishing House, 1943–1946), 4 vols.

—— *Attack upon "Christendom."* Transl. by Walter Lowrie (Princeton: Princeton University Press, 1944).

—— *Either/Or: A Fragment of Life.* Transl. by David F. Swenson, Lillian Marvin Swenson, and Walter Lowrie (Princeton: Princeton University Press, 1944).

—— *The Concept of Dread.* Transl. by Walter Lowrie (Princeton: Princeton University Press, 1944).

—— *Works of Love.* Transl. by Lillian Marvin Swenson (Princeton: Princeton University Press, 1946).

Koht, Halvdan, *The Life of Ibsen* (New York: The American-Scandinavian Foundation, W. W. Norton Co., 1931), 2 vols.

Kuhn, Helmut, *Encounter with Nothingness* (Chicago: Henry Regnery Co., 1949).

Levinas, E., *En découvrant l'existence avec Husserl et Heidegger* (Paris: Vrin, 1949).

Lotz, Johannes B., S.J., *Das christliche Menschenbild im Ringen der Zeit* (Heidelberg: Kerle, 1947).

Löwith, Karl, *Kierkegaard und Nietzsche oder philosophische und theologische Überwindung des Nihilismus* (Frankfurt a.M.: V. Klostermann, 1933).

—— *Von Hegel bis Nietzsche* (Zurich: Europa Verlag, 1941. 2 ed., Stuttgart: W. Kohlhammer, 1950).

Lowrie, Walter, *Kierkegaard* (New York: Oxford University Press, 1938).

—— *A Short Life of Kierkegaard* (Princeton: Princeton University Press, 1942).

Lubac, Henri de, S.J., *Surnaturel. Etudes Historiques* (Paris: Aubier, 1946).

—— *The Drama of Atheist Humanism* (New York: Sheed and Ward, 1950).

Lukacs, Georges, *Existentialisme ou Marxisme?* Transl. from the Hungarian by E. Kelemen (Paris: Nagel, 1948).

Marcel, Gabriel, *Le Coeur des autres* (Paris: Grasset, 1920).

—— *Journal métaphysique* (Paris: Gallimard, 1927).

—— *Le Monde cassé, suivi de Position et Approches concrètes du Mystère ontologique* (Paris: Desclée de Brouwer, 1933).

—— *Etre et Avoir* (Paris: Aubier, 1935).

—— *Du Refus à l'Invocation* (Paris: Gallimard, 1940).

—— *Homo Viator* (Paris: Aubier, 1944).

—— *La Métaphysique de Royce* (Paris: Aubier, 1945).

—— *Existentialisme Chrétien.* Edited by Etienne Gilson (Paris: Plon, 1947).

—— *The Philosophy of Existence* (London: The Harvill Press, 1949).

—— *Being and Having.* Transl. by K. Farrer (Westminster: Dacre, 1949).

—— *The Mystery of Being: I. Reflection and Mystery,* The Gifford

Lectures, 1949. Transl. by G. S. Fraser (Chicago: Henry Regnery Co., 1950. — *II. Faith and Reality*, The Gifford Lectures, 1950. Transl. by René Haguel (Chicago: Henry Regnery Co., 1951).

Maritain, Jacques, *Court traité de l'Existentialisme et de l'Existant* (Paris: Paul Hartmann, 1947). *Existence and the Existent*, English version by Lewis Galantiere and Gerald B. Phelan (New York: Pantheon, 1948).

Meyer, Hans, *Die Weltanschauung der Gegenwart* (Paderborn and Würzburg: Ferdinand Schöningh, 1949).

Michel, Wilhelm, *Das Leben Friedrich Hölderlins* (Bremen: C. Schünemann, 1949).

More, Paul Elmer, *Nietzsche* (Boston and New York: Houghton Mifflin, 1912).

Morgan, G., *What Nietzsche Means* (Cambridge: Harvard University Press, 1941).

Mounier, E., *Existentialist Philosophies. An Introduction.* Transl. by E. Blow (London: Rockliff, 1948).

Müller, Max, *Existenzphilosophie im geistigen Leben der Gegenwart* (Heidelberg: Kerle, 1949).

Nahm, Milton C., *Selections from Early Greek Philosophy* (New York: Crofts, 1941, 2 ed.).

Nietzsche, Friedrich, *Gesammelte Werke.* Musarionausgabe (München: Musarion, 1920 ff.), 23 vols.

——— *The Works of Friedrich Nietzsche* (New York: Macmillan, 1909 ff.), 18 vols.

——— *Gesammelte Briefe* (Leipzig: Insel Verlag, 1902–1909).

Pfeiffer, J., *Existenzphilosophie: Eine Einführung in Heidegger und Jaspers* (Hamburg: F. Meiner, 1949).

Pourrat, Henri, *Le sage et son démon* (Paris: Albin Michel, 1950).

Przywara, Erich, S.J., *Hölderlin* (Nürnberg: Glock und Lutz, 1949).

Reyburn, H. A., Hinderks, H. E., and Taylor, J. G., *Nietzsche. The Story of a Human Philosopher* (New York: Macmillan, 1948).

Ricoeur, Paul, *Gabriel Marcel et Karl Jaspers* (Paris: Editions du Temps Présent, 1947).

Rosteutscher, J. H. W., *Die Wiederkehr des Dionysos* (Bern: A. Francke, 1947).

Ruggiero, Guido de, *Existentialism. Disintegration of Man's Soul* (New York: Social Science Publishers, 1948).

Sartre, Jean-Paul, *La nausée* (Paris: Gallimard, 1938).

——— *Les mouches* (Paris: Gallimard, 1942).

——— *L'être et le néant: essai d'ontologie phénoménologique* (Paris: Gallimard, 1943).

——— *Huis-clos* (Paris: Gallimard, 1944).

——— *Les chemins de la liberté* (Paris: Gallimard, 1945), 3 vols.

——— *Morts sans sépulture. La Putain respectueuse* (Paris: Gallimard, 1946).

—— *Existentialism.* Transl. by Bernard Frechtman (New York: Philosophical Library, 1947). This is a translation of *L'Existentialisme est un humanisme* (Paris: Les Editions Nagel, 1945).

—— *The Psychology of Imagination* (New York: Philosophical Library, 1948).

Siegmund, Georg, *Nietzsche, der "Atheist" und "Antichrist"* (Paderborn: Schöningh, 1946).

Steinbüchel, Theodor, *Existentialismus und Christliches Ethos* (Heidelberg: Kerle, 1948).

Swenson, D., *Something about Kierkegaard* (Minneapolis: Augsburg Publishing Company, 1941).

Thomte, Reidar, *Kierkegaard's Philosophy of Religion* (Princeton: Princeton University Press, 1948).

Tonquédec, Joseph de, *L'Existence d'après Karl Jaspers* (Paris: Beauchesne, 1945).

Troisfontaines, Roger, *Le Choix de J.-P. Sartre. Exposé et critique de L'être et le néant* (Paris: Aubier, 1945).

—— *Existentialisme et Pensée Chrétienne* (Paris: Vrin, 1948).

Vietta, Egon, *Theologie ohne Gott. Versuch über die menschliche Existenz in der modernen französischen Philosophie* (Zurich: Artemis, 1946).

Waehlens, A. de, *La Filosofía de Martín Heidegger.* Transl. from the French by R. Ceñal, S.J. (Madrid: Instituto Luis Vives de Filosofía, 1945).

Wagner de Reyna, A., *La Ontología fundamental de Heidegger* (Buenos Aires: Losada, 1939).

Wahl, Jean, *Petite histoire de l'Existentialisme* (Paris: Editions Club Maintenant, 1947).

Welch, E., *The Philosophy of Edmund Husserl: The Origin and Development of his Phenomenology* (New York: Columbia University Press, 1941).

Würzbach, Friedrich, *Das Vermächtnis Nietzsches* (Graz: A. Pustet, 1943).

Wust, Peter, *Ungewissheit und Wagnis* (München und Kempten: Kösel, 1946).

—— *Der Mensch und die Philosophie. Einführung in die Existenzphilosophie* (Münster i.W.: Regensberg Verlag, 1946).

INDEX